EDITING BY DESIGN

This page is traditionally kept blank,
but I persuaded the publisher to let me use
the space to show several fundamental
characteristics of multi-page publications:

1) The black bar flows from left to right,
overleaf, page to page.
See the chapter on "SPACE."

2) It is the first link in a chain that ties the
product together.
See "PARADE."

3) It is at the top of the page, because that's
where people look.
See "MULTI-PAGE MEDIUM."

4) It repeats at all the chapter starts, so it
becomes a recognizeable roadsign.
See "SIGNALS."

5) It bleeds at the top-right edge of the pages
and the titles in it are as close to the edge as
can be, to help page-rifflers find what they
are looking for—fast.
See "MARGINS."

All these factors are as much design
decisions as they are editing decisions:
How to break up the material (editing);
how to identify the segments (design);
how to assemble them to make the most of
the capabilities of the medium in order to
expose the intellectual content most vividly
and effectively (product-making).
Hence the title: "EDITING BY DESIGN."

For
designers,
art directors,
and
editors

The classic guide to winning readers

EDITING BY DESIGN

Jan V. White

COMPLETELY REVISED
THIRD EDITION

ALLWORTH PRESS

NEW YORK

07 06 05 04 03   5 4 3 2 1

Published by Allworth Press
An imprint of Allworth Communications, Inc.
10 East 23rd Street, New York, NY 10010

Cover design by Derek Bacchus

Page composition / typography by Jan V. White

ISBN: 1-58115-302-3

Library of Congress Cataloging-in-Publication Data

White, Jan V., 1928–
        Editing by Design : for designers, art directors, and editors : the classic guide to winning readers / Jan V. White. — Completely rev. 3rd ed.
                p.cm.
        Includes Index.
        ISBN 1-58115-302-3
        1. Graphic design (Typography) 2. Laypout (Printing) 3. Magazine design.
4. Editing. I. Title.

Z246.W578 2003
686.2'2—dc21

        2003052427

Printed in Canada

CONTENTS

For my grandchildren (in order of appearance)

Morgan Jessica White
Courtney Alexandra White
Alexandra Brandeis White
Emma Boland White
Andrew Mallon White
Reis O'Neill White

Also by this author

EDITING BY DESIGN (FIRST AND SECOND EDITIONS)

DESIGNING FOR MAGAZINES (FIRST AND SECOND EDITIONS)

MASTERING GRAPHICS

USING CHARTS AND GRAPHS

GRAPHIC IDEA NOTEBOOK (FIRST AND SECOND EDITIONS)

ON GRAPHICS: TIPS FOR EDITORS

THE GRID BOOK

THOUGHTS ON PUBLICATION DESIGN

GRAPHIC IDEA TRIGGERS

GRAPHIC DESIGN FOR THE ELECTRONIC AGE

COLOR FOR THE ELECTRONIC AGE

GREAT PAGES

COLOR FOR IMPACT

LEARN GRAPHIC DESIGN (VIDEO)

ACKNOWLEDGMENTS

When you pontificate in seminars to editors, journalists, art directors, designers, publishers—fellow working-professionals all—you are forced to observe, analyze, and promulgate principles that had better make sense for them in their practical world. That is why every one of my clients is part author of this tome: they forced me to figure things out for them. Without such challenges, this compilation of observations, exhortations, opinions, warnings, and recommendations would never have happened. Are they idiosyncratic? Yes and no. All are based on experience. Are they proveable? No. Everything our professions produce varies (that's why it is such fun) but the underlying constant is to make the most of the What by exploiting the How (that's what this book is about).

As far as the illustrations are concerned: The little guardsman who starts marching on page 15 is by Feliks Topolski.* The gentleman on horseback on page 171 and the rhino on 175 are from woodcuts by Albrecht Dürer. The column and doughnut on 184 are by William Wirt Turner.** The devils on 108 and legs on 156 are details from Gustav Doré's illustrations to Dante's *Divine Comedy.* Drawings on pages 145, 146, 147, 152, 153, 156, 175, and 177 are by Emil Weiss. The prolegomenon overleaf was assembled from mediæval woodcuts. I apologize to Leonardo da Vinci for page 224, and must take the blame for the rest of the scribbles.

My thanks to Nicole Potter and Liz Van Hoose, my editors at Allworth; it gets very lonely being a one-man-band, coming up with the idea for a book, writing, designing, illustrating, setting the type, and assembling the pages. You need a pal to see the big picture as well as save you from yourself. They even queried the tiny type dropped out from yellow on page 212 with a note "I can't read this." That is above and beyond the call of duty, because you're not supposed to be able to read it. It's an example of what not to do.

Without the tranquility and confidence that my Clare has given me, I doubt I would have had the energy to tackle this rodomontade. The task has been daunting. How can I leave out the names of the Whites who appeared in my other acknowledgments: Toby and Caroline, Alex and Lilian and Paula, Greg and Dana, Christopher, and Bentley? Thanks for being you.

---

* *The London Spectacle*, 1935, The Bodley Head, London
** *Shades and Shadows*, Ronald Press, New York, 1952

OUR PUBLISHING ANCESTORS

A montage of 16th and 17th century woodcuts showing some of the occupations working together to produce a printed product.
In the distance, the writer, (working at home).
A typefounder,
a cartographer,
an illuminator who colors and gilds illustrations (that's a stencil, not a mouse in his hand),
an apprentice,
a production organizer,
the art director,
a woodcut artist,
and a courier from the outside printer's.
At left, the editor.
Not shown:
our customer—
the reader.

The drawing of the self-satisfied writer is a throwback to my first year in publishing. It was an illustration for an article in *FYI*, our TIME INC in-house newsletter. Typewriters, scrunched-up paper, overflowing wastebaskets, cigars, feet on desk, the newly-invented ergonomic chair…

Not much has changed in publishing in the last fifty years—or the last four hundred, for that matter. Technology, perhaps. And maleness. And fear of lung cancer. Then along came Scotch tape… Letraset rub-off lettering… Xeroxes… offset printing and flow-through color… and Macs! Despite the ever-improving marvels of technology, the worst leftover dreg we seem unable to change is the traditional attitude that pits *editors* VERSUS *designers*. It remains as misguided today as ever. What can we do about it? Deliberately build bridges of understanding, personal liking, and professional appreciation of each other's contribution to the common effort.

Start with the only thing we can control: ourselves as "editors" or "designers." Grow up. Stop guarding one's little personal empire of "The Word" or "The Picture." Quit defending them against imaginary intruders. Realize how interdependent they are and how they can't exist without each other.

If we are to capture and hold our audiences, add value, establish a brand with brand-loyalty (buzzwords, yes, but how apt and vital in today's competitive situation) we must combine the two warring aspects of our printed product:

> the **physical** vs. the *intellectual*
> the **form** vs. the *content*
> the **design** vs. the *journalis*m
> the **product-making** vs. the *story-telling*

Product-making sees the publication as an object-for-sale and is concerned with overall character, appeal, personality.

Story-telling is the technique of communicating a specific message within the context of that object-for-sale.

We must seduce the uncaring page-flippers to pay attention by flaunting the relevance of the material to their interests. Then we must guide them through it. Therefore we must understand and exploit both the physical attributes of the medium as well as viewer psychology. That is why each chapter of this book starts with a reminder of how PRODUCT-MAKING and STORY-TELLING interconnect. There are some overlaps (and there may be some internal disagreements) because some elements are referred to in different ways under several rubrics to cover the various aspects of the subject. There are four sectors.

1. The physical attributes of the medium and how they affect the product. (THE MULTI-PAGE MEDIUM, starting on page 3)

2. How to appeal to the reader. (INDUCEMENT, starting on page 9)

3. How-to tips in the bulk of the book. (Starting on page 15)

4. Practical worries that bedevil our profession as communicators in print. (APPENDIX: Q AND A, starting on page 231. Glossary and Index are also devised to respond to questions.)

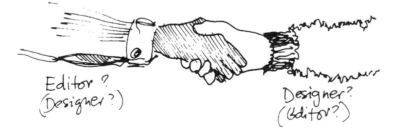

Editor?
(Designer?)
Designer?
(Editor?)

Warning and disclaimer: there is no such thing as The Correct Way to do anything in our profession as communicators. It is all a matter of analysis and judgment. Nothing in this book claims to be The Truth or the Only Way. It is all just the result of a lifetime of trying to figure out what fundamental techniques seem to work for the editor / designer team.

STORY-TELLING │ A true story about how common sense runs up against entrenched habits of thought. A few years ago I was asked to suggest improvements for technical documents for a *very* large company. One enormous subset were the manuals for field use. They weighed a ton, so the technicians preferred to have them miniaturized and attached to clipboards.

Discussion:

Where are the pages held together?
By the clips at the top.

How must one flip pages to find things?
At the bottom.

What do technicians need to find fast?
The titles of the material on the pages.

Where are the titles?
Under the clips at the tops of the page.

So can you see them?
No, they're under the clips. So the technicians have to use the tiny page numbers at the foot of the pages to find what they're looking for.

That's crazy! Doesn't it make sense to move the titles to the foot of the page so they pop out at you?
Sure, but we can't do that, because our Manual on Manuals decrees that TITLES SHALL BE AT THE TOP OF THE PAGE and that's where they had better be, or else...

MORAL: *don't be a consultant.*

PRODUCT-MAKING │ **The physical object and the users.**
How do they hold it?
What do they see?
Where do they look?
How do they proceed?

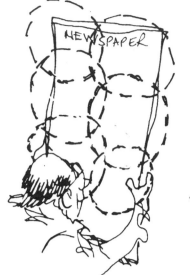

Page size affects what people see and in how many "takes" they look at it. A broadsheet newspaper is examined in several takes. The magazine spread can be absorbed in one because our peripheral vision encompasses the entire thing at normal viewing distance. The closeness at which we hold it to read it also affects the scale of the things we put on the page. But whatever the trim size, our paper or monitor screen is a miniaturized world.

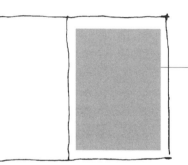

The single page isn't a stand-alone unit like an old-fashioned sheet of letterhead (or a one-page ad), even if we often think of it as a single piece. It is delivered to the recipient as just one-half of the dominant shape of the product—a spread.

The spread isn't flat, like a painting to be hung on the wall, or like the image on the monitor screen. Beware of that phony flatness. It is a trap. (The only time it is seen like that is when it is mounted on cardboard and submitted for a design award.)

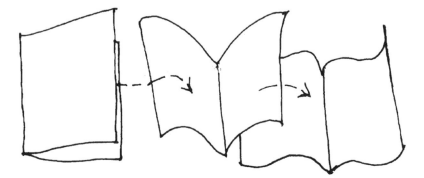

The spread is split in half, and no matter how hard we may wish it were unbroken and pretend the gutter doesn't exist, it does. The thing is folded in the middle. And it is made of a material that is floppy and curved—and as paper gets ever more expensive, it becomes ever thinner, flimsier, and floppier.

Something on the cover arouses curiosity. The potential readers must pick it up to find out more... check the table of contents... flip through to find the story. Other elements may beguile them on the way. Some readers search for something interesting by page-flipping. In any case, the physical process of handling paper pages is combined with the reactions to what is noticed on those pages.

The object is floppy, folded, bound, three-dimensional. It is held by the spine, so the inner half stays hidden until flippers decide to open it all the way and reveal the full spread. What they see on the outer halves motivates them to do that.

Put your best stuff where skimmers look, on the outside, so they can't miss it. That's where the most fascinating images and provocative words should go, because that's where they will be seen. Never hide your headlines in the gutter.

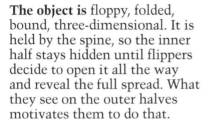

The most valuable areas of real estate on the spread are the top-left corner and the top-right corner, because those are the areas where people look most.

The least important part of the spread is at the foot near the gutter. Who ever looks down there? That is why footnotes are called footnotes and tucked out of the way down there.

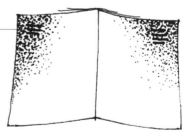

Viewers concentrate on the upper parts of the pages when they are examining a magazine or newsletter. As they flip the pages, they stare at the tops and swivel their heads sideways, because it is faster, easier, and less of a pain in the neck than up-and-down. Try it. That is the reason why logical makeup is horizontal rather than vertical, as in the following example.

Logical page makeup responds to the way people look at the product. Present your menu of choices horizontally across the page tops to help scanners decide what to bother with. Don't insist on aligning columns at the foot of the page for "neatness." Let them hang as they come because nobody looks down there (or cares about neat alignment, if they do).

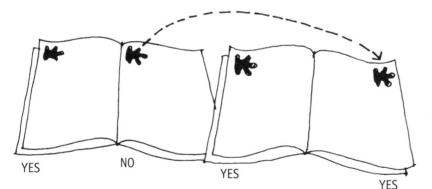

YES NO YES YES

Lefts must be laid out differently from rights to make the most of the potential eye-catching areas. The logo that makes sense at top-left on a left-hand page or on a stand-alone single (which is probably the way you see it on-screen) is hidden in the gutter, if it is in the top-left corner of a right-hand page. Move it to the far outside right, where it can be seen and can do its job of signaling.

Rights are preferred by advertisers because as people hold a magazine and flip pages, they tend to concentrate on the right-hand pages, because the left hand does the holding, the right controls the flipping. The right-hand pages are held steady, left-hand ones move and flop. Besides, as the magazine lies flat on the table and pages are turned, the heavier part remains flat while the lighter part—the front of the book—is curved. After the centerfold, the left-hand part stays flat, while the back of the book is curved.

Lefts are ideal as editorial spaces. The advertisers' preference for right-hand pages plays directly into our editorial hands: by getting the rejected left-hand leftovers, we can display our best stuff out at the far left, where the first words of our headlines and irresistible pictures can hook them in. ——————

Rhythmic placement creates expectability and accumulates into strength. So long as our pages are *all* on rights or *all* on lefts, *the sameness* outweighs the preference of whether they are lefts or rights. If ad placement is allowed to dictate placement and results in arbitrary scatter, the product is weakened because the rhythm is disturbed.

Readers hate having to jump somewhere into the back of the book to follow a story to its end. It interrupts thinking, destroys concentration, jeopardizes the stories that have to be leapfrogged. (Worse: Usually page numbers are so small and often left off because of the ads.) If we know that we infuriate our readers that way, why do we continue doing it?

Work from the top down, not bottom upwards. The page tops need to be controlled, so they become part of a visual chain. Do not begin layout by placing the end of the text at the foot and working backwards, allowing the tops to fall at random. Instead, control the top and let the bottom fall as it may.

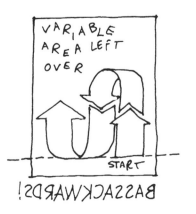

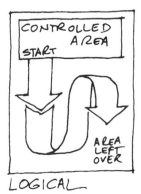

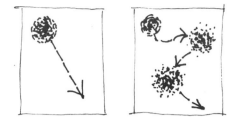

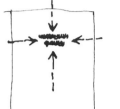

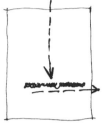

The looker begins a single page at top-left and scans diagonally downward, unless something pulls his attention away. The designer manipulates the neutral background by positioning elements in it.

How a line of type affects the space on the page

Centered, perfectly balanced, the words lie immobile like a jewel on a tray. Standard, static.

In a single line off-center, the left-to-right reading direction forces the eye to right edge and overleaf.

Forcing the eye downward, the pull towards the right is even stronger than if the line is at top.

Hanging the wording off the very top of the page, the eye moves upward and then to the right.

With the wording at the foot of the page, the eye sinks downward and is directed to the right.

The way we organize elements in space affects the readers' reaction as they look at the page. Too often, however, we override the need for simplicity, shoehorn material onto the page, "pour in" the text, then try to "break it up" with pictures. Instead of controlling the space to encourage the flow of looking and reading, we create artificial barriers as in this example:

before

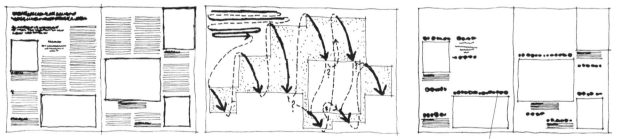

Pictures dropped in higgledypiggledy... do we really want the reader's eye to jump around this way?... look at the hurdles it has to vault over.

...but by simplifying, massing the text and aligning the tops of columns, readers will go where we hope they will go: i.e., first check the pictures, then settle down to read:

after

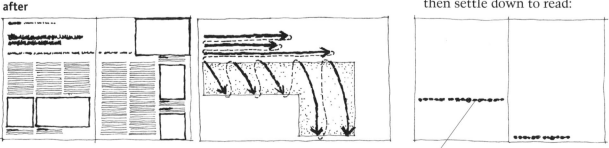

Pictures pushed to the outer edges, text shape simplified... smooth reading with no worrisome barriers to jump over except at foot of columns.

PRODUCT-MAKING

People resist getting involved. They are afraid. They seldom want to read or study. They are in a hurry—yet so much print clamors for their attention simultaneously. They weigh the

cost/benefit ratio of the effort and time invested against the payoff gained. *"Is this sufficiently interesting?"*

They start flipping the pages seeking the What's-In-It-For-Me value. If they get hooked, they may well start to read, but few start where we assume they will—at the beginning. Instead, they are pulled in by something somewhere else which may well seduce them to return to the beginning.

STORY-TELLING

We must edit and design on two tracks:

1: **The fast track,** where we show the value of the message by *revealing its significant bits at first glance.*

2: **The slow track,** where we go into depth. Nobody wants to read everything. Making it obvious that it is skippable implies permission *not* to read, which is psychologically comforting. In any case, they'll have gathered the gist of the ideas from the fast-track they did already glance at.

If the piece looks bland and uninvolving, it will be skipped. If it is only marginally interesting or if it looks too long, they'll say *"I think I'll come back to it later"* which is the kiss of death, because the issue will be put on top of the TO-BE-READ pile and when tall enough, the whole stack will go to the dump for recycling. That is why we must use every psychological, intellectual, and visual (i.e., *editing*) trick to get them to react the first time they see the story. It must be so irresistible that they feel they would be missing something if they didn't read it *now*.

So this is all about **inducement,** using psychological strategy:

> Habit—what are they accustomed to?
> Expectations—what is normal or abnormal?
> Curiosity—what will startle or fascinate them?

Hence the need to build in hooks. Snares. Traps. Display. The more of them there are to pull them in with the better, even if the pages look "messier." We have to persuade page flippers to stop, look, and listen. The "display" is what makes the publication magnetic and pulls them in. Though hooks can take any shape (examples are shown on the next few pages) the most obvious ones are verbal.

Exploiting display

Headlines are unabashed, proud sales-copy and ought to be written first (*What?*) (*Yes!*) to ensure that the hooks are baited with the best bits of irresistible stuff. Yet they, and the other display elements, especially captions or cutlines, are written last, as a nuisance-job after the enthusiasm for the story has worn off, when it's too late to whip up fervor because the writer and editor are bored, tired, rushing to close. Writing headlines and captions first forces the writer to figure out why the story is worth publishing. Retrofitting—the usual procedure—is harder, but we don't realize it, because we are so used to doing it that way.

The most involving display is meaningful to the individual readers. It gets them excited about the what's-in-it-for-me, how-does-it-affect-my-life implications of the article. The headline is obviously the most important display element. To work most effectively, every headline ought to have:

1. An active verb. That forces the writer to think in terms of action and results.

2. The magic word YOU in there somewhere somehow, spoken or implied. That forces the writer to tailor the story to the reader.

To test the effectiveness of a headline, read it out loud, then ask *"So what?"* If the answer is *"So nothing"* or *"Not much,"* then it isn't involving enough and the story must be re-analyzed to find the right ideas, so the headlines can be rewritten. Dead titles are products of lack of thought—taking the easy way out—regardless of the puns or cleverness of wording. If the story has no angle of self-interest for the reader, it'll remain unread. Why publish it?

Our pages in magazines, books, newsletters, magapapers, wherever, are editorial products. They aren't advertisements. Yet both edit and ads are looked at, examined, *and reacted to* the same way. So here's how successful single-page ads have worked ever since ads were invented. ADVERTISING 101: Viewers are pulled in in a logical sequence 1, 2, 3, 4.

1 The picture attracts attention and arouses curiosity. Since everyone interprets an image her own way, because every viewer has her own history and interests, words are needed to define the Idea—the purpose—behind the visual.

2 The headline highlights the Idea... then promises a benefit that is intended to motivate readers to find out more (to get them to delve into the text). **The headline needs to be long enough to say all that.** The newspaper dictum that heads should be short and snappy may be true, but it is often limiting. Unless you can find brilliant wording, opt for more words.

3 The text is where the details lie. The words are so exciting and captivating that the skeptical readers are persuaded to take action, now that they understand how much more fulfilling their lives will be.

4 The coupon is right there to be filled out and sent in to get a free sample. A more up-to-date version of audience participation (which is what the whole purpose is): visiting the www address.

Images involve the viewer by means of emotion and curiosity. Manipulate them to trigger understanding at first glance but exaggerate them graphically only if that clarifies meaning.

Use infographics to replace long descriptions with fast visual explanation. Find the statistical comparisons in the text, so you can turn them into pictures and make them easier to understand. Transforming words into images helps you to edit tighter.

Put the picture above the headline, so it pulls the viewer in. The image and its explanation are a twinned unit of information. Put the headline under the picture as though it were a caption and tell the viewers what the picture is about. It will pull them into the text much more irresistibly.

Never run a picture without a caption, and always place the explanation where the viewer is used to finding it: **under the picture.** Captions hook the already curious lookers into the story if they (the captions) are baited with irresistible what's-in-it-for-me information.

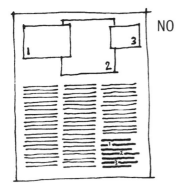
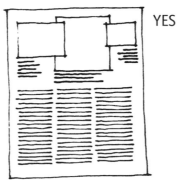

Never ask readers to look for explanations somewhere else on the page. It frustrates them and can make them angry because it demands time, effort, concentration, and study. Part of our service is to do this work for them. The look of the page is less important than the speed and clarity with which we communicate. Avoid ganging captions, even if it looks neater.

Every page should have a welcoming entry point, dominant enough so it isn't missed. It can be anything—verbal, pictorial, diagramatic— but it has to identify to the still uninvolved page-skimmers what subject this space is devoted to and why they should want to find out more about it.

Clusters of short elements pull better than long essays. Short bits are less threatening than long ones, because they demand less commitment of time or effort. Sidebars break out supportive material into subsidiary stories. Define each box with its own heading, and add its own pictures. Here is a story about a volcanic eruption. One subsidiary box covers where, the other when.

Speed is of the essence. The skimmer should gather **the gist of the story from the headline, deck, and subheads.** Subheads should define the subcomponent parts of the text. They must be actively useful, not just afterthoughts to "break up the text." Make them more visible, longer, more informative. (Then readers may skip the text if they are only moderately interested, but they will know what the story is about.)

Turn your publication into a source of useful references. Not only are addresses, schedules, dates, or other such information appreciated as unexpected bonuses, but their long-term utility extends the shelf-life of your product.

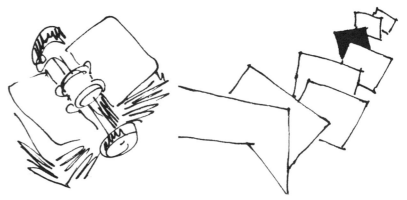

NO DUMPING VIOLATORS WILL BE PROSECUTED

Never assume that the readers understand. They are not dumb, just ignorant about what we want them to know (until they've read it). Therefore read the display from the recipient's viewpoint. We have written it and therefore understand its purpose, but does it actually say what we believe it says? Does its visual presentation expose it the way we want it understood?

Some faceless state vehicle department bureaucrat perpetrated this sign. He could not have read it because he probably doesn't read, which is not to be wondered at, given what he has to write.

What does it really say?

NO DUMPING!
VIOLATORS WILL BE PROSECUTED.

The intention, of course, is to warn people against dumping.

NO DUMPING-VIOLATORS
WILL BE PROSECUTED

That isn't the only way it reads. It could be interpreted as its unintended opposite.

No!   (Don't you dare!)
DUMPING VIOLATORS WILL BE PROSECUTED

Stretching it a bit, you could read it this way.

NO DUMPING VIOLATORS WILL BE
PROSECUTED   (as opposed to something else).

Or you could be led to substitute words.

Each interpretation depends on the way the words would sound if they were spoken. To make it intelligible, spoken language uses intonation and pauses —i.e. phrasing. Written language has their equivalent:

1. Punctuation, invented to act as visual clues when the speaker isn't there to be heard.

2. The way the thoughts are broken at the end of each line.

Read the copy out loud according to the clues given by the way it is arrayed on the page. Hear it like they may. **Fix it.**

Paper… background… emptiness… space-between…
the terrain we print on… white space… this stuff:

PRODUCT-MAKING

It is valuable, marvellous, miraculous, and its capacities are
FREE, because they are built into our medium. They are part
and parcel of the material and physical object we make when
we produce a book, magazine, newsletter, paper, Web page.

Nobody really covets a drill bit, yet millions are sold, because
people need holes. Few subscribers want your publication as
an object, but all of them want and need the information in it.
They want it fast and clear. They want to access it easily and
hassle-free. This is where space comes in. Using the terrain
actively does not mean wasting a lot as "white space." Nor is
it a matter of inventing clever tricks. Space is a raw material
ready to be used actively and imaginatively.

*It is not static but kinetic,
plastic, fluid, flowing from
left to right and then
overleaf.* Curious about
where this fist is pointing?
Go ahead and turn the
page.

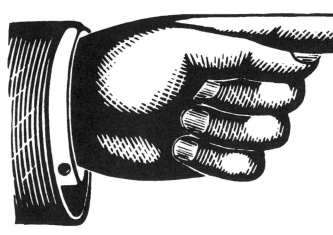

*There's a lot of it and its
muchness costs nothing.*
Over on the right in the corner stands
a Buckingham Palace guard, ramrod straight
and immobile. Watch him come to life when you
flip the pages. Isn't it marvellous what repetition
in sequential-space-coupled-with-time can do?
Publication-making is like directing movies.

The relationship between words and form. The finger forced you to turn the page because its tip flows overleaf. The curiosity engendered by the words on the preceding page also helped. The verbal and the visual must work in harmony, reinforce each other, and lead you to look from one side of the paper to the other.

DON'T WASTE THE SPACE

The relationship between the two sides of a page. See how "transparent" the paper appears? (That's a trick: the words here are printed in a 20% screen of black.) For a moment you might think that it is the "show-through" from the words on the next page or the next one after that.

DON'T WASTE THE SPACE

The relationship between the two pages across the gutter. Did the black letters opposite rub off on this page when the pages kissed each other as the publication was closed? Pages are not individual stand-alone units. Each is merely one half of a conjoined twin unit, linked at the gutter.

DON'T WASTE THE SPACE

DON'T WASTE THE SPACE

The relationship between the size of the empty page and what is printed on it. Here are examples of the usefulness of unexpected scale to startle and get attention: the tiny object floating in a tremendous ocean of space or the overwhelmingly enormous object shoehorned into a tiny cell.

DON'T
WASTE
THE
SPACE

White space is not *blank* space.

Here it is functional: it creates

the illusion of enormous sky.

The message couldn't be conveyed without it.

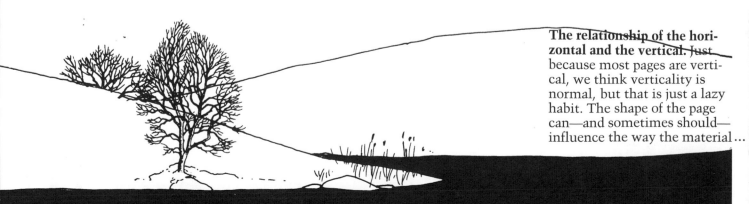

The relationship of the horizontal and the vertical. Just because most pages are vertical, we think verticality is normal, but that is just a lazy habit. The shape of the page can—and sometimes should—influence the way the material…

DON'T WASTE THIS SPACE

...is placed on it, which will persuade the reader to turn the page sideways. A potentially useful characteristic, rarely used because turning the page is thought to be a nuisance. It is therefore reserved for functional problems like pictures of skyscrapers or type tables that are too wide to fit onto a page, so we turn it sideways. But what a surprise a change of direction can pack, and what a waste to reject it when the subject calls for it.

Are you faced with producing a publication but don't feel confident about your judgment? Are you about to make decisions you are not trained for? Welcome to the club: you are in company with thousands who suddenly find themselves writers, editors, proofreaders, designers, production managers, and everything else rolled into one. Courage! It is not nearly as difficult as it seems.

Chances are that the first things you start thinking about are type, pictures, color, and page arrangements that are pleasing to the eye. Isn't that the stuff you control? Indeed it is, but Whoa! You are putting the cart before the horse. Have you forgotten about the other part—the background on which the stuff will be printed? That is probably just what you have done, but relax. Why should you be different from everybody else?

Perhaps "forgotten about" is an overstatement. "Taken it for granted" is probably more accurate. It is quite normal not to think about it. Obviously print cannot exist without its substrate. Printing and paper are like yin and yang. That is why you must take the object's physical attributes into account in order to produce excellent communication in print. The paper you print on is not just a neutral, empty surface waiting to be covered. It must be used as an active participant in the communication process.

Take it a step further: when you begin thinking about it, the paper is not merely the physical sheet from which your product is made. More important, if subtler, the paper carries *the space* in which printed matter is arranged. It is vital to take both space and its paper carrier into account in planning, editing, and designing printing.

All this is simply an extension of the most fundamentally obvious realization that if you are to communicate words in print, you have to turn them into little black marks on paper (TYPE). Once the words have been turned into these visual symbols, you have to arrange them in logical groups in the available space. That means you have to organize them on the pages (DESIGN, LAYOUT). The physical attributes of the materials you are working with are inescapable. The words, the type, the paper, the space are all part and parcel of communication. They are the physical, visual aspect of writing and editing. None exists alone.

I said earlier that communication in print isn't as difficult as it appears but I didn't say it is *easy*. Of course, you can follow the patterns based on traditional wisdoms. Many of the software templates are based on them. If the result appears a bit boring, there is an advantage to that: readers will understand it because they have seen it a million times before. By taking the audience's expectations and habits into account, you help them interpret what you say in a cogent way. The speaker (the writer/editor/designer) and the listener (the reader) must speak the same language. But, just as the spoken word can either be monotonously soporific at one end of the scale, or evocatively and even thrillingly compelling at the other, just so can its translation into visual terms be banal or stimulating.

Attack the problem with lateral thinking. What you see on the page can actually be "listened to." See it that way, and you begin to see the complexity of the task as well as the direction to aim in. Doing it well-enough requires following tradition and normal practice. Doing it brilliantly demands self-confidence and insight. Much can be defined and learned. The various insights are interconnected and you need to understand them all in order to use them well. You need to be aware of the *background*, in order to use it actively. You must understand *space* in order to control it.

Everybody examines a printed piece twice, if it has more than a couple of pages. The first time is little more than a fast flip-through. It is a scan to determine size and content, to find the what's-in-there-for-me and to gauge the effort and time its study is likely to take. The second time is when they actually settle down to pay attention and read.

The first overview is vital because that is when the concept of usefulness and value is communicated. That is what makes them *want to* do the studying. Once the reader actually starts reading, then the information takes over. Its fascination speaks for itself, so the piece sells itself. Bringing the potential readers to the point where they realize how well they will be served is the first challenge. This is when the object's physical attributes—especially space—come into play. Space is only remarkable when it is well used. Used generously, luxuriantly, it adds an aura of value. Used strategically, it catapults ideas off the page into the reader's mind because it clarifies and dramatizes them. *The way the text overfills this page cancels out its own large size.*

The relationship of thickness to lightness. Shoehorning so much into a space that nobody will want to read it is false economy. *It isn't what is put on the page, but what comes off that page into the reader's mind that matters.* A bit of empty space helps.

Are you faced with producing a publication but don't feel confident about your judgment? Are you about to make decisions you are not trained for? Welcome to the club: you are in company of thousands who suddenly find themselves writers, editors, proofreaders, designers, production managers, and everything else rolled into one. Courage! It is not nearly as difficult as it seems.

Chances are that the first things you start thinking about are type, pictures, color, and page arrangements that are pleasing to the eye. Isn't that the stuff you control? Indeed it is, but Whoa! You are putting the cart before the horse. Have you forgotten about the other part—the background on which the stuff will be printed? That is probably just what you have done, but relax. Why should you be different from everybody else?

Perhaps "forgotten about" is an overstatement. "Taken it for granted" is probably more accurate. It is quite normal not to think about it. Obviously print cannot exist without its substrate. Printing and paper are like yin and yang. That is why you must take the object's physical attributes into account in order to produce excellent communication in print. The paper you print on is not just a neutral, empty surface waiting to be covered. It must be used as an active participant in the communication process.

Take it a step further: when you begin thinking about it, the paper is not merely the physical sheet from which your product is made. More important, if subtler, the paper carries *the space* on which printed matter is arranged. It is vital to take both space and its paper carrier into account in planning, editing, and designing printing.

All this is simply an extension of the most fundamentally obvious realization that if you are to communicate words in print, you have to turn them into little black marks on paper (TYPE). Once the words have been turned into these visual symbols, you have to arrange them in logical groups in the available space. That means you have to organize them on the pages (DESIGN, LAYOUT). The physical attributes of the materials you are working with are inescapable. The words, the type, the paper, the space are all part and parcel of communication. They are the physical, visual aspect of writing and editing. None exists alone.

I said earlier that communication in print isn't as difficult as it appears but I didn't say it is *easy*. Of course, you can follow the patterns based on traditional wisdoms. Many of the software templates are based on them. If the result appears a bit boring, there is an advantage to that: readers will understand it because they have seen it a million times before. By taking the audience's expectations and habits into account, you help them interpret what you say in a cogent way. The speaker (the writer/editor/designer) and the listener (the reader) must speak the same language. But, just as the spoken word can either be monotonously soporific at one end of the scale, or evocatively and even thrillingly compelling at the other, just so can its translation into visual terms be banal or stimulating.

Attack the problem with lateral thinking. What you see on the page can actually be "listened to." See it that way, and you begin to see the complexity of the task as well as the direction to aim in. Doing it well-enough requires following tradition and normal practice. Doing it brilliantly demands self-confidence and insight. Much can be defined and learned. The various insights are interconnected and you need to understand them all in order to use them well. You need to be aware of the *background,* in order to use it actively. You must understand *space* in order to control it.

Everybody examines a printed piece twice, if it has more than a couple of pages. The first time is little more than a fast flip-through. It is a scan to determine size and content, to find the what's-in-there-for-me and to gauge the effort and time its study is likely to take. The second time is when they actually settle down to pay attention and read.

The first overview is vital because that is when the concept of usefulness and value is communicated. That is what makes them *want to* do the studying. Once the reader actually starts reading, then the information takes over. Its fascination speaks for itself, so the piece sells itself. Bringing the potential readers to the point where they realize how well they will be served is the first challenge. This is when the object's physical attributes—especially space—come into play. Space is only remarkable when it is well used. Used generously, luxuriantly, it adds an aura of value. Used strategically, it catapults ideas off the page into the reader's mind because it clarifies and dramatizes them. *This type size is smaller, but even so, people are more likely to read it, because it is set in a comforting white frame.*

The relationship between pages on a spread, and spread to spread. The shape of the spread is horizontal, bigger, wider, and more impressive than just two individual pages stuck together at the gutter. Don't just see pages as stand-alones. Each page is a conjoined twin in a flowing continuum of space.

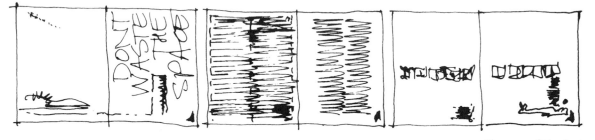

Diagram of the last
thirteen pages
to dramatize
the fact that
the publication
is a medium
that encourages
the deliberate
placement of
one impression
after the next.
The effects
accumulate
synergistically
into a whole
that is greater
and more powerful
than the sum
of its individual
parts. Think
horizontally.

More on this
thinking as a flow
on pages 30–31.

(THIS PAGE LEFT INTENTIONALLY BLANK)

The relationship interrupted.
Few things are more infuriating
than this legal statement on a
blank page in official documents. Forget the annoyance.
Instead, realize how a quiet
moment (a "rest") in music
contrasts, separates, raises
consciousness. Wonderful
blank space acts the same way.

PRODUCT-MAKING

The only printed piece that exists by itself is a single-page envelope stuffer. Stop thinking in single-page terms. Start thinking of pages as a series of events in a sequence, passing by like a parade. Check it out: take any magazine and flip the pages and *become aware of the relationships*. Better checking technique: dismember a couple of copies and then hang the pages in left-to-right sequence around the room. Stand back a bit, so you can see it as a whole.

Assembling a publication is like making a stop / go filmstrip. But a publication is even better than a film strip because each recipient is in personal control, skipping forward, going backward, studying or flipping at her own speed and interest. We must help, orient, guide readers. A magazine is a *collection* by definition, and the whole must be greater than the sum of its parts. That is why we have to rise above the normal single-impression-stuck-to-the-next-single-impression assembly technique and start to exploit its consecutive flow through space. A novel may not need this, but all other print does.

Space flows the way we read, from left to right, across the gutter, and overleaf. It is not static, even though we see it immobile on-screen or as hard-copy. Exploiting the potentials in this underlying motion helps us communicate more vividly and make the product more lively.

STORY-TELLING

To make this concept even more exciting, viewers' reactions to a page are affected by the memory of what they just saw, as well as curiosity about what might be following. Canny communicators exploit this fourth dimension—*time*—to "pace" the product and build in surprises, emotional highs and lows.

This is the sequence shown on pages 26–27. The thinking is analogous to the other examples of **the space/time continuum** shown on these pages. They differ in form, yet they all share one vital characteristic: movement... change... development...

Watching a parade march past: it approaches slowly, files past, the music vibrates, then inevitably they all disappear. You are standing, while they are moving past you, but the marshall has set up the sequence to create contrasts, surprises—i.e., "pacing."

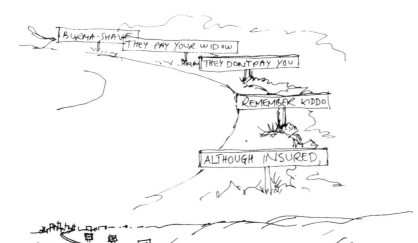

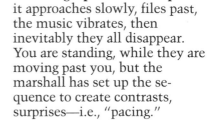

Reading billboards alongside the road. You whizz by them; they just stand there and wait. When traffic was slow and local, BurmaShave were famous for their funny rhymes. Now each sign is carefully honed to make an immediate impression as you drive past—fast.

The business presentation is consciously planned, building up toward climaxes whose bells and whistles are chosen to catch, hold, and persuade you. You are sitting captive to the presenter's timing and emphasis in both voice and images.

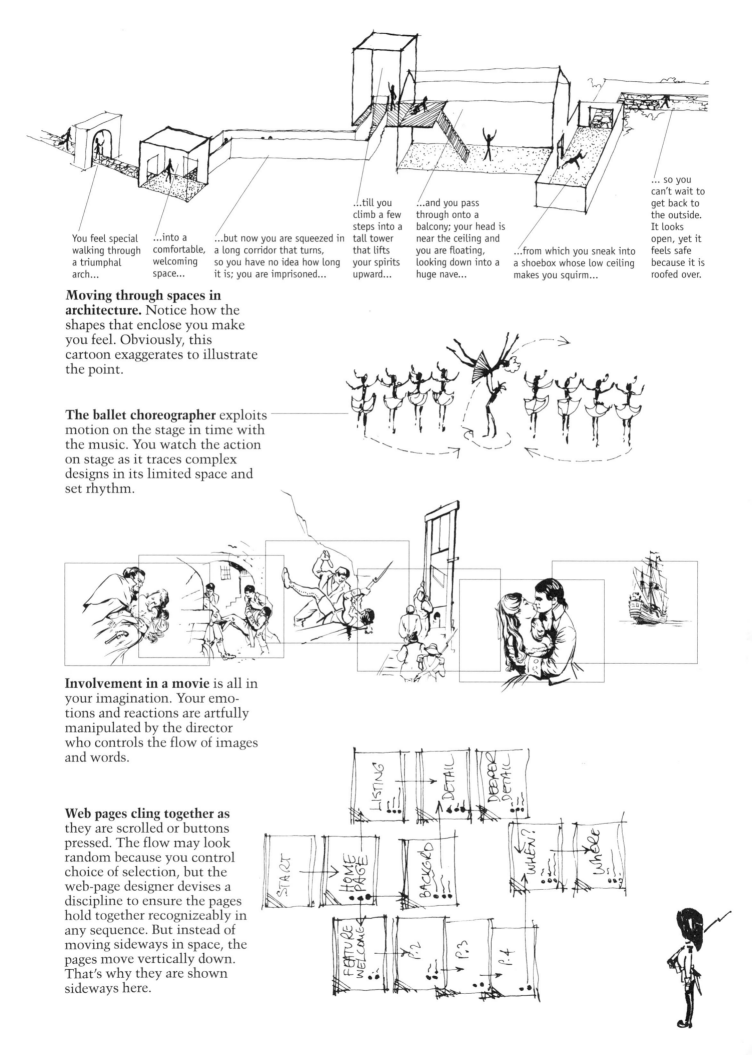

You feel special walking through a triumphal arch...

...into a comfortable, welcoming space...

...but now you are squeezed in a long corridor that turns, so you have no idea how long it is; you are imprisoned...

...till you climb a few steps into a tall tower that lifts your spirits upward...

...and you pass through onto a balcony; your head is near the ceiling and you are floating, looking down into a huge nave...

...from which you sneak into a shoebox whose low ceiling makes you squirm...

... so you can't wait to get back to the outside. It looks open, yet it feels safe because it is roofed over.

Moving through spaces in architecture. Notice how the shapes that enclose you make you feel. Obviously, this cartoon exaggerates to illustrate the point.

The ballet choreographer exploits motion on the stage in time with the music. You watch the action on stage as it traces complex designs in its limited space and set rhythm.

Involvement in a movie is all in your imagination. Your emotions and reactions are artfully manipulated by the director who controls the flow of images and words.

Web pages cling together as they are scrolled or buttons pressed. The flow may look random because you control choice of selection, but the web-page designer devises a discipline to ensure the pages hold together recognizeably in any sequence. But instead of moving sideways in space, the pages move vertically down. That's why they are shown sideways here.

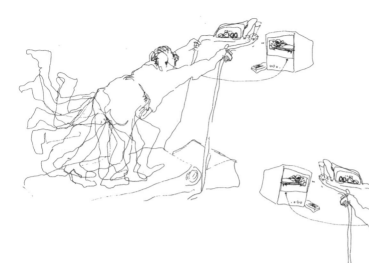

The left-to-right direction flows faster and more naturally than the right-to-left direction. It is only habit—a trained response because we learn to read left-to-right from babyhood. You can run much faster on a left-to-right treadmill. It is more of a workout on a right-to-left one. (Not so in real life, it just feels that way in print).

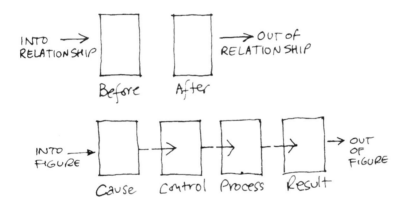

INTO → RELATIONSHIP

→ OUT OF RELATIONSHIP

Before   After

INTO → FIGURE

Cause → Control → Process → Result → OUT OF FIGURE

Flow from left to right would just be an interesting concept, if it were not much more useful. It can be developed to denote

progression…
change…
development.

As such, it can be applied to make editorial meaning clearer. The principle is shown here by means of theoretical little rectangles but it can be expanded to picture-strips or even the handling of full-size pages.

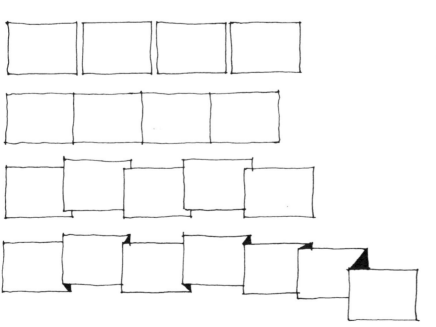

Numbering is made unnecessary when the relationship is shown clearly by alignment and tight spacing. The sequence of steps is faster and the flow between units smoother by butting them.

Overlapping is smoother and faster still. The second overlaps the first, and so on. Folding and blending the units into a single ribbon is done by filling in the corners.

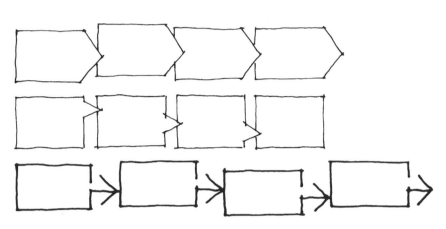

Change in tonality shows progression by controlled steps —in black or in color. Darkest looks closest.

Change in shape (such as combining rectangles with arrows) points up the direction. Pointers can overlap and move up or down to add further emphasis. The arrows themselves can enclose the shape of the boxes.

Change in size implies shrinkage or growth, deterioration or improvement. Overlapping is not necessary but it can dramatize the point.

Change in the rate of repetition indicates speeding up or slowing down. It is shown here as arrows to make the point obvious. It could equally be achieved with rectangles of increasing or decreasing widths.

Change in direction upward means improvement, downward deterioration. Combined with the rate of repetition, you have a promise of hope or warning of impending disaster.

 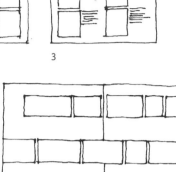 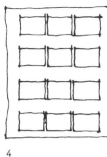 

1 2 3 4 5

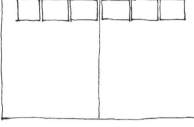

6 7

The left-to-right direction applied to picture strips on the page. There is no clue in **1** because shapes and spacing in both directions are equal. In **2**, shapes and spacing create vertical columns flowing downward. In **3**, captions are attached to each picture. In **4**, the sequence is obviously left-to-right. In **5**, captions explain each step. In **6**, the principle of proximity in sequence jumps the gutter—a safe trick if the horizontal rows are clearly articulated. In **7**, the strips can even be broken into unequal units and the flow continued by the way the bleeds are used.

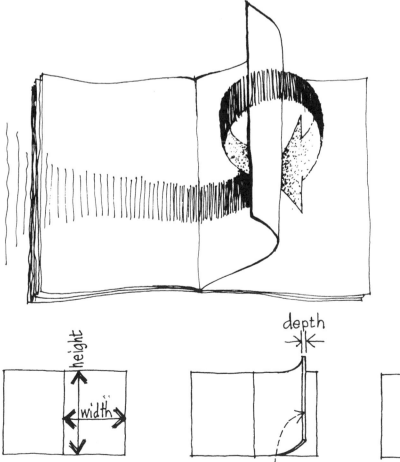

Motion—resulting from the interrelationship of pages to each other—is one of the most useful attributes to making more interesting publications. It is unfortunately seldom used, because we consider our pages to be individual and static. But they aren't. What is on one side is affected by what is on the other: continuation ...or SUR-PRISE! (And that's why this diagram is so large: the point is so important.)

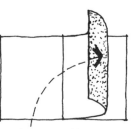

The flat two-dimensional page...   ...has thickness...   ...and a reverse side.

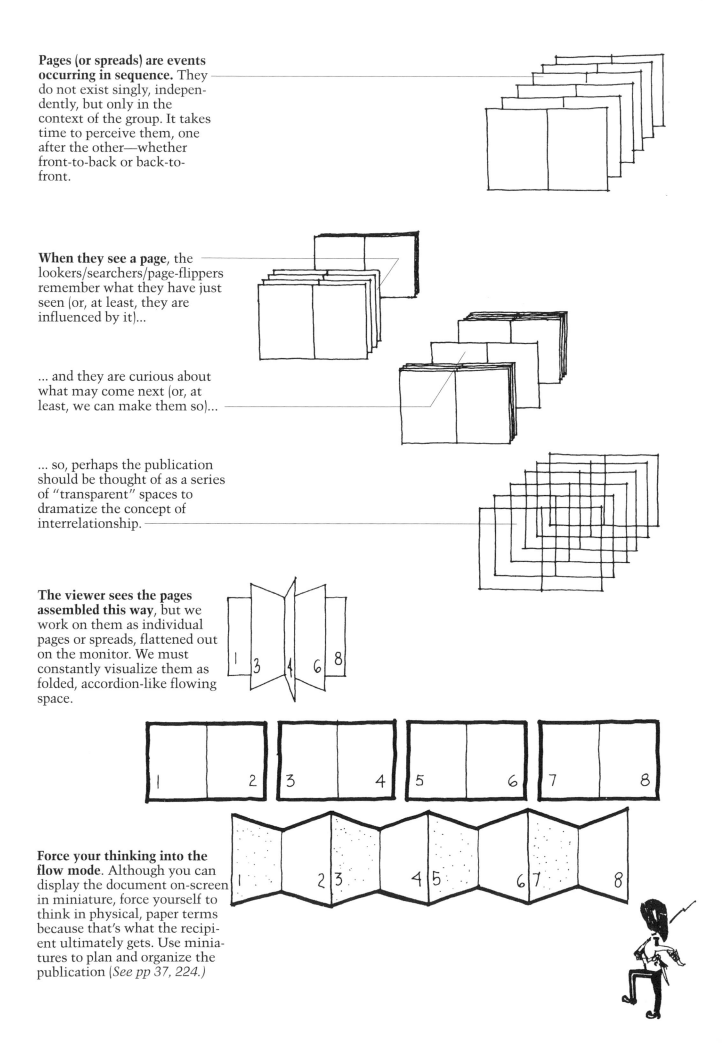

Pages (or spreads) are events occurring in sequence. They do not exist singly, independently, but only in the context of the group. It takes time to perceive them, one after the other—whether front-to-back or back-to-front.

When they see a page, the lookers/searchers/page-flippers remember what they have just seen (or, at least, they are influenced by it)...

... and they are curious about what may come next (or, at least, we can make them so)...

... so, perhaps the publication should be thought of as a series of "transparent" spaces to dramatize the concept of interrelationship.

The viewer sees the pages assembled this way, but we work on them as individual pages or spreads, flattened out on the monitor. We must constantly visualize them as folded, accordion-like flowing space.

Force your thinking into the flow mode. Although you can display the document on-screen in miniature, force yourself to think in physical, paper terms because that's what the recipient ultimately gets. Use miniatures to plan and organize the publication (*See pp 37, 224.*)

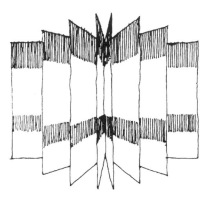

Pages are little vertical units like little soldiers on parade. Emphasizing their verticality is stultifying because the scale of the page is always the same. Break the monotonous sequence of verticals by thinking in spreads: suddenly everything grows in size. Do not think page-by-page or even spread-by-spread but whole-story-by-whole-story. (*See WIDENESS*). That means patterning, repetition, and alignment.

Patterning and repetition are not boring. They create strength and identity. Where every page is different, you perceive chaos and babel. Instead, develop the right format for each story type (*see COLUMNS AND GRIDS*) and play them against each other.

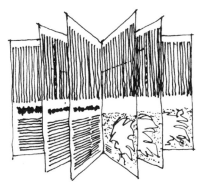

Align tops along a "magic line" to define spaces. The top edge of pictures is the easiest to control and is the most visible. The top of the text area is even more vital to demarcate: not only does it define the space, but the reader is encouraged to continue reading because the top of each column either begins the text or continues it from the previous one.

Think of pages as frames in a cartoon strip and construct the strip frame by frame, impression by impression. Use progression to develop the sequence and tell the story as a flow.

How to exploit flow to make the most of a simple four-page story:

Each page is a separate vertical unit: end of previous story | opener | text | mugshot group | text | independent box. Where is the big 4-page story?

Disintegrating mugshot group, spreading them across page tops, cutting text a bit—sorry about that—aligning column tops unifies the four pages.

Moving box allows 4-page story to start on a left (stronger than a right-hand opener) and close on a right (stronger than a left-hand ender). POW!

Making a story an important event in the issue demands thinking in 3-D. Exploit the flow and horizontal alignment to display interesting stuff across page tops and—most important—shifting things sideways.

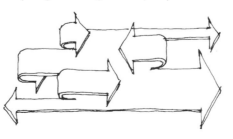

Do you start with the words or pictures? Opening on a spread is more impressive than starting on a right. The physical product also affects the *editorial* decision about starting with text or pictures. Assume the story is about Benjamin Franklin's preference for the Turkey over the Eagle as National Bird.

1. Starting with headline and introduction means this is a treatise on turkeyhood, and the picture is just a sidebar illustration. Worse: the picture is a huge hurdle to jump in order to continue reading text on page 3.

2. Placing picture first couples the left-to-right eye motion with picture-to-text preference. Picture has pride of place, and headline acts as glorified caption. Text flows smoothly overleaf without interruption. Much better than solution 1.

3. When you add the eagle page, the sequence begins to be trickier. Here the story begins and ends with strong images and the text flows smoothly overleaf. Not a bad solution.

4. This starts with theory, interrupts the text, and the pictures can't be compared dramatically because they're back-to-back. The worst of everything combined, yet it is done so often for "variety"—*"If the picture is on the right here, let's put it on the left on the next spread."* Lousy.

5. This utilizes the magazine's flow most effectively: the two birds are seen one-after-the-other for most dramatic comparison, but story still starts with the boring text. However, the story does end with a bang.

6. Here we start with an intriguing picture, then echo its power in a one/two punch on the next left: turkey/eagle. But the text is split and the end is weaker. None is "correct," or ideal, but I'd vote for this, because it makes the story a strong event—**good for the issue**.

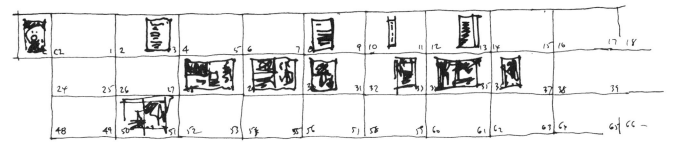

Make hardcopy printouts,
reduced to about 40%, small
enough to lose detail, large
enough to discern patterning.
Crop away excess paper so only
the page is left. Pin them in
their correct numbered cubby-
hole on the pinup wall. Make
the wall as wide as possible, so
you force your thinking into
the left-to-right horizontal flow.

The miniature planning wall
becomes the heart of the
publication-making process,
because it shows not only the
physical object as it is being
assembled, but also scheduling
progress... and lateness!
(Avoid arranging pages vertically
like production and ad-people do,
because they don't need to think
sideways, whereas we do).

**Exploit "pacing" to make the
issue interesting**. When it is
nearly complete, study the wall
display for how the stories
relate to each other. Look for
stories that are "fast" (basically
pictorial) or "slow" (basically
textual) and shift them around
to make the most of their
contrast. This can't be done
ahead of time before the stories
are finished. It is essentially a
visual comparison.

Chart the excitement index.
Assign each story a score between
10 and minus 10 for its degree of
interest. Then swap them around
to make the most of contrasts.
(*See* CHECKING)

**Yes, some people examine a
publications backwards,** but
ignore them, because it is
impossible to please everybody
with a product that has physical shape. Do give them a fun
"start" in the back by placing
something interesting opposite
"cover 3" (the inside back
cover).

Ads placed on successive right-hand pages in the front of the book—each as different as it can be to catch attention. Lefts open for editorial.

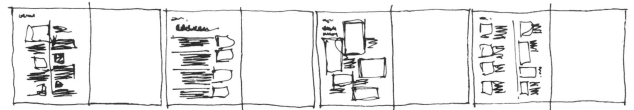

Ambitious editor/designers make each page as different as they can (for variety) despite the fact that they are all the same new products reports.

Put them together and the editorial non-pattern swims into the advertising non-pattern and together they become an indistinguishable blob.

Repeating a pattern (no matter which pattern so long as it is obvious enough) makes editorial stand out against the ads, for the good of both.

Pages scattered among the ads in the front and back need thinking in 3-D even more than multi-page self-sustained feature stories. The more isolated each editorial space is in such "flow-through makeup," the more vital does rigid disciplined repetition become, because it helps editorial spaces to stand out and be recognized. The more ads there are to interrupt the editorial flow, the less "variety" there should (or needs to) be in the look of the editorial pages.

Even carefully controlled rhythm—successive lefts is ideal—requires standardized placement of elements on the left-hand edge. That is the most visible area, so the more steady the effect there, the greater the linkage. This is a mess.

Link pages together with a strong visual trademark. The design of the mark can be anything you wish—in terms of size, color, shape, icons, typography, direction, angle... The only thing that matters: repetition and placement. *(See SIGNALS)*

Plan for only a few major acts
in the issue and keep the rest
cool and quiet. The publication
as a whole is more important
than any of its individual
segments, so it may be necessary to hold back on a particular element for the sake of that
whole. Always view the issue
as a totality, and don't make
the "special" so special that it
no longer belongs to your
product.

Which mountain is tallest?
Each vies for attention so none
is dominant (but it is probably
the far one way in the distance
over at far left). If each page or
spread or story is treated like a
mountain, competing for
attention with its neighbors,
they'll cancel each other out.
You may produce an impressive
mountain range, but if you
want variety by pacing, it is
better to have some mountains
that tower over the others.

A mountain is at its most
impressive when it stands on a
contrasting plain. That plain is
like the grid-like regularity in
our pages—which is what
makes it possible to get a
special story to stand out by
inserting that strategically
placed inconsistency into an
expected context.

**Build in surprises where they
will do you the most good.**
Precede them with quiet pages,
so they stand out best. Arrange
the sequences so as to lead the
reader quietly up to them.

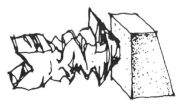

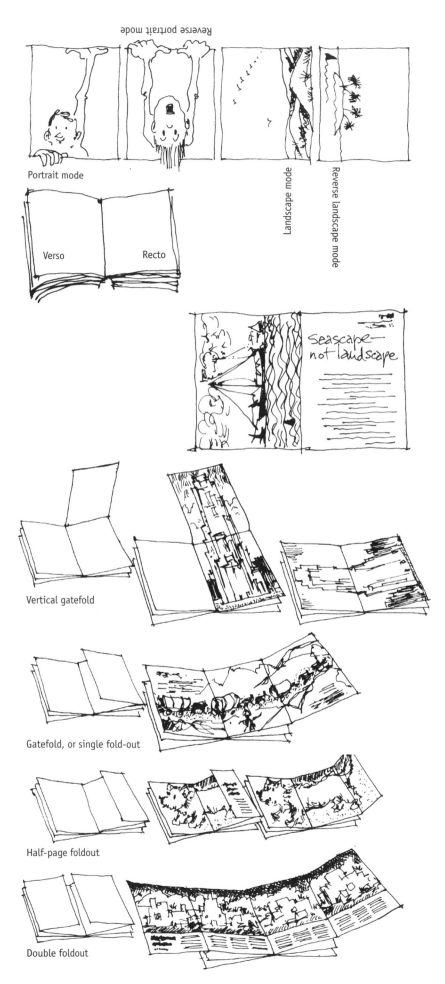

Reverse portrait mode

Portrait mode

Verso   Recto

Landscape mode

Reverse landscape mode

Vertical gatefold

Gatefold, or single fold-out

Half-page foldout

Double foldout

Flow of space in the magazine is predicated on the sequence of page-sized rectangles.

Pages are normally used vertically (in portrait mode). Nonetheless, it is useful to know the nomenclature of the other directions, as is the fact that right-hand pages are called RECTOS (right in Latin), and lefts VERSOS (backward in Latin, like the word reverse).

Landscape format for single pages is rarely used because it is a nuisance to turn the page sideways—unless the material screams for it. The design surface is identical, but the sideways effect is completely different. *(See p. 23)*

Gatefolds seem to be the answer to size and shape, but they are expensive. A vertical gate fits a skyscraper, but requires diecutting, so forget it and settle for the picture sideways across the gutter. Exploit the investment in foldouts to make major editorial points with appropriately impressive visuals.

PRODUCT-MAKING

The essence of multipage (print) or multi-impression (Web) design is the rhythmic repetition of a basic pattern that gives the product its consistent visual character. The structure lends predictability so the viewer/reader intuits the fundamental organization of the piece, feels a sense of order, and even deduces ranking of comparative values of the material.

Developing systematized spatial organization is not difficult for books or products without advertising, but the ads limit the makeup of magazine pages. Standardized column widths are indispensable to accommodate ads of standard widths. As a result, the structure and hence the scale of most magazines look interchangeable and so they look so much alike that superficial distinguishing subtleties have to be added.

A more serious downside of standardization is that it displaces original analytical thinking. It is so much easier to rely on pat solutions, than it is to break away and invent something original when the material justifies it. We think of "pouring stuff into columns" as if they were old bottles. As a result, rigidity dulls the creativity of the editor and designer, gives the publisher an excuse to discourage risk-taking, and engenders boredom in the viewer.

The ideal solution is to resist imprisoning your thinking in the standard format, if you are stuck with one. Instead, treat each article as a separate, distinct unit of varied pattern, within the all-encompassing continuum. The product will hold together if you retain typographic consistency in terms of the fonts, sizes, and line-spacing.

STORY-TELLING

If you devise a pattern that visually reflects and exposes the structure that underpins each story, you'll gain not merely variety for the publication (which is desirable) but it will be sense-making variety (which is even better) and you'll be communicating the ideas in each article more effectively (which is best of all).

Both rigidity and freedom have their own advantages. Why not mix and match?

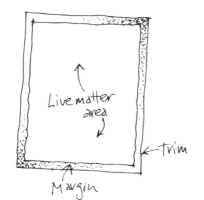

The live-matter area of the page is the area within which the text is printed. It is framed by margins of about half an inch. They serve a practical purpose: to make sure that nothing important gets chopped off in the trimming of the printed product. (The margins can be crossed by images, of course. Elements that go out to the trim and are indeed chopped off are said to "bleed"—for obvious reasons).

Dividing the space into columns of equal width is normal, and since everyone uses it, it is the lowest common denominator. It results in a standardized look because its own simplicity encourages standardized thinking.

Columns can be more than abstract, mathematical subdivisions of a larger space. Their geometry should be a response to *editorial* needs, so there is no reason why column widths should not vary as needed.

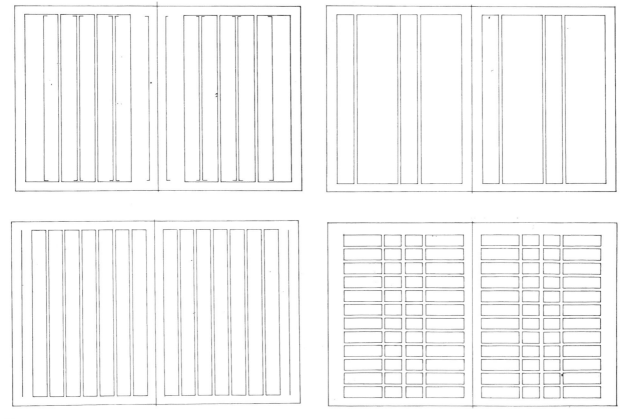

Varied type size and column widths create functional "variety" which guide the viewer to understanding. The bigger the text looks, the more important the viewer assumes it to be. The smaller, the less important. Big type in wide columns is right for pronouncements. Tiny type in narrow columns is right for informal bits and pieces. Clever communication plays off one against the other. *(See p. 97)*

Combining columns of various widths on the same page, within the same story, or between stories is permissible—in fact encouraged—if it helps makes sense. That, in turn, depends on what you are saying and how loud it ought to be.

What the text says and how strongly you want it to be listened to should determine type size and hence the column width. Column widths are more than just mathematical subdivisions of a wider space. The type, its size, the length of the lines (i.e., column width) and spacing between the lines are interconnected. The bigger the type, the wider the column in which it is set should be. The longer the lines, the more space between the lines there should be. Gutters between columns should also vary in proportion. *(See p. 97)*

12/14 Times Roman, 22 picas wide, justified

This type is so large because what it says is believed by the editors to be worthy of being played big and loud. Large type belongs in longer lines than small type does, and it deserves extra spacing between the lines to give it dignity.

This type, on the other hand, represents lesser value in terms of information, news or instruction. It is not set as small as a footnote might be, but it is clearly different from the stentorian pronouncement in the example above, which stands there and orates in a self-important way, bloviating its views and opinions to the four winds. The very texture and appearance of the typography —its size and its column width and its line spacing—create an impression the viewer understands at first glance without even thinking about it. That is an immensely valuable attribute that ought not to be wasted.

8/8.5 Times Roman, 7 picas wide, ragged right

Accommodate functional needs of the wording when assigning column widths; e.g., chemical formulas must have wide columns to avoid breaking them up. So must mathematical equations. By contrast, newspaper stories need narrow columns for quick reading (to reduce the saccadic jumps (sideways eye movements).

The heat-transfer coefficient, U_F, for the fouled exchanger becomes:

$$U_F = 247,500/A\,(24.7) \simeq 10,020/A$$

Hence, the ratio $U_F/U = (10,020/A)/(21,429/A)$, or $U_F \simeq (1/2)U$.

To understand how fouling comes about, let us calculate U empirically from the following equation:

$$\frac{1}{U} = \frac{1}{h_o} + r_o + r_w + r_i\left(\frac{A_o}{A_i}\right) + \frac{1}{h_i}\left(\frac{A_o}{A_i}\right) \qquad (4)$$

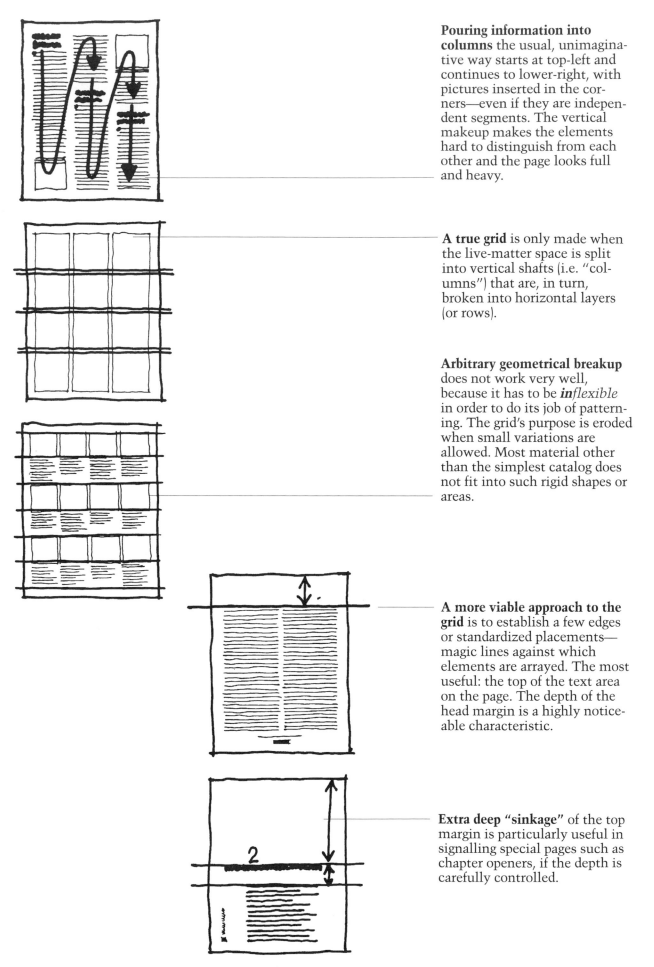

Pouring information into columns the usual, unimaginative way starts at top-left and continues to lower-right, with pictures inserted in the corners—even if they are independent segments. The vertical makeup makes the elements hard to distinguish from each other and the page looks full and heavy.

A true grid is only made when the live-matter space is split into vertical shafts (i.e. "columns") that are, in turn, broken into horizontal layers (or rows).

Arbitrary geometrical breakup does not work very well, because it has to be *inflexible* in order to do its job of patterning. The grid's purpose is eroded when small variations are allowed. Most material other than the simplest catalog does not fit into such rigid shapes or areas.

A more viable approach to the grid is to establish a few edges or standardized placements—magic lines against which elements are arrayed. The most useful: the top of the text area on the page. The depth of the head margin is a highly noticeable characteristic.

Extra deep "sinkage" of the top margin is particularly useful in signalling special pages such as chapter openers, if the depth is carefully controlled.

Breaking the space on the page into horizontal blocks, the viewer recognizes the three separate information segments at first glance. (The first one to be read will be the shortest, because it demands the least time and effort.)

Space is the essential ingredient. There are two distinct, self-contained stories on this page. We are used to crowding, because that is the way newspapers used to be assembled, therefore, typically, very little space is used to separate them from each other. It is easy to separate stories from each other on the page in the *north-south* direction. All you need to do to dig a moat of space between them is to skip a few lines. The articulation of the elements is immediate, obvious, and helpful.

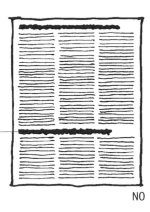

NO   YES

Separation of elements in the *east-west* direction is impossible, because the column structure is rigid if all the space is used, as it normally is, no matter into how many columns the page may be subdivided. But if the columns are slightly narrower than the maximum, (i.e. if some space is "wasted"), extra space can be added to the margins, or the extra slivers of space can be accumulated and used actively to separate story from story—sideways. Result: clarity of organization in both directions. The sketch is exaggerated to make the point clear. You don't need more than a pica or two for this clarifying trick to work in real life.

Extra wide column-gutters allow vertical placement of identifiers or topic subjects.

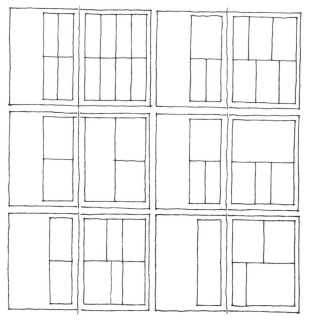

Variety: Grids must not be straitjackets. They should be helpful tools. There is no reason why a publication should not be constructed on a basis of several related ones, each of which is appropriate for a specific use.

Grids can be any shape, any size. This one is unusual because it only covers three-quarters of a spread. It also illustrates the variety of shapes even such a simple set of divisions as this can conjure up.

ONE COLUMN

All available space is used, but it looks like a letter. The page feels heavy and the type is hard to read unless it is made larger and generously linespaced to compensate for the overly long line length. Therefore it accommodates less material than one might have hoped.

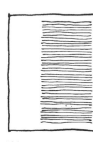

This narrower type column is much easier to read, because the lines are shorter. It can probably contain as many words as the full-page version, because the type can be smaller. The off-center look is dynamic.

Centered column: looks serious and "dignified" enough to seem stodgy.

Exposing headings in space attracts attention to them. Using the "wasted" space at left for "hanging indents" is the ideal way to make the material easy to scan.

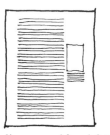

Since we read from left to right, material at left is perceived to be more important than at the right. Placing the empty, narrow column to the right of the main text is perfect for secondary matter such as annotations, comments, small pictures, mugshots, biographies, cross-references and so forth.

The centered narrow column leaves space on either side for hanging indents at left and marginalia at right. It may look busy, but it is active and easy to take.

TWO COLUMNS

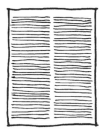

The space used to the maximum: two columns squeeze in a lot of information, but it looks dull and uninviting, unless the text is broken up with display material.

Two columns set a trifle narrower than the maximum leave a narrow space in which to hang indents...

...or insert paragraphs of text at maximum width. The "color" (boldness) of type can be varied. Set the right-hand edge justified or ragged, to help distinguish the two sets of materials.

Extra-wide margins can be invaded by headings that hang to the left or the right. To tie the headings to text, underline them with column-wide rules.

Two narrow columns placed at the center: dramatic use can be made of the space added to the margins.

Two very narrow columns placed off-center leave spaces that encourage active exploitation and unexpected arrangements.

REE COLUMNS

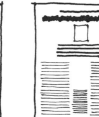

e columns:
nal, expected,
nary,
xciting but
 to work with,
gh this
ngement
ourages
ovative page
ngements.

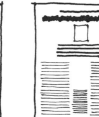

Type set ragged-right to make it easier to read (by keeping the word- and letter-spacing predictably standardized). Vertical column rules are needed to make the pages neat and precise.

Three columns slightly narrower than the maximum: the saved space is added to the outside margin to make space for a rule, decorative feature, page number, catalog-label etc.

FOUR COLUMNS

Reducing column width to four per page calls for smaller type size. Leaving one column empty creates unexpected and dramatic results and uses less space than the same effect in three-column makeup.

Doubling up two adjacent columns and inserting larger type gives opportunity to emphasize important matter.

Four columns allow many layout variations, yet retain a crisp, neat feel. Picture and type sizes can be made to vary quite dramatically for emphasis and variety.

COLUMNS

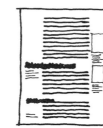

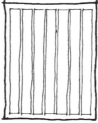

page is
d into five,
ery narrow
ns demand
e of tiny
But this
ement allows
ive doubling
ling of
ent columns.

In this formal arrangement the two outer columns have been combined and filled with medium sized type, distinguishing the single central column with tiny type. The bold deck uses the three central columns.

Combining columns allows an infinity of unexpected variations. This simple one combines the central three using large type, to contrast with the outer ones that carry small sidebar matter.

SEVEN COLUMNS

A single one-seventh is too narrow for type, but if you think of combining columns, a flexible tool is at your command.

Two columns use doubled-up sevenths, and the third column combines the remaining three. The wider the column, the larger the type size can (should) be.

Four columns are combined into a single wide one to give voice to an extremely important statement. One column is left empty except for a tiny mugshot and bio. The farthest right combines two sevenths and carries normal-sized type.

amples of flexibility (seven-column page)

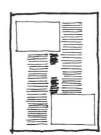

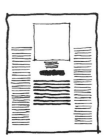

These six page diagrams illustrate flexibility of a particular struc-tural scheme. The important point is not that they provide an *infinity of arrangements*, but that they make a *variety of expression* possible. **Flexibility is only significant if it is put to use expressing and clarifying the content of the story...**

YES

1: A "READ":

Ten examples of formats to show off story structures

If the publication's usual grid needs breaking to make the story more vivid, break it. If typefaces remain consistent throughout, the issue will hold together.

This looks like a good "read" and it will be read if the subscribers are already sold on the subject, if the catchy headline is provocative, or if the respected author is worth listening to. But you aren't too likely to convert too many nonreaders—which is OK! You can't expect everyone to cotton to everything. Not everything can or should be exciting, especially not if the excitement is artificially hyped. Phony excitement is recognized immediately and the credibility of the entire publication becomes suspect.

NO

YES

2: A PROVOCATIVE MESSAGE:

Catching the viewers and persuading them to *want to* read is normally done by the headline. If the subject is important, the headline is made to scream very loud. Then the message itself is buried down in the normal text. The importance of the message would be exposed more dramatically, if the words that contain it were allowed to be the dominant. Let them do the screaming and let the headline merely define the topic. Too many headlines nowadays are too big anyway, so their size has lost implied value.

NO   YES

3: A Q&A STORY: This also looks like a good, smooth read. At first glance it has the same shape as the flowing text above. But it isn't running text, it is a string of twinned units: question/answers. How often have you found yourself skipping around among questions to find just the one you are interested in? Few plough through from start to finish of anything, let alone when it's made up of small bits.

Rearrange the space to make them look the way the piece is written: Pull the questions out of the mainstream into columns of their own. The columns can be narrower, because questions are usually shorter. The result will look startlingly different, showing two equals conversing side-by-side. Also it can be scanned fast to find that interesting question.

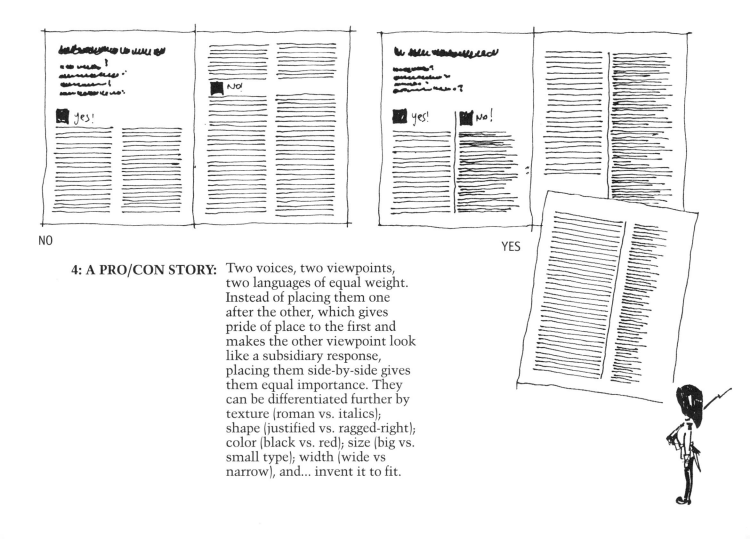

NO   YES

4: A PRO/CON STORY: Two voices, two viewpoints, two languages of equal weight. Instead of placing them one after the other, which gives pride of place to the first and makes the other viewpoint look like a subsidiary response, placing them side-by-side gives them equal importance. They can be differentiated further by texture (roman vs. italics); shape (justified vs. ragged-right); color (black vs. red); size (big vs. small type); width (wide vs narrow), and... invent it to fit.

5: TEXT WITH COMMENTS: Footnotes and cross-references are usually at the foot of the bottom of the page (the "foot"—that's why they are called footnotes). What a nuisance they are to find and link with their referents, if there are many, even if the cross-reffing symbols are large enough to recognize and understand. Why not run them alongside the text at the right, in the tiny type often seen in the exegeses in many Bibles?

The format will look different, learnèd, and intriguing. Lots of people will start with one of the footnotes in tiny type, just because they are cute and tiny, and such an unusual treatment arouses curiosity. And the story definitely does not look like the running text of a novel.

6: TEXT WITH QUOTES: Imagine a three-page Round Table report, with mugshots of the participants and an interesting comment from each. Instead of busting up the running report with inserted mugs and quotes, give the text journalistic importance and intellectual dignity. Display it as clean, clear, running text. The subject is worth it (else why run it?) Give the story heft with a big overall photo.

And the quotes and mugshots? They go where they will do the issue the most good: where they will be seen—across the page tops—in a "discussion" sequence. Readers love short bits: use them to get them involved in the substance— which they will have to find in the text, below.

7: TEXT WITH SIDEBARS: A four-page story on an important large topic can well be improved by breaking out subsidiary topics into sidebar boxes. That reduces the apparent text length, and it gives the editors additional opportunities to catch readers by means of interesting headlines on each box. It can, however, look like a disorganized mess, with pages peppered with uncoordinated bits and pieces. Solution: Break the space into two parts, the dominant, upper part carries the main thrust of the story with big, imposing pictures and smooth, easy-to-read text. Below a hairline rule separating the two areas go the various bits and pieces in a much smaller, more intimate, more informal contrasting scale. Two-tiered information in two separate tones of voice.

NO
YES

8: TEXT CLUSTERS: At first glance this looks like an article consisting of running text with subheads thrown in "to break it up." (The newspaper axiom: a subhead or crosshead every six inches—whether it makes sense or not). On closer inspection you discover that this is just an "umbrella" headline over a cluster of short, related items. Running them vertically makes them harder to scan, identify, and choose. Explaining their commonalities in the deck and displaying the choices horizontally is an immediate clue to what the "story" really is: it is not one long broken-up entity, but four separate individual items, related to each other in some way. The choice of which to read first (if any) is far easier and it is made in the light of understanding the context.

NO

YES

9: TEXT AND PICTURES: Far too often, the text is reduced to a neutral gray background invaded by the "interesting stuff," the pictures. Pictures are always more powerful than text, but it is normally the text that contains the information. Instead of "breaking it up" to make it look "shorter," we must coddle and protect the text, because it is valuable. It does not look very important here. Organize the material in the space differently: group the pictures into a self-contained cluster, then set them off against the self-contained text. That way they can fulfill their function of arousing curiosity and attracting attention. The text gains authority and dignity by being treated as a worthy element in its own right—which is precisely what it is. It is something to be displayed with pride, not cut up and camouflaged.

YES,
but only
if it is
really
well done

10. RANDOM PAGE LAYOUT: You can indeed forget all about the discipline of grids and assemble the pages using each information unit as a separate rectangular area. Here, the four-page presentation is constructed in such a way that each unit is discrete and can be noticed and identified as itself. Undoubtedly, this can make for interesting-looking pages. But it is extremely difficult to do—far more difficult than simply fitting things into pre-existing boundaries. It is also far more time-consuming. Doing it well, so the pages don't look like an unkempt heap of uncoordinated bits and pieces, demands uncommon skills that combine editing with layout. Also essential: enough lead-time and patience.

Margins are more than just that sliver of dead paper framing and surrounding the live-matter area. The temptation is to keep them down to the minimum width, in order to waste as little space as possible, but they can add value if they are used purposefully.

PRODUCT-MAKING

Margins contribute actively—if perhaps subliminally—to the effect the overall product has on the skimmers and page-flippers when they riffle the pages. The white spaces' steady, expected regularity creates a sense of comfort and belonging. They also act like picture-frames, defining, enriching, supporting, embellishing what they enclose.

The outer perimeter of what we look at is a vital clue to our recognizing what it is. It is not a conscious process but simply there, built into the way we perceive.

What is this?

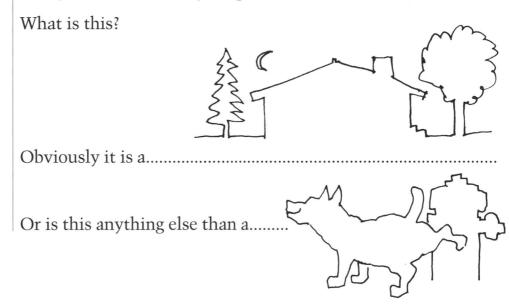

Obviously it is a..

Or is this anything else than a.........

STORY-TELLING

Repetition (from page to page) makes this recognition of shape an effective tool, because it welds the parts into a whole. Paradoxically, it can also add surprise by breaking that very steadiness. When the pattern of expected framing is interrupted, the margins can be used deliberately to tickle the viewers' curiosity and so pull them into the story on that page.

Head or top margin

Back or gutter margin

Outside, side or fore-edge margin

Tail, foot or bottom margin

½"

Margins don't have to be the standard half-inch wide. That's only the rule-of-thumb minimum to make sure that nothing important gets trimmed off after the publication is bound.

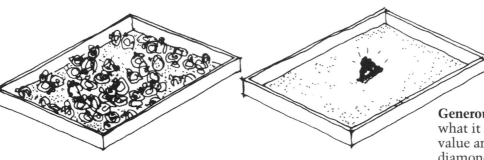

Generous framing dignifies what it encloses with an aura of value and a sense of luxury. A diamond ring looks special, displayed alone on a velvet-lined tray. A unique, isolated object looks more important (and costly) than if it were sunk among dozens of others.

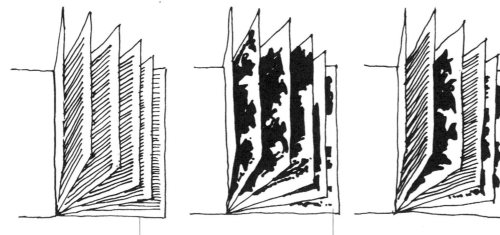

The outer margins create a pattern of expected framing as pages are flipped and scanned. Their controlled, consistent regularity defines them as part of the larger editorial package. That contrasts with the ads, whose perimeters are usually much more irregular.

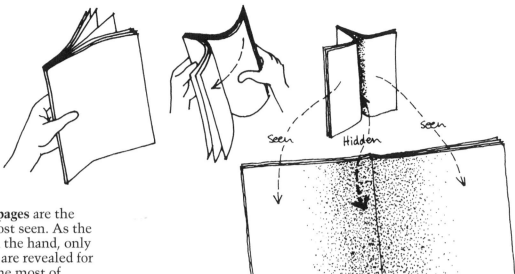

The outsides of pages are the areas that are most seen. As the pages are held in the hand, only the outer halves are revealed for flipping. Make the most of them. Put the best stuff where it will be most visible and will therefore do you the most good. People are attracted by pictures, display type (that says something interesting) and short bits of all kinds. That's where they ought to go.

The width of the inner margins is affected by the way the piece is bound. Make it easy for the reader: prevent the type from hiding in the gutter in very thick publications by making the inside ("gutter") margin wider than normal. Saddle stitched and perfect bound publications can have the narrowest inside margins, but sidewire needs nearly as generous a space as three-hole punch or mechanical binding.

saddle stitched   side-wire   mechanical

Bleeding creates an illusion in which the image seems to extend off the edge of the page into the space beyond. The printed part is perceived as just a small slice of a larger whole. Bleeding enlarges the page in the viewer's imagination, and that strengthens the impact not only of the page, but also of the subject of the picture. So don't waste bleeds on product shots, whose bland background is just background. Reserve it for uses where such expansion is meaningful. Here, the sky continues upward off the page, the foreground downward, the horizon sideways, left and right.

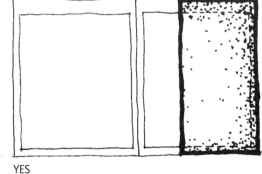

NO   YES

Get attention with a strong bleed. It destroys a portion of the frame and thus eliminates a small piece of the pattern the viewer expects. The value of the image justifies damaging the pattern. So avoid insignificant minibleeds and bleed big.

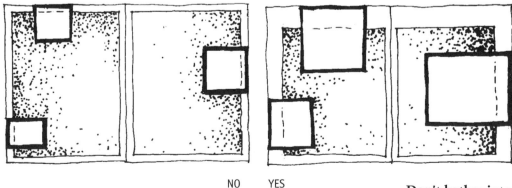

NO   YES

Don't bother interrupting a narrow frame with a small picture—there is little point to pulling a special stunt that nobody notices. To achieve maximum effect jump big pictures across a deep frame.

Make the top margin deeper than you think it need be. That isn't a waste of space, even though it could be filled with an extra couple of lines'-worth of words. The higher up the page the text goes, the more oppressive and aggressive the page is seen to be. A generous top margin ("deep sinkage") creates a light and relaxed feeling for the editorial product. It is also a better background for signals, which are more noticeable in more space.

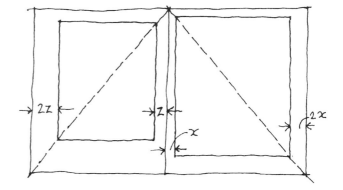

The traditional way to determine well-proportioned book margins: 1) draw diagonal lines; 2) place the outside margins where you want them to be; 3) where they hit the diagonals are the foot margins; 4) the gutter margin is half the width of the outside margin; 5) where its lines hit the diagonals are the positions for the head margins. Two variations illustrate the method.

Leave an extra-wide swath of space (like the old "scholar's margin" for making notes in books) as open space for ancillary material such as the mugshot of the author, bio, byline, footnotes, cross-refs, locator maps, etc.

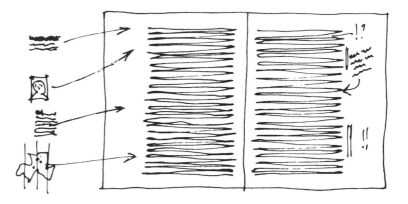

Break out of the framed area into the surroundings to pull the eye to the dramatic element hanging out there. As a pokeout from a graph focuses the eye on the displayed element, so the page can be manipulated to take advantage of this curiosity-arousing trick.

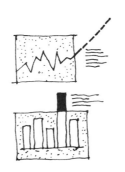

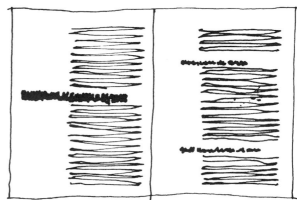

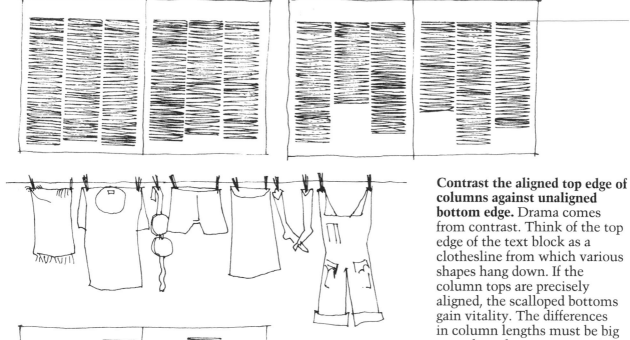

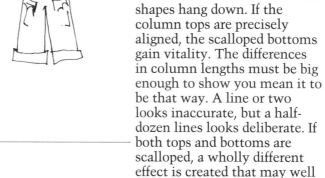

Contrast the aligned top edge of columns against unaligned bottom edge. Drama comes from contrast. Think of the top edge of the text block as a clothesline from which various shapes hang down. If the column tops are precisely aligned, the scalloped bottoms gain vitality. The differences in column lengths must be big enough to show you mean it to be that way. A line or two looks inaccurate, but a half-dozen lines looks deliberate. If both tops and bottoms are scalloped, a wholly different effect is created that may well be another useful pattern.

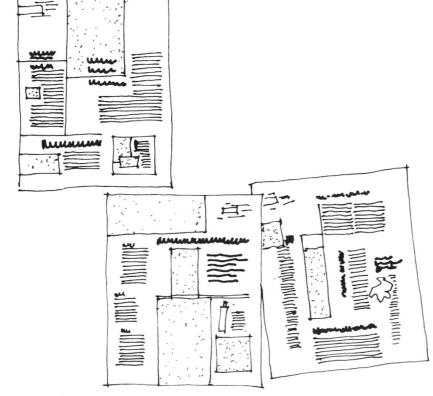

An alternative to controlled margins: ignoring them. They can simply flow into the rest of the white space as neutral background on which to place pictorial and/or textual units in random arrangement. Each unit is seen as a separate information zone. This technique is particularly popular now that page makeup is free and no longer depends on the column structure that metal (and even photographic) page makeup used to dictate. Breaking away from the patterned restriction of column structure is fine, if it is done carefully—which isn't as easy as it looks. However, when you cancel the recognition that standardized margins give, you run the risk that such harder-to-recognize editorial spaces will look like ads. Weigh the pros and cons, then decide.

Don't think of space (i.e., blank area) as though it were neutral, unimportant background. It is a valuable potential resource. Like the yin and yang, the printed bits cannot exist without the blank ones.

PRODUCT-MAKING | Space is always there, ready to be used—not just as swaths of white emptiness (elegant though they might be) but as an active participant in the process of clarifying ideas. As such, it is invaluable. It is an infinitely flexible tool and doesn't cost any more than just the paper itself. Bring it to the foreground and see it as a functional partner in communicating ideas.

This space is working

as an active

separator between

the PRODUCT-MAKING text above,

and the STORY-TELLING text below.

Obviously, it is far deeper

than it need be,

but that's acceptable

because it is just

an exaggerated example.

Narrower wedges separate

the four ideas

in the numbered list

down below.

STORY-TELLING | Our greatest service to readers is to do as much of the thinking-work for them as possible—simply put, *presenting the information they need **clearly**.* Therefore:

1. Concentrate on relevance to the target audience.

2. Edit to pick out the elements that will fascinate them.

3. Design to show them off.

4. Use space to organize the information.

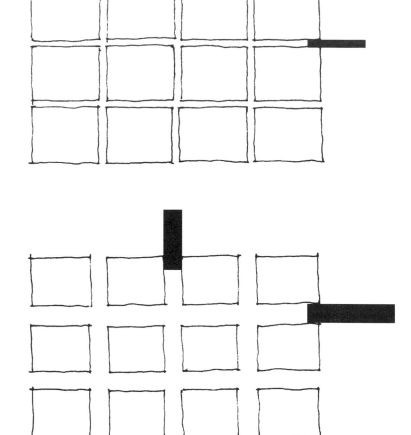

Equal spacing, narrow. A group of a dozen units, with equal spaces between them, looks like a single rectangular block. If the units represented a series of actions (one-two-three) would you read the units from left-to-right in rows, or up-and-down in columns? There is no certainty, since the geometrical arrangement gives no clue and equal space between things is neutral, clueless, not helpful. (Only study of the objects themselves would give the clue what the serial logic might be.)

Equal spacing, wide. Has that additional space made any difference to understandability? No—other than making a larger and looser conglomeration and forcing the units to be smaller than perhaps they need be. The rectangular block-as-a-whole is still the dominant element.

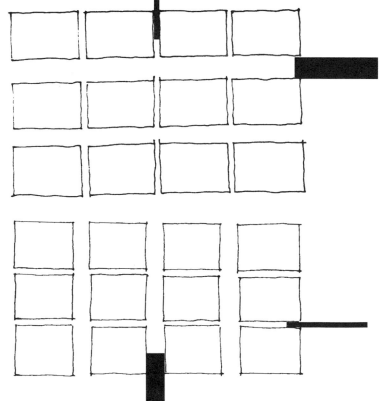

Unequal spacing. Without thinking or analyzing—or counting—you just know at first glance that there are three separate layers of units and that you would read them from left-to-right. Or below, you know there are four columns of three and that you would read them from top-to-bottom.

Isolation in space creates value. The object displayed in lonely splendor is perceived as important because all competition has been pushed aside, outside the confines of the frame that encloses and defines the space. The larger the area reserved for it and the smaller the object, the more dramatic the contrast and therefore the greater the perceived value.

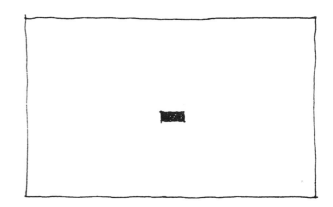

Crowding devalues the individual unit. Each widget is not particularly valuable here—look how many of them there are! Their very number and agglomeration makes them common and unimportant. But much depends on context and what you are trying to say; a vast number of unimportant widgets could also be perceived as an impressive mass.

Random placement. The spaces-between need not be strictly aligned or placed in geometrically precise parallels. The effects are just as discernible in irregular relationship as in regular ones, if the units that go to make up the whole are more or less of equal shape. Here the group has been broken into four obvious "columns," despite the fact that the units dance around.

Exploit the contrast between vertical and horizontal. Both directions are essential parts of the makeup of a page. Playing them against each other creates interest, variety, surprise. Which is *better*? Neither. Choice of shape depends on the pictorial material (landscape versus giraffes), its meaning, its purpose. Tiny type in narrow columns, big type in wide ones.

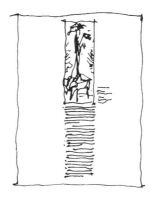

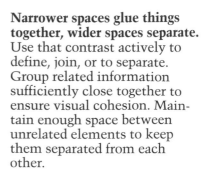

Narrower spaces glue things together, wider spaces separate. Use that contrast actively to define, join, or to separate. Group related information sufficiently close together to ensure visual cohesion. Maintain enough space between unrelated elements to keep them separated from each other.

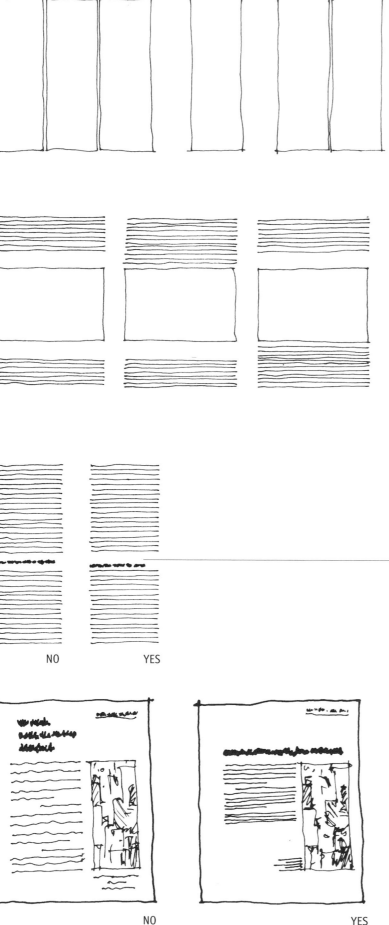

Closeness explains relationships. The picture at far left floats halfway between the text above and below it. Since the space is identical, the picture "belongs" to neither. In the middle column it belongs to the end of the upper text as an afterthought or postscript. In the example at right, it belongs to the text below it. (Pictures attract attention, so they should be exploited as "thought-starters." Which of these three is most useful that way?)

More space above headings and less space beneath them makes them belong to the text below. A subhead in a column of running text is neutral, if it is inserted halfway between the preceding paragraph and the following one. Yet the function of the subhead is to draw the reader into the text below. It succeeds if the spaces are unequal and it is obviously closer to the start.

NO   YES

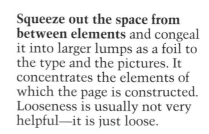

Squeeze out the space from between elements and congeal it into larger lumps as a foil to the type and the pictures. It concentrates the elements of which the page is constructed. Looseness is usually not very helpful—it is just loose.

NO   YES

Set headings flush-left to create a worthwhile wedge of white space at right. The blackness of the type stands out better when it is contrasted against that larger area of "empty" white space. Centering the head over the columns divides that valuable white space into two insignificant halves.

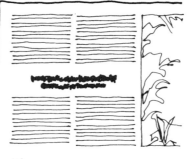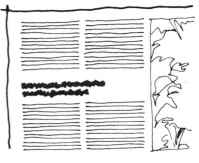

NO   YES

Don't center the headline atop type that is set ragged right. Balancing it on a column whose right-hand edge looks as though it had been nibbled away not only looks uncomfortable but it leaves empty spaces that look very untidy (and can't even be fixed with a vertical rule).

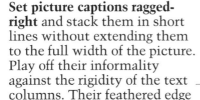

NO   YES

Set picture captions ragged-right and stack them in short lines without extending them to the full width of the picture. Play off their informality against the rigidity of the text columns. Their feathered edge lets in a little air that lightens the page. The arrangement adds sparkle by contrast of dark against light, solid against void.

What about that old bugaboo of "Trapped Space"—one of those sins one has been taught never to commit? Forget rules because they can mislead. By definition, a hunk or strip of space used as an active separator is obviously "trapped," since it is a barrier between things. If a barrier is what you need, then go ahead and put it in, whether it is trapped space or not. Use common sense.

Yes, this is trapped space that does nothing but draw attention to itself. Avoid that.

Use spacing to highlight value.
It is not essential to have a lot of space surrounding an object to give it its own special importance. You just need a little bit more than normal or slightly wider than the spaces that can be seen separating the other elements on the page. The trick is merely to compare the slightly wider against the normal narrower.

The space surrounding an object must be geometrically and precisely defined if it is to create dramatic contrast. The perimeter of the space can't be fuzzy. The edges have to align and the corners need to be neatly squared off, if it is to have the desired visual impact.

NO

YES

Use spacing to guide the viewer.
Pages that contain several stories need to be composed to help the reader navigate. The more regular the spacing between things—the blander the mosaic—the more unhelpful it is, and therefore the less welcoming the page seems to appear.

However, the more varied the spaces-between are, the more obvious do the individual clusters of information become. The big mass is broken down into its component parts and the viewer understands instinctively what belongs to what (which is always helpful) and how long something may take to read.

The small quick in-and-out segments get highest readership. People always read the short bits first because they demand the least effort. The short bits are made obvious by the space that isolates them.

Pages are not lonely little objects hung on the wall to be admired like paintings. They are events in a series or links in a chain, because a multi-page publication is a *collection*, and the flowing whole is (or should be) greater than the sum of its parts. Yet, as you flip through magazines, you become conscious of a monotony due to the sameness of scale—that constant repetitive single vertical page shape.

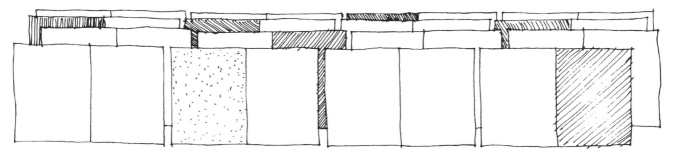

PRODUCT-MAKING | Break the tyranny of the single-page vertical proportion and build in surprises of unexpected scale at crucial nodes in the stream. If nothing else, jump the gutter with a big picture in order to break that vertical proportion. It will help to make the product more varied and thus more interesting.

Where Web rather than paper pages are concerned, the horizontal proportion is there at the start. The continuity is not horizontal—sideways—but vertical—scrolling down. The same principle applies to both kinds: the whole must be handled to exploit its muchness.

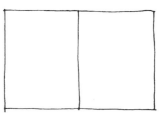

STORY-TELLING | Focus attention on important elements by making them bigger and noticed. Assemble the material horizontally in wide, deliberately more impressive spreads to emphasize key points and make the story more vivid. Big images are also remembered better because they are more powerful.

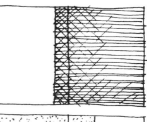

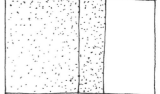

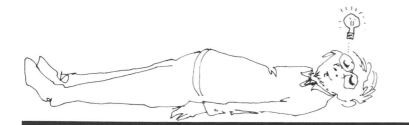

The examples of techniques on the next five pages follow no logical sequence. Each communication problem carries within itself the seeds of its own solution. The one essential they all have in common is just to think horizontally.

There is an infinity of examples and variations on thinking sideways. Each situation is different, because each story is assembled from different raw materials and each has a different purpose. Since they all demand different emphasis and proportions, there can be no rules, but that is what makes publication-making such fun. Here are a few "layouts" from the CONTRAST chapter where each is analyzed individually. They are bunched here just to emphasize the point of variety.

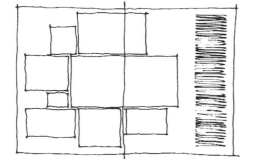

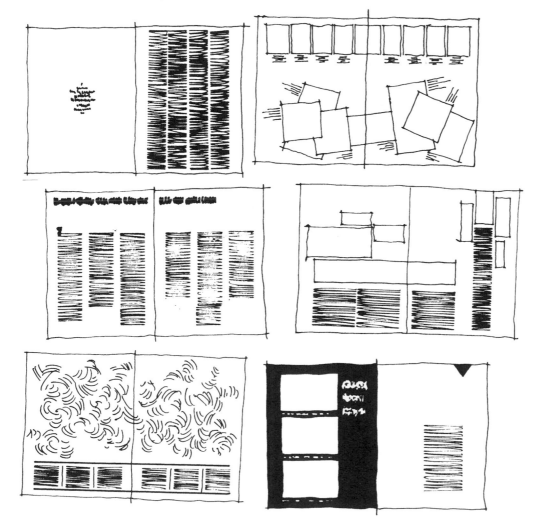

Align the eye level of people, even if the picture shapes do not align. The horizon (or eye-level, when there is no obvious horizon) is a vitally important reference point for us as humans. It may be subconscious in nature, but in the illusion that printed pages are, you can use it consciously to create a feeling of comfort, rightness—and width.

Echo or mirror a shape on both pages. It needs to be small so that the background emptiness in which it is to be noticed can be generous. The shape should also be geometrically simple in order to make the relationship evident. If the shapes are obviously identical, then neither the content of each shape nor the color of the background need be identical. Picture versus text... white versus black... it is the *"versus"* that gives life to the linking.

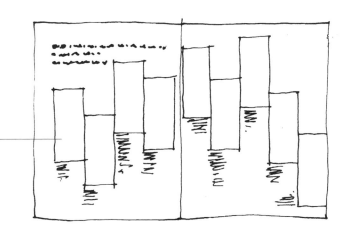

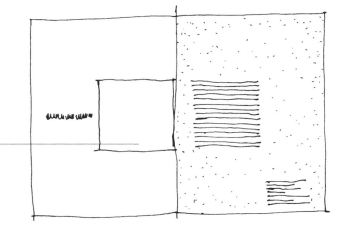

Jump the gutter with a string of like-shaped, like-sized elements. So long as the shapes themselves are sufficiently recognizable, alignment is unnecessary. (It would probably be visually boring, if the little boxes weren't dancing up and down.) The horizontal linkage is more obvious still, if the subjects inside the shapes are also related (tall pots, full-length portraits, a family of giraffes).

A full-bleed photo is impressive because the vastness of the space within it seems to spill out beyond the confines of the paper. Increase its impact by contrasting it with a smaller image insrted into it.

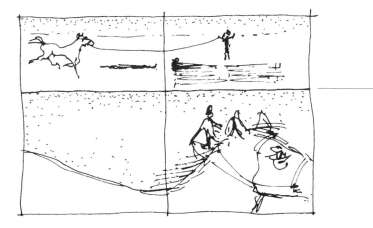

The drama of an extra-wide panorama is more than twice as strong when the **space is split into two horizontal strips**. Their pull is increased if the images can be made to work together in a one-two punch, as in this case, where the upper is a long shot of a horse being trained and the lower is an exaggerated close-up.

Demarcate the head and foot of the page with a graphic element such as a swath of color or bold rule to emphasize the horizontality of the spaces. If you then also use that upper space for a frieze of tiny images of some sort, the contrast becomes powerful. A square hole in each of the text doughnuts gives a contrasting play of squareness to the horizontality that makes the spread come alive.

Horizontal alignment from side to side is the most fundamental, simplest, most basic, obvious width-creating technique of all.

Color links intuitively. If you have a red heart on one side and a red lobster on the other, their shared redness will imply belonging to each other whether that makes sense or not. Turn this instinctive capacity to advantage to tabulate and organize information. It works best when there are no competing colors around to confuse the intended linkage.

Exploit the fact that we read left-to-right so that there is a built-in sense of direction: from... to... and... before... after. There is an inherent logic to the left-towards-the-right flow that communicates intuitively and in the process helps create an awareness of horizontal size—width.

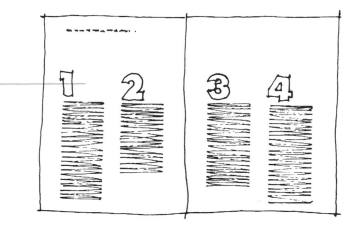

Leave the left- and right-hand edges empty to make the spread look wider. Use the inner area of the spread for a dramatic image. Here the silhouetted figure captures its surrounding white space, thereby turning it into an active background. The effect is heightened by the text wrapping around the edge of the figure.

Two smaller pictures can achieve the impact of width, if their subject is closely and obviously allied, so that their CONCEPT (rain and umbrella) is unified. But don't fall in the page/page trap as at left. Jump the gutter with the dominant.

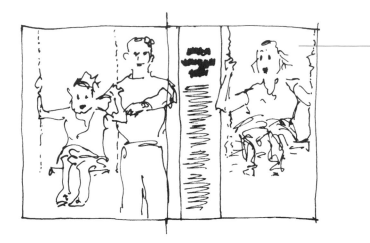

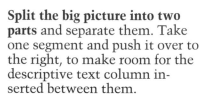
Split the big picture into two parts and separate them. Take one segment and push it over to the right, to make room for the descriptive text column inserted between them.

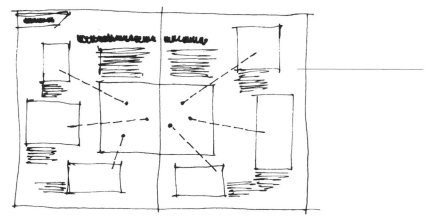

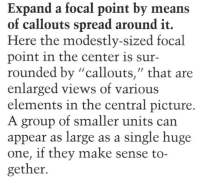
Expand a focal point by means of callouts spread around it. Here the modestly-sized focal point in the center is surrounded by "callouts," that are enlarged views of various elements in the central picture. A group of smaller units can appear as large as a single huge one, if they make sense together.

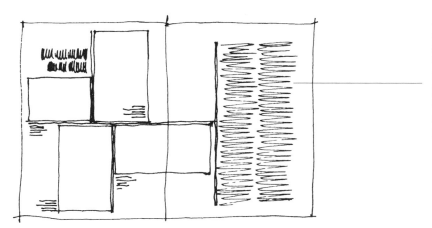

Jump the gutter with a part of a graphic element that is easily and clearly recognizable as part of a greater whole (such as this piece of a whirligig). That demands enough white space to make the device noticeable at first glance.

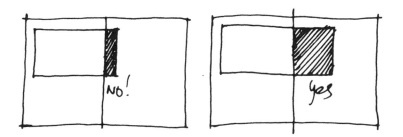

Jump the gutter with a part of a graphic element that is large enough to be visible. A thin sliver is hardly worth it, though it may well be better than nothing.

Use the implications in images to link the two pages. People-pictures speak for themselves, especially when they show faces (with EXPRESSIONS) and hands (with ACTIVITY). There is no mistaking the tension between this lady and her henpecked spouse.

TOP-RIGHT-DOWNWARD-TO-THE-LEFT reverses the normal left-to-right flow of viewing a page. So it is less dramatically effective than the...

...TOP-LEFT-DOWNWARD-TO-THE-RIGHT flow which follows the normal direction of viewing. Everything depends on which direction the people are looking.

Latch on to the curiosity factor. People wonder what other people are looking at, so they follow the direction other people are looking— even in pictures. If they happen to be glaring at each other from opposite sides of the spread, the pages are stapled together in the viewer's mind.

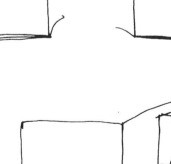

Extend the curiosity principle by deliberately having the person look off the right-hand page. That expands the spread by having it flow over onto the next. This breaks another of those publishing axioms: that people are s'posed-to look into the spread. Sure, but...

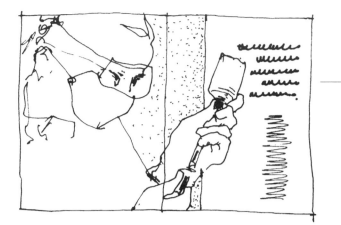

Exploit the left-to-right direction—and then some. The left-to-right photo is partially silhouetted to allow the focal point (the hand holding the medicine) to poke out beyond the confines of the photo at right. It spills out and overlaps into the white space and also bumps into the headline so the intimate interplay between the visual and verbal becomes vivid.

Link pages by intellectual curiosity. The photo is a picture of a kid looking... the headline uses the word "Look" as the first word... so it is both a visual and an intellectual linkage. Remember that the viewer who sees it for the first time, and whom it is intended to capture, has no idea what you are trying to say; so you had better say it simply and clearly, or they won't get it.

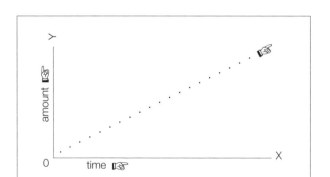

Use the whole spread to plot a "graph." The left-to-right direction which we usually interpret as the X axis of a chart (normally representing time from zero at the left end), is enhanced by the Y axis (normally representing amount, from zero upwards). The flower grows upwards and blooms over time from left to right. We take this for granted, because it is part of our visual language.

PRODUCT-MAKING | Bigness is like shouting. The louder you shout, the more important does the hearer think your message is. In print we assume that anything that is big (especially in type) must therefore be important. This implication of value is a vital means of emphasis that must never be wasted, lest it lose impact and the publication lose credibility.

Scream! *Whisper*

Imagine how loud the word SCREAM would sound and how puny the whisper of *Whisper* would be, if you used size as measure of loudness (i.e., importance). The word Scream would "sound" even louder if it were set in bold and printed in black. But this example's purpose is just to compares **sizes**, so it is made as light and pale as possible to prevent it from overwhelming the page.

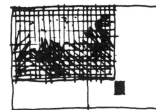

Picture sizing has the identical implications. The bigger it is, the more important we assume its subject to be. The smaller it is, the more subservient it becomes to the dominant image.

STORY-TELLING | Reserve loudness/bigness for the things that matter, because they are significant to the story, helpful in getting its point across, and relevant to the reader. But don't assume that making things bigger is the only way to add emphasis. Instead, think laterally: to call attention to an object, don't puff it up bigger, but make the surroundings smaller instead.

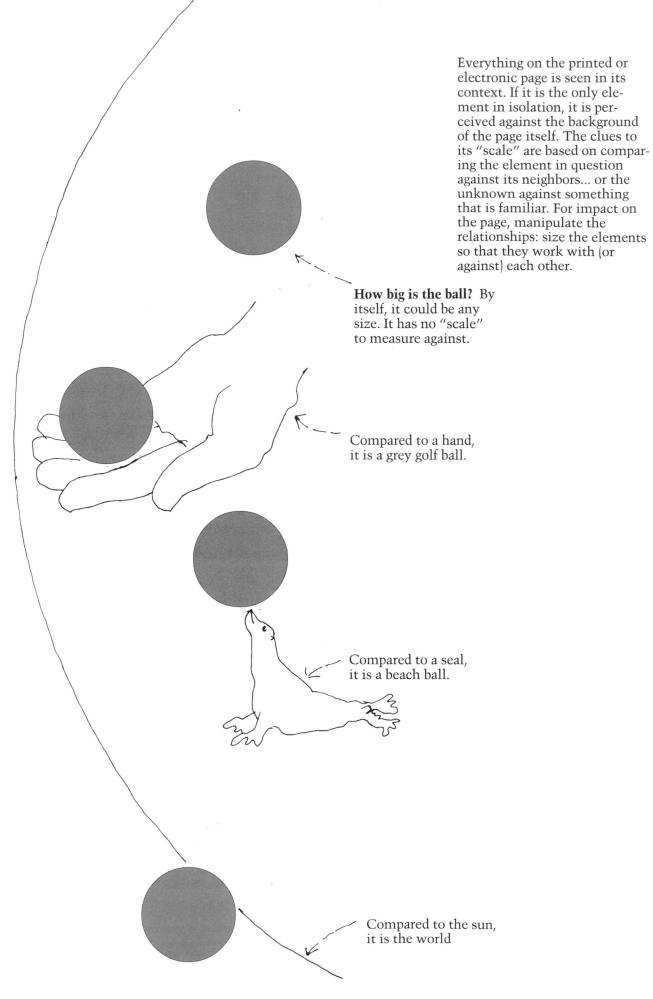

Everything on the printed or electronic page is seen in its context. If it is the only element in isolation, it is perceived against the background of the page itself. The clues to its "scale" are based on comparing the element in question against its neighbors... or the unknown against something that is familiar. For impact on the page, manipulate the relationships: size the elements so that they work with (or against) each other.

How big is the ball? By itself, it could be any size. It has no "scale" to measure against.

Compared to a hand, it is a grey golf ball.

Compared to a seal, it is a beach ball.

Compared to the sun, it is the world

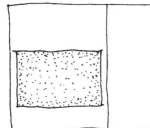 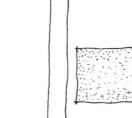 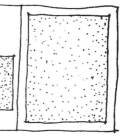

Bigness exists by contrast to smallness. The picture at the left lacks size, scale, and impact because it is not compared to anything. It is just there. To make it look big and impressive, place a small one next to it and suddenly it will appear to have grown, even though its dimensions remain the same. If, on the other hand, you want to reduce its apparent size, place a big picture next to it and it will shrink as if by magic.

(Problem: only pictures of fog are plain grey rectangles like these. You also have to take the **scale** of the subject shown inside the picture into account.)

Use the whole space to create the illusion of size. The word can be made very tiny and isolated in such a large area of space that it becomes a jewel and the surrounding space its setting. Or it can be blown up to such enormous size that the space in which it is displayed can apparently not contain it. Both effects depend on the relationship of the object in the foreground and its background.

Life-size image. In an article about tea, don't show a miniature teacup and tea bag, if you have the space to show it life-size. The full-size image will have an overwhelming impact seen in the miniaturized context of the page. That unexpected contrast gives it its power and surprise.

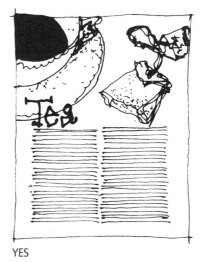

NO   YES

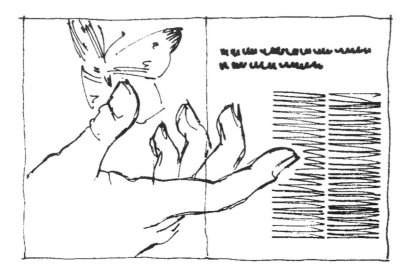

Larger-than-life-size subject. Even more powerful than life-size is the incongruity of enlargement. The larger-than-life-size technique applied in an unexpected context can be startling: imagine a serious technical report on light materials published in a Learned Journal using this butterfly to illustrate "lightness." (We are used to seeing this in fashion magazines, where gigantic closeups of eyes showing makeup are not just dramatic but functionally essential in showing the how-to details.)

Display type / text type. The headline summarizes the gist, the text gives the details of the story. The display is fast, the text slow. The headline catches attention, and hooks the reader. The text communicates the plodding details. The bigger the display type and the louder it screams, the more important the event is understood to be. The event had better be worthy of the screaming, or its attention-getting loudness loses its value and becomes mere noise, crying "Wolf!" Obvious, but often ignored—because large type looks exciting in itself.

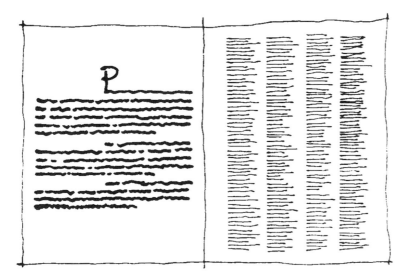

Large type / small type. You know—without having to study or think—that the left-hand page has far more important information on it than the right-hand page. Its type is bigger, the texture darker, the lines long and so it overwhelms the itsybitsy insignificant little stuff at right.

Size as indicator of importance.
Pick out the nub of the argument, emphasize it, and bring the central issue to the reader's attention. If everything is about the same size and visually bland, more likely the story will be passed over and ignored *because its worth-whileness has not been made noticeable.* Its value to the potential reader hasn't been "sold" either in the editing or the layout. It has just been arranged without explanation. The readers have to find the value for themselves.

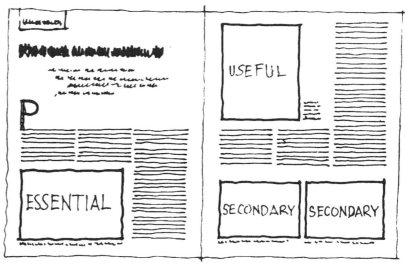

before

Editing and designing work together. Make the Big Idea with the Big Picture as dominant as practicable. Flesh it out and add details with smaller, ancillary, explanatory pictures. The spread brings its message more forthrightly and dramatically, but it also looks more dynamic, more interesting, more captivating. Yet everything that was squeezed into the feeble version is accommodated here. The text is the same, as is the "useful" picture. The "secondaries" have been reduced, and the space around the headline squeezed. The "essential" photo bleeds.

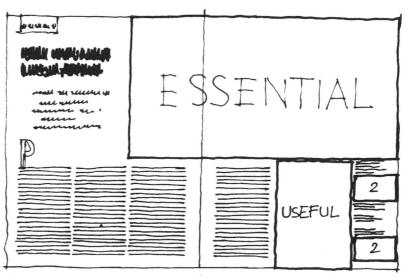

after

Don't blow up anything just to fill a hole. Viewers become accustomed to interpreting significance by certain sizes as pages are turned or scrolled and new images revealed. They should not be misled by something unworthy of their attention being blown up just because space is available.

Never size type to fit an arbitrary width. The bigger the type is, the louder the word screams. The smaller it is, the quieter it whispers. Listen to the clues the size gives and always use it to emphasize sense, never as a graphic design trick just to make a neat rectangle. Is the word "THE" more significant than "UNDERSTANDING"?

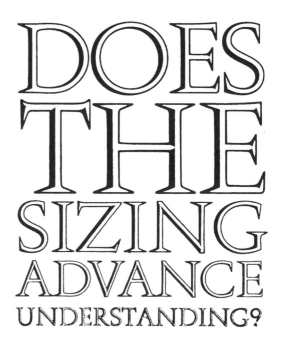

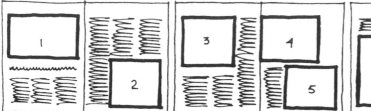

before

Don't make everything about the same size. Where are the comparative values in this homogenized mass? Nothing is duller than neutrality without a point of view. The editor must guide the viewer to a conclusion—and size is an indicator of value. So be choosy (i.e., edit) and *don't make everything as big as possible, if you want to avoid bloat.*

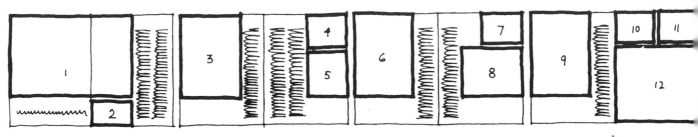

after

Take advantage of varied picture-sizing, as well as alignment and bleed. The same material as in the example above is shown here rearranged and re-sized to exploit size variety and expose value.

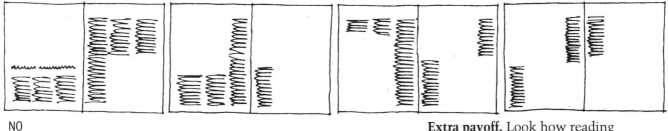

NO

YES

Extra payoff. Look how reading flow is simplified: instead of weaving the text among and around the pictures, it stands in clear, dignified columns.

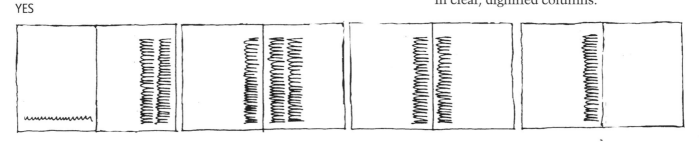

PRODUCT-MAKING

Think of the page as though it were a billboard by the roadside. To do its work, it must attract attention and get its message across not just at first glance but at 60 mph. The viewer speeding by who doesn't know about the subject on the billboard—and probably couldn't care less—must be

struck by it...

captivated...

interested...

and hungry for more...

STORY-TELLING

Once page-flippers or scrollers settle down to read, contrast and all the other attention-getting techniques don't matter any more. They have accomplished their work of pulling the potential reader in.

How contrast works: nothing on the page exists in a vacuum. Viewers glance at it and see everything mixed up and related to everything else: the page itself... the logos... the type... the images... the empty spaces... their interrelationships... the pages that went before... and those that follow. They have to sort through this mass of stuff—*FAST*.

That's why it is essential to make the important elements stand out, and to push the supporting materials into the background. Whose responsibility is it to decide what those materials are to be? Is the decision design-driven or content-driven? Obviously: cooperative editor/designer understanding produces the most striking result. Should there be arguments? Of course. But that's where the fun lies.

The obvious ploy is to make the headline big and black, so it is conspicuous by comparison to the surrounding type, but that's primitive. There's an infinity of ways of doing it more imaginatively. They grow out of the material of the message itself. Nine examples illustrate the variety...

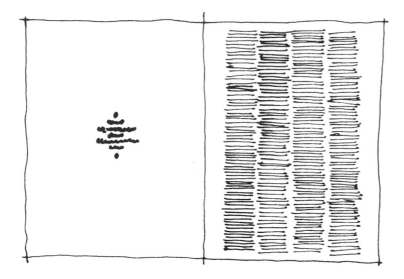

Emptiness / fullness. The huge, luxurious white space in the middle of which the short message floats is set off against the full-to-the-edges thick texture of the page at right. The left-hand page will get 100% attention. If the contrast is dramatic enough, it will also get 100% readership—there's little enough there to be scanned quickly. Use what it says to lure people into the right-hand page.

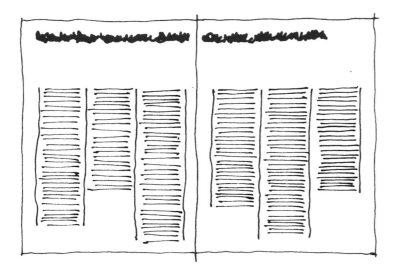

Alignment / randomness. The top of the text columns aligns precisely. It is made vivid by contrast to the generous white space above. The text in the columns hangs like clothes from a clothesline, variegated in length. The clear hard edge versus the irregular edge, shown off against enough white space to make them both noticeable; if you are going to do something, do it boldly.

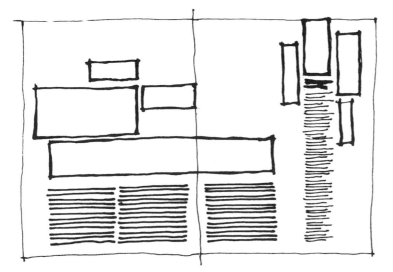

Horizontality / verticality. Juxtaposing the direction of the elements on the page creates drama, especially if the pictures mirror the subject: pictures of giraffes want to be vertical, but snakes call for horizontal treatment. (That is unless the giraffe just died or the cobra is rearing up for an attack. In that case the unexpected direction increases the drama and adds to the effect.)

Flatness / angularity. The expected right-angled geometry of the printed page is vertical/ horizontal, because we are used to seeing it that way. (On-screen it is horizontal/vertical, but the right-angle dominates there, too). When printed pages were hand-assembled in metal, it was difficult to insert anything at any other angle. Non-vertical/horizontal elements are still somewhat startling. The contrast between the expected horizontal units and the unexpected angled ones creates interesting tension.

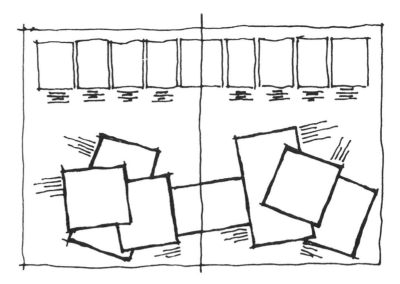

Pictures / text. Images are fast shots to the brain and the emotions. On the other hand, words need time to be read, absorbed, and understood. They are two separate languages that complement each other so we can tell a story more powerfully. Their visual and intellectual difference can be exploited to increase both the story's own drama and the publication's overall impact.

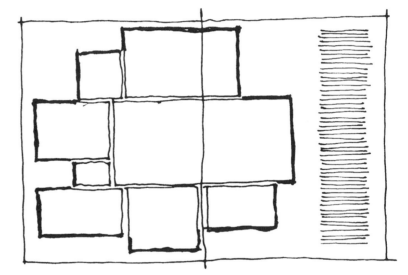

Darkness / lightness. In your mind's eye, turn the pages of a boring, monotonous user-manual. Page after page continues in that same repetitive black type on white paper. Imagine the shock of suddenly coming to a page that reverses the expected pattern: white type on black. Pow! (But avoid too much white type on black, because it is hard to read).

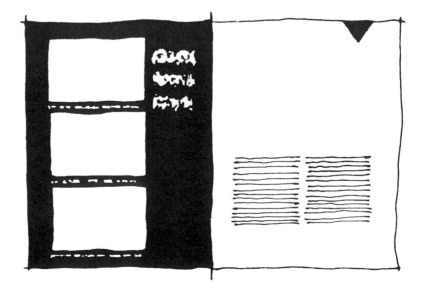

Looseness / tightness. Careful rectangularity… equal spacing… walled-in edges… tightly controlled corners… are normal and fine. But they are dull when rigidly applied. Contrasting looseness is called for. It does not have to be as large as it is shown here.

Looseness / tightness works equally well in miniature. In a context of tight text columns, a feather-edged picture-caption or a ragged-right pullquote let in a touch of informal air that contrasts

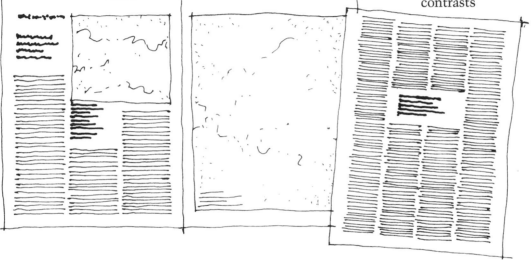

cheerfully with the surrounding rigidity. It may not be as obvious as larger-scaled contrasts, but when you hold the publication at intimate reading distance, it comes into its own.

Colorfulness / black+whiteness. Flip the pages of a typical magazine: cheerful color everywhere—till you come to pages that are plain old black-and-white. Are they conservative? Dull? Boring? Not at all. Startling. The absence of color merely creates contrast to be used with material that will gain from its monochromatic subtlety. But dull and boring material remains dull and boring, whether it is presented in full, glorious color or just in shades of grey. Visual fireworks can never substitute value if the message they convey is empty.

PRODUCT-MAKING

The ideal image of any publication—periodical, book, daily, newsletter, Web site—should transmit a feeling of controlled, deliberate, well-crafted unity. Yet, in the working world (never enough time, never enough people), it is often impossible to organize material in that ideal, orderly arrangement on the page. Bits of text have been written at different lengths—and they must remain that way because cutting or filling would destroy the story. Or you are faced with a collection of diagrams, photos, and drawings all meriting equal size and attention yet unsympathetic in style to each other. That is the reality you are stuck with.

Ingenuity is called for: You have to devise an arbitrary pattern (and use it courageously) so that IT becomes the dominant effect on the page while the problematic material slotted into it becomes less noticeable. The pattern must accommodate the largest as well as smallest unit and do it so subtly that not only do they "belong," but they look as if they were always meant to be that way.

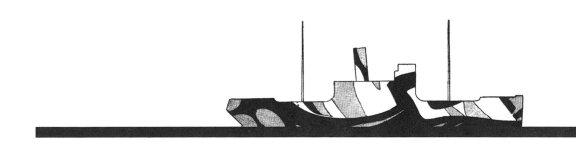

STORY-TELLING

Think camouflage: break up big things, cluster small ones, make something else scream so loud that it outshouts the background. Think magic: the conjuror makes you look over here, while doing something unnoticed over there.

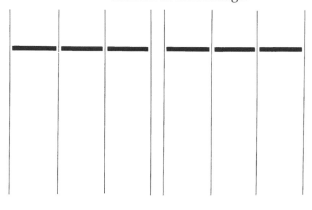

Six hunks of copy and headlines all of unequal lengths look like this, if the aligned top of the text is used as datum. The inequality of lengths is striking, but the subject determines whether that is acceptable. It could be. But what if it isn't? Then you can build a cage of vertical rules (long enough to accommodate the longest unit plus a bit over) and strong horizontal bars. The unequal pieces of copy slot into an all-encompassing whole which creates the visual impact. The unequal hunks disappear because their inequality has been masked. That's the essence of camouflage.

A bunch of varied picture sizes and text lengths can be a real mess. Fit them into a simple geometric shape subdivided into precise boxes. The whole is so strong that it absorbs the various bits-and-pieces of which it is assembled and they disappear within it. (But they had better make sense together as a group. Devise an umbrella headline to give the viewer an immediate clue to their commonality.)

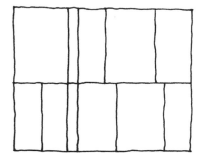

Balance unequal text blocks by using ragged-right typesetting. It doesn't really—it merely looks as if it did. Setting text justified is tighter and more limiting, so the unequal number of lines shows vividly. Unjustified setting allows lines to be set at any length, so the *total number of lines can be forced to be equal.* When the text is set rag-right, the discrepancy is less noticeable even though the lines are much shorter than those in the column at left.

NO   YES

This piece of text demonstrates the flexibility of text set ragged-right. The same words placed in longer lines in a wide column can be squeezed into shorter lines in a narrower column. The capacity of squeezing allows you to vary the number of lines into which the text is broken. So you can specify the number of lines you need and their length will correspond. By virtue of the ragged-right edge, the difference in line length is less noticeable than the difference in column lengths, if you insist on retaining equal line length.

This piece of text demonstrates the flexibility of text set ragged-right. The same words placed in longer lines in a wide column can be squeezed into shorter lines in a narrower column. The capacity of squeezing allows you to vary the number of lines into which the text is broken. So you can specify the number of lines you need and their length will correspond. By virtue of the ragged-right edge, the difference in line length is less noticeable than the difference in column lengths, if you insist on retaining equal line length.

This piece of text demonstrates the flexibility of text set ragged-right. The same words placed in longer lines in a wide column can be squeezed into shorter lines in a narrower column. The capacity of squeezing allows you to vary the number of lines into which the text is broken. So you can specify the number of lines you need and their length will correspond. By virtue of the ragged-right edge, the difference in line length is less noticeable than the difference in column lengths, if you insist on retaining equal line length.

This piece of text demonstrates the flexibility of text set ragged-right. The same words placed in longer lines in a wide column can be squeezed into shorter lines in a narrower column. The capacity of squeezing allows you to vary the number of lines into which the text is broken. So you can specify the number of lines you need and their length will correspond. By virtue of the ragged-right edge, the difference in line length is less noticeable than the difference in column lengths, if you insist on retaining equal line length.

(The question of how long the lines should be for easy reading is something else. See page 100.)

Ragged-right typesetting can make pages look untidy, when several columns are placed next to each other. The wiggly edge at right (which is what makes the text easier to read, because it allows regular word-spacing) creates messy white spaces there.

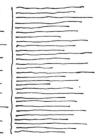

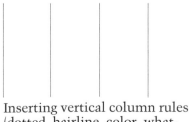

Inserting vertical column rules (dotted, hairline, color, whatever) creates a geometric sense of order and solves the problem.

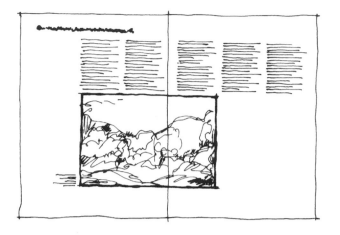

To make anything maximally visible, place it at the top of the page, because that has pride of place, since people look there first. Put just small-scale, plain text up there, if that's what you want to draw attention to, despite a picture you fear will pull attention away from it. (Exploiting the magnetic quality of the picture somehow might be better, but if it really makes no sense, then put the text above the picture).

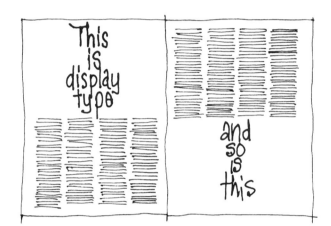

Sharp and unexpected contrast draws attention away from minor elements and to itself, if it is dramatic. Just the exaggerated drama of layout and composition creates a smoke-screen and you notice the drama, not the substance. Given these huge white spaces within which the enormous headlines sit, who cares what is happening in the text? (The author does, and the reader does, but in the communiction business there are lots of different purposes and... who knows?)

To hide something you don't want noticed, place it near the gutter down at the foot of the page. That's the ideal Siberia for award-receiving and grip-and-grin photos. (Make them small, too.)

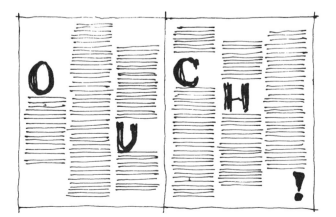

The focal-point trick draws the eye toward an "interesting" element that overwhelms its surroundings that then tend to be ignored. Big initials, out-of-scale numerals, or any unexpected graphic spot that is decorative or symbolic can, if startling enough, mask the shortcomings around it.

PRODUCT-MAKING | If you want to impress with formal dignity, use the traditional, standardized, symmetrical, balanced layout format. Symmetry's controlled rigidity impresses by its bulk, size, familiarity. It implies seriousness, thoughtfulness, credibility, and importance. It works well for legal briefs, contracts, and rigid material that must follow strict formats, such as learnèd journals.

STORY-TELLING | Symmetry is a non-thinking solution based on the principle that *"it works, it's normal, and besides, they expect it that way."* In fact, symmetry impedes fast, active communication because balance is *equilibrium* whose essence is lack of motion. It is a straitjacket whose shape steals attention from the message and directs it to the container. More serious than looks, though, is the fact that it makes it more difficult for us to allow important thoughts to jump off the page.

Asymmetry—*imbalance*—is much more flexible, besides being more fun to look at, even if that palatial residence up there is more impressive, grandiose, authoritarian, pretentious. That's why asymmetry is more appropriate to the variety of arrangements needed to combine ideas, words, and images in the most meaningful and effective ways.

In this
symmetrical stack of lines, the ideas
that are embodied in the words-in-type are arbitrarily forced into a shape that
has nothing to do with the meaning or the flow
of
the
thoughts, let alone
the phrasing of the language. If it
looks like a psychological Rorschach test, let
it. Maybe it looks cute, a bit like a butterfly
but what a job it is to decipher.

RIP
VISUAL EXPRESSIVENESS
WE
HAVE
ALWAYS
DONE
IT
THIS
WAY

Words-in-type are not congealed lumps to be stacked like bricks. They are fluid symbols the eye follows across the page left-to-right or west/east. **Symmetrical type arrangement** stacks words regardless of the phrasing or meaning and forces them into an arbitrary shape. The central axis about which it revolves is merely an æsthetic device placed in an arbitrary position (the middle), there for its own sake. It often runs counter to the meaning of the thoughts. Worse, the shape makes the text more difficult to absorb quickly. Read the example aloud, pause where the lines end, see how that affects the sense.

The ideal application of symmetrical format is on tombstone inscriptions. Perfect for dignified, quiet contemplation. They were never meant to be scanned or understood fast.

This asymmetrical arrangement of words \\

is arrayed flush-left/ragged-right. \\

The left-hand edge is the leading edge \\

to which the eye returns, \\

when it searches for the start \\

of the succeeding line. \\

Each line represents a complete phrase, \\

reflecting the way we speak out loud, \\

which makes the meaning \\

that much easier to decipher, \\

understand, and remember. \\

Asymmetrical type arrangement enables lines to be broken at the ends of phrases, reflecting the natural way we speak. Thoughts are transmitted in a natural way, each line representing visually the shape of the phrase it contains. Read it aloud, pause where the lines end, notice how the message is easier to understand. Here the axis has shifted from the center to the left, the leading edge of all type lines. Not only does that help to find the start of the next line, but it helps to encourage the smooth rhythm of reading—and keep the reader going along happily.

Subhead placement affects reading. Thoughts flow from line to line in steady rhythm. Subheads (or crossheads) are inserted to "break up the text" (i.e., to make it look shorter) which is a wrong thing to do. It is much better to exploit their presence functionally and signal a change in the information.

 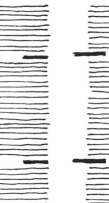

Centered subheads interrupt the flow of ideas (which you want) but they also interrupt the continuity of the flow of steady reading (which you don't want, because such major disturbances in the rhythm are tempting opportunities for the reader to stop reading).

Flush-left subheads signal a new direction of the thinking in the text (which is good), but they avoid disturbing the left-to-right rhythm of reading because they themselves are placed flush-left. They remain part of the continuum of eye motion, so they don't discourage the reader from continuing to read quite as much as if they were centered.

Flush-right subheads are so far away from the leading edge of the reading process (the left-hand edge of the column) that they are lost. They don't work very well, which is why they are seldom used.

Hanging indent subheads (poking out beyond the left-hand edge of the column) emphasize their presence by far greater visibility. Their unexpected intrusion into the space that is normally defined as a clean left-hand edge of the column exaggerates their presence—an effect you may well want.

Find the most compelling thoughts and display them, to pull the potential reader into the text. The ideal way is to lay out the goodies sideways—west/east—like dishes at a buffet, to follow the natural west/east eye flow…

…but unfortunately most print pages are vertical. The vertical equivalent of fast west/east scanning is to pull the fascinating stuff into the white space at the left for **quick scanning north/south.** This is the main reason for using asymmetry, because balanced symmetry makes such arrangements impossible. This is also the most natural technique for encouraging flow from page to page on screen.

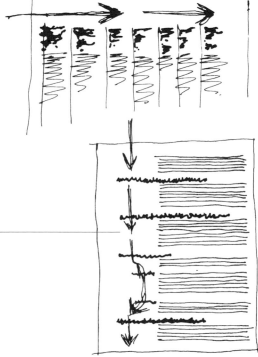

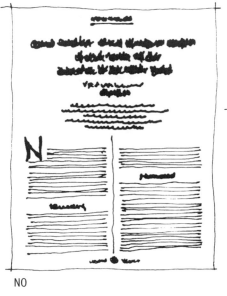

NO

YES

Asymmetrical page architecture's rationale is based on the principle of greater noticeability by means of placement of elements in space. Emphasis (and de-emphasis) can be used to clarify ideas and transmit thoughts arranged in classified categories. **Symmetrical page architecture** has an official, serious, authoritarian look—grandiose and imposing. It could be pretentious if it weren't so ordinary. By contrast, **asymmetrical page architecture** is informal and therefore flexible. Because it is so versatile and malleable, it can be responsive to the specific needs of each story. Because it is unconstrained, it is reader-friendly.

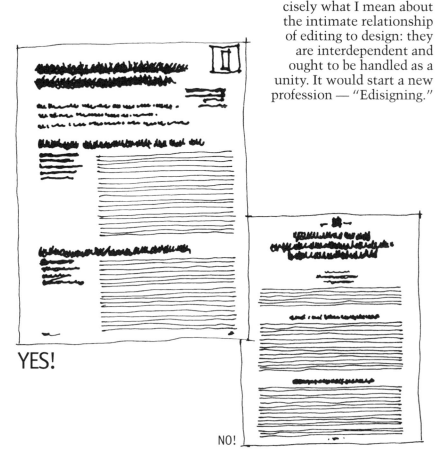

YES!

NO!

If only one could make up new words like "EDISIGN"? It says precisely what I mean about the intimate relationship of editing to design: they are interdependent and ought to be handled as a unity. It would start a new profession — "Edisigning."

Editing/designing pages:

1. Break the information into its component info-units.

2. Separate each unit into a fast/slow stream. The fast stream displays the nub of the idea in what's-in-it-for-me style, big and bold in space. The slow stream concentrates secondary and supporting information that fleshes the idea out in smaller type.

3. Exploit the advantages provided by the left-to-right direction of reading and the top-to-bottom direction of scanning and apply them to the layouts.

That way you assemble a vibrant, moving, magnetic page which the viewer finds "interesting" because you have emphasized the most magnetic bits and placed them so they are noticed. The cost? The formal dignity that symmetrical layout imparts.

PRODUCT-MAKING

The choice of Font (what used to be called "face") obviously affects the character and personality of the piece, so publishers worry about that. The sad reality is that regardless of whether it is set in Centaur or Optima, Times Roman or **Helvetica**, to casual readers the type we worry about is just "PRINT" and they see it as either *"too damn long"* or *"too damn small."*

Few journalists or editors are more sophisticated, for to them what the words say is uppermost (as it should be) and the typography is an "Artistic Decision," which they judge by traditional axioms passed down as Revealed Truth, whether they make sense or not.

STORY-TELLING

Many nonreaders excuse their reluctance by claiming that it is *"hard to read."* What they really mean is that it is hard to get into… hard to understand… hard to find what they are looking for… and, most important, hard to know why they should bother. As editors and designers together, we must use the type so well that we succeed in persuading them to want to read. That's why we must distinguish type as:

SPEECH MADE VISIBLE: This affects display (i.e., headlines, decks, captions, pullquotes, etc.) more than text, because that's where we catch their interest most directly. This type has to be arrayed so subtly that it expresses spoken language in its phrasing, shouting, whispering.

STORY-TELLING: This is the steady, long-term reading. It is a slow, thoughtful, flowing process, sequential and lineal, just like listening to a speech.

EXPLANATION: This takes facts and groups them visually by reflecting the organization and structure of the writing: listing, tabulating, cataloging information for easy understanding and fast retrieval.

IMAGE: This plays on the emotions and curiosity of the viewer/reader by creating word-pictures. Like concrete poetry, it uses words handled as though they were images.

You can't go wrong with any of these: Times Roman, Baskerville, Garamond, Goudy, Bodoni, Bembo, Caslon, Janson, Palatino, Helvetica, Akzidenz, Gill, Franklin, Frutiger, Univers, Futura, Interstate, Meta, News. (For a showing of sixteen text faces *see Appendix*, starting on page 231.)

The best text type is so comfortable that it is invisible... transparent. The reader should never become aware of the act of reading, lest they stop. All normal fonts in general use are "easy to read." We misuse them in order to be "original" and "creative" and often ruin their readability by overriding the original designer's purposes. Just because it is possible to alter their proportions on the computer doesn't mean it ought to be done.

War declared! Finest lace

CLASSICAL DIGNITY

High-tech precision

Friendly relaxation

Pushy aggressiveness

Pick a face (or "font") that is appropriate to the subject. The look of the type ought to make sense with the words. It is clearly more critical in headlines, but text type, too, has a "feel." Some types are academically impressive, others fanciful and playful, hard-edged and high-tech, or old-fashioned and comfortable. Be conservative: you are choosing for an audience, not for yourself.

Formulas for "Good Type" don't exist. There are no laws or rules, except common sense. There is no such thing as "correct" or "incorrect." If it works well, it is "correct." If it doesn't work, it is "incorrect."

This is about as normal a face as you can find. It is called Century Schoolbook, for the simple reason that it was devised and used for schoolbooks, to teach kids to read. That's why it is so familiar and comfortable.

This is a piece of text that looks dark, surprising, cool, unusual, and it may be exactly right for some special occasion, but there is no doubt that every single reader will be aware of the struggle to decipher it. Weren't you? Fine for a couple of lines, but imagine facing a column...

Readers are most comfortable with what they are used to. Depart from it only deliberately, because every departure from the norm will cost you. Not that you must never do it. Just do it with circumspection and when it makes sense, never arbitrarily or to show off. Avoid weird, self-conscious faces just because they are new or cool.

Sans-serif type is harder to read than serif type, though it should not be too dangerous, if your readers are used to it. Make sure that it is easy by adding extra space between the lines to compensate for the lack of serifs (which help move the eye sideways, as well as separating lines from each other.)

These are the serifs

Sans-serif means "without serifs"

All-capitals are hard to decipher in bulk. That is proven fact, so avoid using them that way. A few words for special emphasis or character are, obviously, fine. But that vital information you want to emphasize is sure to be skipped if you set it in all-caps to give it emphasis. Besides, it takes that much more space!

This is nothing but good old Times Roman, one of the best fonts ever designed. It is so good that it is universal and nobody even notices it. They take it for granted. But when even such a great face is set in all-caps, you lose the reader by the third line, assuming they ever started in the first place.

THIS IS NOTHING BUT GOOD OLD TIMES ROMAN, ONE OF THE BEST FONTS EVER DESIGNED. IT IS SO GOOD THAT IT IS UNIVERSAL AND NOBODY EVEN NOTICES IT. THEY TAKE IT FOR GRANTED. BUT WHEN EVEN SUCH A GREAT FACE IS SET IN ALL-CAPS, YOU LOSE THE READER BY THE THIRD LINE, ASSUMING THEY STARTED IN THE FIRST PLACE.

The Up-And-Down-Style That Capitalizes Initials Of Words Is Harder to Decipher And Demands More Work Of The Reader To Plough Through. It Is More Common In Display Than Text, But It Is Worth While Decrying It Here, Too.

Just Because We Are Used To Seeing This And We Pay So Little Attention To It, Does Not Mean That It Makes Sense, Does It?

Just because we are used to seeing this, and so we pay little attention to it, does not mean that it makes sense, does it?

Italics are unpopular in bulk. People find them less comfortable because they slant, so why risk alienating them? Use italics sparingly: reserve them for special occasions. They are often beautiful, decorative, and full of character. They are also often lighter than the roman, so they do not stand out well as emphasizers. They don't shout, they whisper.

Italic is also called oblique—for good reason

Boldface is harder to read than regular in bulk. It looks too massive, heavy, stodgy. Bold can be useful for emphasis in a line or two, of course. If you must use it, add generous line spacing to help the eye move from side to side. This text is set 10/11.

Boldface is harder to read **than regular in bulk. It looks too massive, heavy, stodgy. Bold can be useful for emphasis in a line or two, of course. If you must use it, add generous line spacing to help the eye move from side to side. To dramatize the point, this is set in Trump Bold, without extra leading or 10/10. It is a chore to wade through. Compare it to the regular text set 10/11 at left.**

Boldface is harder to read **than regular in bulk. It looks too massive, heavy, stodgy. Bold can be useful for emphasis in a line or two, of course. If you must use it, add generous line spacing to help the eye move from side to side. To illustrate, this is set in Trump Bold, with three points of lead, or 10/13.**

Functional typography is invisible because it goes unnoticed. The aim is to create a visual medium that is so attractive, so inviting, so appropriate to its material, that the process of reading (which most people dislike as "work") becomes a pleasure. The type should never stand between the reader and the message. The act of reading should be made so easy that the reader concentrates on the substance, unconscious of the intellectual energy expended in absorbing it. Ideally, it should be so inviting that the reader is sorry when the end of the piece has been reached—though the subject may have a little something to do with that, too. 10/11 Times Roman.

TYPOGRAPHY IS A MEANS OF TRANSMITTING THOUGHTS IN WORDS VISUALLY TO SOMEONE ELSE. AVOID THINKING OF IT AS ANYTHING ELSE. IT IS MERELY A MECHANICAL MEANS TO A DISTINCT END— CLEAR COMMUNICATION. 11/10 HELVETICA. N O T H I N G E L S E M A T T E R S.

Readers have to understand the form and absorb the substance of your printed piece at the same time. This is no small task, especially if the information is complex. Keep in mind that people scan the piece quickly for its length in order to gauge the time and effort to be invested relative to their interest in the subject. Few sit there and figure out its format, structure, or how headings fit into a hierarchy. The truly committed ones may start at the beginning and stay with it to the end. Some may start at the beginning and then hop around, pecking here and there as bits strike them. Others may be caught by a detail somewhere and be hooked by that snippet into returning to the start. Every potential reader is enticed differently. 12/11 Oficina bold.

It is wise not to make the piece too intimidating. People tend to shy away from the visual complexity of five levels of headings coupled with three degrees of indentions accompanied by subparagraphs, footnotes, extracts, and quotations. Wouldn't you? The simpler the arrangement, the greater the likelihood of the potential audience bothering to pay attention. Too many minor variations are self-defeating, even if they do tabulate the information. If you must provide instructions on "How to read this article," better rethink. 12/13 Centaur italic.

Keeping it simple pays off, as long as you don't go overboard and oversimplify. That is as dangerous as making it look too complicated. The happy medium to aim for is a condition in which the piece looks easy, yet everything that needs to stand out does so. The capacity of type to mirror the human voice is one of its most valuable properties, because it can be helpful to the reader. Always think of the publication from the user's viewpoint. Make it reader-friendly by giving visual clues (the equivalent of raising your voice or changing its pitch) so they know what not to miss, but without having to figure it out. They just know because you have shown them, guided them, enticed them. Typography must be used to show where readers are, how the elements fit together, which items are dominant and which ones matter a bit less and are perhaps even skippable. That is an aspect of editing as much as of designing. That is design at the behest of the editor. 10/15 Gill Sans light.

In other words, help readers save time and energy by suggesting where they can skim and skip. With your cunning visual clues, they won't have to figure it out for themselves. Ideas will catapult off the page into their minds effortlessly. They will reward you by "liking" your publication, and announcing that it is "easy to read."

They will never realize how much work and thought went into getting it that way. 6/18 Trump Mediaeval.

Would you read it if you hadn't written it?

The texture of text type is a vital criterion for choice. Look at the variation in color and texture in these examples. The visual effect it has in bulk on the potential reader can be beguiling and attractive or depressing and repulsive. It affects the feel and look of the product. Is this an æsthetic, art, design choice? Certainly. But it is not High Art. Like everything else in publication-making, it must be a common-sense decision based as much on comfort and feel as on anything else. It is, after all, nothing more than a means of communication, just a visual personality that produces a tone of voice. It certainly is part of who "you" are, but it must also appeal to—and be understood by—your special audience.

Pick one font and use it throughout. Simplicity will give the product character and unity. Pick a font with strong color contrast, so the **bold** stands out well against the normal regular weight.

Use contrasting faces for maximum payoff, if you feel you must add variety. Avoid mixing faces that are similar in design.

Beware of competing against yourself by making some type units friendly, while others are less so. The shorter, easier-to-read units will always get higher readership than the ones that look longer and more difficult.

Text faces are usually from 9-to 12-point in size, but effective "size" depends on its appearance, not arithmetical pointsize. Never rely on pat formulas that maintain "ten-point is ideal for text..." (yes, but also no!) The x-height makes it look big or small. Examine a large sample reproduced to look as similar as possible to the finished product. Judge it visually, and remember that youngsters need—and oldsters deserve—larger sizes.

Both texts are set the same "size" (10-point) but they appear different because of the x-heights. Bembo, top, looks much smaller and takes much less space than the Dominante, below.

apbx apbx

We hold these truths to be self-evident, that all men are created equal, that they are endowed by their Creator with certain unalienable Rights, that among these are Life, Liberty and the pursuit of Happiness. That to secure these rights, Governments are instituted among Men, deriving their just powers from the consent of the governed. That whenever any Form of Government becomes destructive to these ends, it is the Right of the People to alter or abolish it...

We hold these truths to be self-evident, that all men are created equal, that they are endowed by their Creator with certain unalienable Rights, that among these are Life, Liberty and the pursuit of Happiness. That to secure these rights, Governments are instituted among Men, deriving their just powers from the consent of the governed. That whenever any Form of Government becomes destructive of these ends, it is the Right of the People to alter or abolish it...

Reading rhythm must be smooth. The eye moves in "saccadic jumps" from word to word (or word-group to word-group). Irregular spaces between words disturb its rhythm and irregular spacing decomposes the words and makes them more difficult to recognize.

Millions over milleniums attest that deciphering this stuff is more than minimally difficult. You are aware of being forced to decipher it and very few people all of whom are in a hurry have the patience to sit there and bother to go on reading after the first few words of this self-conscious stuff which looks like a smudge on the page

Reverse type (white on dark) is unpopular and it automatically cuts readership by 40%. Why risk that? But if you must, then compensate for the increased difficulty of reading by enlarging it, setting it bold, and increasing line spacing. Shorten the lines, too, if possible.

This text is in a light typeface set quite small and tight, but since it is "dropped out," "reversed," or "knocked out" from a dark background it is harder to read than the version at right.

This is set in a typeface that is bigger and bolder, since it is intended to be "dropped out," "reversed," or "knocked out" from a dark background.

How small can type be? If you are uncomfortable, so will the reader be. There's a big difference between what *can* be read and what *asks* to be read. Make type big enough—and then make it a size bigger.

Now, new! Seven ways to become a sexy millionaire and live to 129!

Who's afraid of the big *bad* wolf, big *bad* wolf, big *bad* **wolf** ?

*Ah'm gowna hurff an' Ah'll **purff**, an' Ah'll blo*

Type is speech made visible, so open your eyes and listen to it. Read it out loud, using the clues it gives. It can help transmit thoughts as expressively as does the human voice. The way it looks can reflect loudness by boldness, whispering by smallness, shouting by size, emphasis by contrast, dialect by its visual character.

This type is very small so it looks as if it were far away and it sounds very quiet,but it sounds louder and looks bigger as it comes closer towards you and as its size grows the more attention it commands and the louder it shouts **the more attention it gets**

Big type shouts an important thought, tiny type whispers a footnote. Use size to emphasize what is essential and play down what is secondary. Establish norms, so size itself is a signal. If you have too much copy, don't squeeze it in by reducing type size or altering the horizontal scale. Cut text or add space. Don't cheat yourself or the reader.

Reading is lineal, flowing word after word, like speaking. If we were ticker-tape machines instead of hot-air machines, our words would come out as type on a strip of paper. We would have to cut that tape into a series of short bits which we would stack as "lines" in vertical **columns**. Columns are nothing but an artificial compromise to squeeze a lot of horizontally-flowing words into a vertical area. To encourage the flow of reading (listening?) we must encourage that horizontal flow.

Don't be imprisoned by the three-column or two-column page. Don't squeeze everything into a format that was developed as the lowest common denominator for news weeklies. Arrange material on the pages in patterns that reflect the structure of writing. *(See Columns and Grids).* **Or consider these possibilities** ☞

This eight point Trump Mediæval is small. But it is in scale with the narrow column, which it fits quite naturally. Since it only yields about 24 characters per line, it would be hard to read, if it were set justified: the word-spacing would be too irregular, and that is too great a sacrifice to make for the sake of neat edges to the columns. So it is better set unjustified. But it does show how small scale type naturally fits into narrow columns. It is better set text unjustified, or ragged right in such narrow columns. However, if the ragged right columns look a bit too untidy, it might be a good idea to insert a hairline column rule between the columns to make the page neater and more geometric, as is shown here.

This is nine point Trump, one size larger than the type in the five-column scheme. It fits naturally into a four-column scheme, and as the column width increases, so ought the type that fills it. There's a logic to relative scales, despite the fact that magazines tend to ignore this important factor in their communication techiques. What they do is to choose a type size—typically ten point—and standardize it throughout, whether the column is narrow or wide seems immaterial. It is far simpler to write, compose, and put the pages together using one simple type size; just let it flow into the spaces. Readers won't know the difference, or will they?

This is ten point Trump Mediæval, set in a three-column measure. It is one size larger than the nine-point Trump used in the four-column measure. The type size grows in proportion to the column width. A coordinated system of typography is a complex æsthetic and functional calculation requiring the balancing of a number of factors. If it is well worked out, it becomes a basic and important visual tool for editorial emphasis as well as a constant definer of the magazine's personality. It is set without extra linespacing.

This is eleven point Trump Mediæval set in a two-column-per-page measure (here 19.75 picas), which leaves a slightly wider gutter between the columns than those shown in the examples above, while filling the same live-matter width of 41 picas. Just as the type size grows with the column width, so should the gutter increase in proportion. This helps readers interpret importance visually.

Disciplined column structure is necessary to accommodate standard-sized ads and to unify the product. But it should also be flexible, with type size coupled to column widths, to enrich communication capacity. Payoff: you can mix widths and sizes to reflect editorial importance, in both type and picture sizing.

Gutters between columns should vary with the width of the columns and the size of type filling them. Tiny type in narrow columns looks out of scale, when its columns are separated by the same gutters as big type run in wide columns. The narrower the columns, the less space between them.

This is twelve point Trump Mediæval set solid and to a measure which is equivalent to three of the five columns in the 5-column page. Big, important.

This is twelve point Trump Mediæval but set to a measure which is equivalent to two out of the three columns in the 3-column page. It deserves an extra point of leading: 12/13.

This is twelve point Trump Mediæval but set to a measure which is equivalent to three out of the four columns in the 4-column page. It demands at least two extra points of leading: 12/14 for comfort.

This is twelve point Trump Mediæval but set to a measure which is equivalent to four out of the five columns in the 5-column page. It needs three extra points of leading: 12/15 to be comfortable for easy reading.

This is fourteen point Trump, the size needed if it is to span across the full page.

This is a very long line of type set in six point, which is a very small size of Times Roman, to show that a single line can be as long as it needs to be. You are reading it because it is worth the bother.

This is a very long line of type set in six point, which is a very small size of Times Roman, to show that a single line can be as long as it needs to be. You are reading it because it is worth the bother. You can even get away with such ridiculously exaggerated long lines if there are two of them, because the reader is aware of reading the upper one, then struggles with the lower one.

This is a very long line of type set in six point, which is a very small size of Times Roman, to show that a single line can be as long as it needs to be. You are reading it because it is worth the bother. You can even get away with such ridiculously exaggerated long lines if there are two of them, because the reader is aware of reading the upper one, then struggles with the lower one. At a stretch, you might even succeed in having three lines like this get their message across, because readers can identify the upper, middle, and lower lines, assuming they are interested enough to bother.

When you present four or more lines like this, you are asking for trouble. The distance the eye has to travel back from the far right to the far left in order to find the beginning of the succeeding line of text is so great, that it is very easy to make a mistake, reread what you have already read or skip a line or two, so the words begin to make no sense and you're forcing the reader to give up in disgust. Don't bother to continue ploughing through this. It is merely a repetition of the previous example. This is a very long line of type set in six point, which is a very small size of Times Roman, to show that a single line can be as long as it needs to be. You are reading it because it is worth the bother. You can even get away with such ridiculously exaggerated long lines if there are two of them, because the reader is aware of reading the upper one, then struggles with the lower one. At a stretch, you might even succeed in having three lines like this get their message across, because readers can identify the upper, middle, and lower lines, assuming they are interested enough to bother.

This is a very long line of type set in six point, which is a very small size of Times Roman, to show that a single line can be as long as it needs to be. You are reading it because it is worth the bother. You can even get away with such ridiculously exaggerated long lines if there are two of them, because the reader is aware of reading the upper one, then struggles with the lower one.

Shorter lines make the same text look less repulsive

How long can lines be? One line can be any length. Even two or three are OK. The trouble starts when you have more than three.

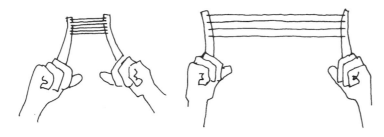

The longer the lines, the wider the line-spacing needs to be

Reading comfort depends on the ratio of type size to line length to line spacing. All three have to be in balance. Who judges comfort? You do: if you feel uncomfortable, add space between lines, increase type size, or both. Best avoid the problem altogether and make the lines shorter.

What do you do about that illegible six-line disaster? Add spacing between the lines. (Here it is doubled: what was 6/6 in the previous examples is here 6/12. That generous white space acts as a handrail for the eye to hold on to while traveling from the east back to the west. Don't bother to continue ploughing through this. It is merely a repetition of the previous example. But when you present four or more lines like this, you are asking for trouble. The distance the eye has to travel back from the far right to the far left in order to find the beginning of the succeeding line of text is so great, that it is very easy to make a mistake, reread what you have already read or skip a line or two, so the words begin to make no sense and you've forced the reader to give up in disgust. This is a very long line of type set in six point, which is a very small size of Times Roman, to show that a single line can be as long as it needs to be. You are reading it because it is worth the bother.

The longer the lines, the larger the type size needs to be

Or you increase the size of the type, like here from 6-point to 12-point Times Roman. In the top part of this example it is set solid (i.e. 12/12). It would be better if it were 12/18 as the last four lines shown here are set. Don't bother to continue ploughing through this. It is merely a repetition of the previous example. The distance the eye has to travel back from the far right to the far left in order to find the beginning of the succeeding line of text is so great, that it is very easy to make a mistake, reread what you have already read or skip a line or two, so the words begin to make no sense and you are forcing the reader to give up in disgust. But you will probably read this part, because it is so easy and even inviting to read. The distance the eye has to travel back from the far right to the far left in order to find the beginning of the succeeding line of text is the same 39 picas but the relationships of line length to leading and type size have changed. That makes all the difference.

Is there an *ideal* line length?
No: There are rules of thumb but no Law, because there are too many variables. Reader-friendliness is not only a factor of the type itself, its design, its size, its boldness, its looseness or tightness, but also of its context.

One two three four five six seven eight words per line (forty characters) is an average rule of thumb for easy-to-read line length. One-and-a-half alphabets. Books are commonly set a bit wider, from fifty-five to seventy characters, but then more interline space is added to facilitate eye flow. But if you use sans serif type, which lacks the strokes that help the eye move sideways, reducing the width helps.

The page is a synthesis of many elements. The only criteria to use to make cogent judgments about line length, are simple visual awareness and common sense.

— Page size
— Number of pages
— Language used... technical, scientific formulae
— "Muchness" of the type to be read
— Coverage: margins and gutters between columns
— How the text is constructed or broken up
— How the printed piece is held in the hand
— Weight, color, texture, shininess of the paper stock
— Color and shininess of the ink on that paper
— Quality and resolution of the printing

Rule-of-thumb text type chart shows normal relationships of line length to interline spacing developed by trial and error. It is just a rough guide, not a rigid standard that must be followed because it is "correct." (There's no such thing). But:

...If you set ragged-right, you can use narrower columns than the minimums suggested here.

...If you are using bold type, double the interline spacing.

...If you are using lots of all-caps, don't.

...If your material consists of short bits like catalog items, you can use narrower leading.

...If you are using type with a large x-height, you need more generous leading than for small x-height. *(See next page.)*

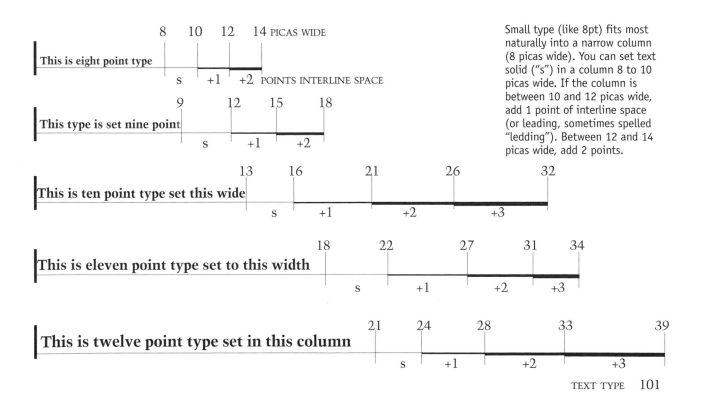

Small type (like 8pt) fits most naturally into a narrow column (8 picas wide). You can set text solid ("s") in a column 8 to 10 picas wide. If the column is between 10 and 12 picas wide, add 1 point of interline space (or leading, sometimes spelled "ledding"). Between 12 and 14 picas wide, add 2 points.

Paragraphs denote new ideas, new trends, changes of direction of thinking. They are shown either by indents or by spacing. **Either technique works, though indents are more usual.** But indents should always be used when there are small bits of self-contained text on the same page. Each little story retains its unity, yet the points signalled by the indenting are still made separately.

This is a headline

This is the first paragraph. It starts a trend of thought and usually contains important information, in order to beguile the semi-curious reader into continuing reading the story.
The second paragraph switches to a second thought that is independent of the first, but flows from it.
The third paragraph changes the direction of the thinking again. The purpose of paragraphing is to signal *change* in the direction of thoughts—a valuable clue to the readers that aids them in comprehending the message and its intellectual organization.
There are some publications that eschew the use of any indention or typographic signaling devices at paragraph starts. Why do they do that? In order to have a neat left-hand edge. There is no question that it makes the page look crisp and carefully tailored. But at what cost? Perhaps a compromise can be worked out at the start of each story?

No ¶ indication

This is a headline

This first paragraph has not been indented. Look how crisp this looks. The first paragraph starts a trend of thought and usually contains important information, in order to beguile the semi-curious reader into continuing reading the story.
　The second paragraph switches to a second thought that is independent of the first, but flows from it.
　The third paragraph changes the direction of the thinking again. The purpose of paragraphing is to signal *change* in the direction of thoughts—a valuable clue to the reader. The first paragraph doesn't change anything. It starts. So why indent the first paragraph? Silly, unthinking habit. Indents are set automatically as a default. (Here the indents are nine points because this is set in 9pt Times Roman. It is set solid, in order to make it thick and grey, to show the indenting clearly.)
　It is a nuisance to remember to override the default, but do it: don't indent the first paragraph.

One-em ¶ indents

This is a headline

This is the first paragraph. It starts a trend of thought and usually contains important information, in order to beguile the semi-curious reader into continuing reading the story.
　The second paragraph switches to a second thought that is independent of the first, but flows from it.
　The third paragraph here changes the direction of the thinking once again. The purpose of paragraphing is to signal *change* in direction of thoughts—a valuable clue to the reader. The first paragraph doesn't change anything. It starts. So why indent the first paragraph? Silly, unthinking habit. Indents are set automatically as a default—here an extra-wide two picas wide to make the point obvious. (Normal indents are one em, the square of the type size: 12 points in 12pt, 10 points in 10pt type etc).
　It is a nuisance to remember to override the default, but do it: don't indent the first paragraph.

Three-em ¶ indents

This is a headline

■ The first paragraph is signposted by means of a solid square. Such a little black spot invites the fast scanning viewer to the beginning of the text. It is a helpful guide, even if it does mess up the clean purity of the page. Compared to the example at far left, it is more visually complicated.
　The second paragraph switches to a second thought that is independent of the first, but flows from it.
　The third paragraph changes the direction of the thinking again. The purpose of paragraphing is to signal *change* in the direction of thoughts—a valuable clue to the reader. The first paragraph doesn't change anything. It starts. So why indent the first paragraph? Silly, unthinking habit. Indents are set automatically as a default. (Here the indents are only nine points because this is set in 9pt Times Roman.)
　It is a nuisance to remember to override the default, but do it: don't indent the first paragraph. Use the space for a signal instead.

This is the first paragraph. It starts a trend of thought and usually contains important information, in order to beguile the semi-curious reader into continuing reading the story.
　The second paragraph switches to a second thought that is independent of the first, but flows from it. The purpose of paragraphing is to signal *change* in direction of thoughts—a valuable clue to the reader.
　The third paragraph changes the direction of the thinking again. The indents shown here are two ems wide, or 16 points, because the type size is eight point.

This is an example of text set ragged right and placed in an excessively wide column, which should be avoided in the first place, but is done here merely as a slightly overdramatized instance of narrow versus deep paragraph indenting.
　This is a one-em indent, and measures eight points from side to side, because this type size is eight point times roman. It is purposely set solid, without any extra line spacing between the lines, to create a thick, dark texture, in order to show off the indented white spaces.
　　　This is a three-em indent, that measures twenty-four points from side to side, because the type is eight point in size, so three times eight is twenty-four. The deeper indent is a broader bay of white space which balances, or at least is not overwhelmed by, the ragged right-hand edge of the text. It draws the eye in more strongly than the puny one-em indent in the paragraph above.

The first paragraph should not be indented. It looks as if a mouse had gnawed the corner. Nor does it make sense. Each new paragraph represents a change in the direction of thought. The first paragraph introduces the story; where's the "change"?

Make the indents deeper to trap the eye in a wider column. Indents ought to look in scale both with the column width as well as the alley or gutter between the columns.

In ragged-right text, make indents deeper, for the uneven right-hand edge makes shallow indents on the left-hand edge practically unnoticeable—especially when the columns are neighbors.

Spaces between paragraphs should be used in long, running text, because they "break up the text" more effectively than paragraph indents. Nonetheless, the integrity of the column must be protected against disintegration. Skipping a full line is too strong an interruption. The ideal is half a line.

This is a headline

This is the first paragraph and it is not indented, precisely because it is the first paragraph. But this is an example of something else: doubling. Excess. Is more always better? This shows the illogic of combining the paragraphing-signalling techniques of indenting with extra spaces between paragraphs.

A second thought starts here in this, the second paragraph, and the new paragraph is separated from the previous one by a full line of space.

That is the most primitive process easily accomplished while setting type on the computer, but it disintegrates the column into a series of short, lonely looking lumps. That in turn threatens the unity of the story.

This is a headline

This is the first paragraph and it is not indented, precisely because it is the first paragraph.

A second thought starts here in this, the second paragraph, and the new paragraph is separated from the previous one only by an extra-deep indent.

That indent says "I am a new paragraph" and thus represents a slightly new direction of thinking. But the columness of the column is retained unbroken.

Is this always necessarily better? There is no such thing as "always" in anything to do with typography, but it does demonstrate that the simplest technique is usually the most effective, especially for that instinctive first-glance reaction. Here, the whole text remains unified, yet its components are clearly evident.

This is a headline

This is the first paragraph and it is not indented, precisely because it is the first paragraph. But this is an example of something else: this text shows the paragraph-signalling techniques of adding extra spaces between paragraphs. (No indents). This shows a *full* line skipped:

A second thought starts here in this, the second paragraph, and the new paragraph is separated from the previous one by a *full line* of space.

Skipping a line is the most primitive process easily accomplished on the computer, but it disintegrates the column into a series of short, lonely looking lumps. That, in turn, threatens the unity of the story. This is, however, less destructive than when it is combined with paragraph indenting, as at far left.

This is a headline

This is the first paragraph and it is not indented, precisely because it is the first paragraph. But this is an example of something else: this text shows the paragraph-signalling techniques of adding extra spaces between paragraphs. This shows only *half* a line skipped:

A second thought starts here in this, the second paragraph, and the new paragraph is separated from the previous one by a *half line* of space.

This is not the most primitive process on the computer, because "the paragraph space after" has to be specified. But it does not disintegrate the column. Instead, it is an excellent, neat, clear compromise.

But half-lines often don't align at column ends. Nonetheless, you gain more than you lose. Who cares about precision down there?

Combining indents with line spaces between paragraphs creates canyons which are not only just too broad, but also look messy. They disintegrate the column and each exaggerated gap is an opportunity to quit reading. *(The text in the examples explains why.)*

Never vary spaces between paragraphs or subheads in order to "force-justify" columns—i.e., to make the columns the same length. It destroys the texture of the typography and looks unkempt. Not mentioned in the tiny text is the worst sin: opening up space between the lines. There is no excuse for such shoddy cheating.

Space between paragraphs must be narrower than the space between the columns, so the page doesn't disintegrate into horizontal bands.

This small and hard-to-read wording merely represents text in columns. It is set very small for two reasons. One is that you should not really want to read it because it takes too much deciphering or a good high-powered magnifying glass. The other is in order to illustrate spacing between things. It is set in eight point Times Roman, tight, no extra line spacing, to an eight pica column width, justified.

Here a half line of space is inserted between paragraphs; that makes the entire column fifteen and a half lines high. What happens when the next column alongside it has two paragraph spaces in it, whereas the first column only has one?

Obviously, the first paragraph space can be accommodated easily, but the problems only happen when you start getting down to the bottom of the second column.

The height cannot be the same, despite the fact that the number of text lines is identical. But what about that extra half-line's space? You can ignore it, or cheat by doubling the space in the left-hand column. Or kill one space. The right way to equalize them is to rewrite the text.

This small and hard-to-read wording merely represents text in columns. It is set very small for two reasons. One is that you should not really want to read it because it takes too much deciphering or a good high-powered magnifying glass. The other is in order to illustrate spacing between things. It is set in eight point Times Roman, tight, no extra line spacing, to a column width of eight picas, justified.

Here is a full line of space inserted between paragraphs; that makes the entire column fifteen and a half lines high. What happens when the next column alongside it has two paragraph spaces in it, whereas the first column only has one?

Obviously, the paragraph spaces can be accommodated easily, so there are no alignment problems when you get to down to the bottom of the second column.

The height can be the same, because the number of text lines is identical. But in this example the columns are very close together, closer than the paragraphs are. As a result, the columns are more broken up and each paragraph appears to stand alone.

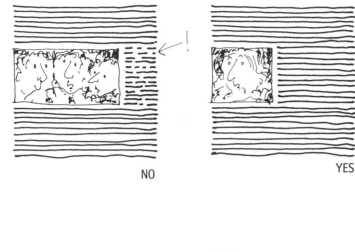

NO   YES

Runarounds are useful but dangerous. The part of the column left after the space for a picture has been gouged out can be too narrow so there are too many wordbreaks at line ends. Also, justification left and right demands that the space between words and characters expand or contract to fit. The type's texture is disturbed, unsightly, and annoying to read. (twenty-five characters per line is a workable minimum.)

NO   YES

Subheads within the runaround look messy and attract attention to something that should not be there in the first place: the fight between the object around which the text is run and the break in the text. The two disparate elements don't belong together. Runarounds should only occur in plain, uninterrupted text areas.

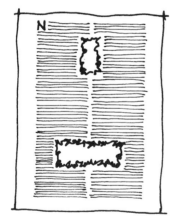

Runarounds between adjacent columns exacerbate fitting problems. See what they do to the text and base judgment on that, because the words are the most fragile element on the page. Design must not ruin reading. But readers probably see the visual objects as jewels on a background. Which is more important: the text or the visual? Controlling contrasts of "color" can help guide them.

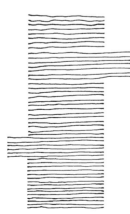

Reverse runaround swells the text outward into the surrounding space.

Crossovers can merge contiguous columns together and visually represent a pro/con, before/after set of opinions. Color or typographic texture added to one of the two sides can enliven and make the discussion vivid.

Lists are popular because the editors have organized the thinking for the reader. They tabulate information and are therefore shortcuts to understanding. They marry content with form, so to work best as a word/picture they must be disciplined and patterned.

The material is written in a pattern that is expressed visually
- The information is segmented into its component parts.
- The different items each start on a new line.
- The typography makes each part visible.
- The type organization on the page shows how the parts fit.

To makes sense, the information needs to fulfill *five requirements:*
1. It must have a clear purpose.
2. It must have a physical shape that organizes the data.
3. It must be typographically clear and legible.
4. It must be neat so its pattern helps communicate the idea.
5. It must make an attractive, easily recognized package.

To produce effective communication, the writer/designer/editor team must
First, understand the problem to be communicated.
Second, analyze and divide it into its component parts.
Third, write the information to fit the segments.
Fourth, invent the best typographic format to fit the material.

The examples of lists in the box tabulate the criteria:

1. Shape	**2. Texture of type**	**3. Visual identification**	**4. Explanatory introduction**
Indented at left	All lines are similarly short	• bullets for random lists	Sentence set in boldface
Ragged edge at right	Each item start with same words	1, 2, 3, for numbered lists	Sentence ending with colon
Extra space above, below	Each line starts with a symbol	1st, 2nd, for sequential lists	Colon implied in the wording

Label or data lists consist of short, self-contained items. The purpose is to identify their group as a group. If the items are just a few words each, then the format allows each item maximum individual noticeability within its context.

Don't indent the paragraph following indented lists (so you don't weaken the effect of the indention's clarity)

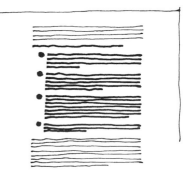

Text lists consist of items each longer than a sentence or two. A pattern of short paragraphs is readily discernible if it has a different color or texture of type and if the left-hand edge is controlled. *Easiest:* allow bullets to hang by indenting turnover lines.

Align bullets and let them hang so they are visible (they identify the list as a list)

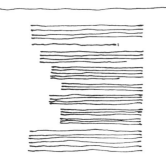

Outline list ranks and tabulates information by layers of subordination. They require more than one degree of indention to explain the hierarchies. *Easiest:* make indents deep enough to discern their differences clearly. They may well need a vertical rule as datum at left against which indents can be measured.

I.   Roman capital numerals
II. Follow numerals with a period and align on it. I II III IV V VI VII VIII IX X
    A. Capital letter (whether roman or *italic*)
    B. Follow capital with a period
       1. Arabic numeral
       2. Follow numeral with a period
          a) Lowercase letter, roman
          b) Follow letter with a parenthesis
             (1) Italic numerals
             (2) Enclose numerals in parentheses
                (i) Lowercase roman numerals
                (ii) Enclose numerals in parentheses

Arbitrary listing of alphanumeric symbols shows the generally accepted series of indents, but there is no "correct" version. Use whatever makes sense, so long as it is understandable at a glance.

Cats	Hippopotamuses	Cats
Birds	Rhinoceroses	Dogs
Giraffes	Chipmunks	Birds
Chipmunks	Giraffes	People
Hippopotamuses	People	Giraffes
Rhinoceroses	Birds	Chipmunks
People	Dogs	Rhinoceroses
Dogs	Cats	Hippopotamuses

Don't make "designs" with lists. Don't force them into artificial shapes, so the shape becomes the tail that wags the dog. The only exception: if the shape explains the subject in some way. (Don't search for deeper meaning in the words in the examples; there is none.)

• Cats miaouw whenever they are hungry, angry, thirsty, bored, or their tail is being pulled.
• Dogs bark whenever they sense that their territory is being invaded by some threatening stranger like a mail carrier.
• Birds twitter all the time, especially in spring, which is very annoying if you're trying to sleep.
• People chatter endlessly, pointlessly, witlessly, and insist on pontificating on chat shows on television. They can be switched off.

    • Cats miaouw whenever they are hungry, angry, thirsty, bored, or their tail is being pulled.
    • Dogs bark whenever they sense that their territory is being invaded by some threatening stranger like a mail carrier.
    • Birds twitter all the time, especially in spring, which is very annoying if you're trying to sleep.
    • People chatter endlessly, pointlessly, witlessly and insist on pontificating on chat shows on television. They can be switched off.

Don't destroy the signalling capacity of bullets, numerals, or other symbols by hiding them in indents or in some shape, or even in running text. Let them disclose the list as a list by standing proudly out there in the left-hand edge in a vertical column.

    • Cats miaouw
      • Dogs bark
       • Birds twitter
      • People chatter
    • Chipmunks squeak
  • Hippopotamuses growl
  • Rhinoceroses bellow
    • Giraffes are silent

• Cats miaouw • Dogs bark • Birds twitter • People chatter • Chipmunks squeak • Hippopotamuses growl • Rhinoceroses bellow • Giraffes are silent but • Cats miaouw and • Dogs bark • Birds twitter • People chatter • Chipmunks squeak • Hippopotamuses growl • Rhinoceroses bellow • Giraffes are silent • Cats miaouw • Dogs bark

• Cats miaouw
• Dogs bark
• Birds twitter
• People chatter
• Chipmunks squeak
• Hippopotamuses growl
• Rhinoceroses bellow
• Giraffes are silent

Break up long, daunting masses into shorter components. Turn a blockbuster story into a cluster of units each of which can stand on its own, but is recognized as part of a whole, under an umbrella headline. Readers prefer short bits, so make it easy for them to enter the article through a doorway of their choice—even if it makes pages busier. Welcome is the aim, not neatness. But do retain unity within each segment, so give each segment a simple outline shape and don't break up the paragraphs too much.

Isolate short stories in space so viewers can see at first glance where each begins, ends, and how long it is. That helps them decide the effort they must expend versus their interest in that subject. Zoning organizes the page. Use space (AS MOATS) or rules (AS WALLS). Squeeze out space from within the story, add it to the surrounding frame.

Fast-scan and slow-study. Organize (edit) the material, write it, and lay it out for deliberate *two-level readership*. Exploit type size coupled with column width to mirror importance. Help readers find those wonderful nuggets by displaying them right on top and making them look important. Add blackness to focus attention and create rankings. (Such forthrightness also allows readers to skip what might interest them less—and they perceive such permission as reader-friendly.)

Encourage fast vertical scanning downpage by poking out display into space on the left-hand edge as hanging indents.

**Made arbitrary arrangements
in which the visual composition
overwhelms the message.**

(Beware of the "original
solution" that will attract
attention to itself
but mislead the viewer.
Will it attract them to *reading*?
If it does, great!
If it is there merely
for its own clever sake,
kill it.)

**Common typographic sins to
avoid.** "The easiest thing in the
world for any reader to do is
stop reading," said Barney
Kilgore, legendary editor of the
Wall Street Journal, 1941-1966.
Enough said.

**Wrote and edited
without keeping typography
in mind while writing and editing.**

(To make the most
of the opportunities
for organization, tabulation,
even simplification,
imagine the type
as it will appear laid out.
Retrofitting is sometimes workable,
but thinking ahead is better.)

A detail from Gustave Doré's illustrations for Dante's *Divine Comedy*.

**Printed type on a background
that vies for attention
and disturbs the viewer's concentration.**

(Worse, if it hampers reading,
the text will be skipped.
What looks cool on screen,
often disappoints in print.
Words must never fight their background.)

**Didn't bother to read,
study, or understand
what the text says.**

(The typography must be crafted
to reflect the way it is written
and how the story is structured.)

**Played with type
just to be different,
inventive, creative.**

(Words are more valuable
as thoughts
than as graphic patterns.
Don't think "DESIGN"
"What does it look like?"
but think "FUNCTION"
*"Are we transmitting
the thoughts clearly?"*).

PRODUCT-MAKING

Each headline is independent, because it refers to its own story. But each is also just a segment of the entire package. Since the purpose of headline type is to be highly visible, the way it looks helps to create (or disintegrate) the visual consistency and personality of the product.

A logical hierarchy of headline sizes and boldness clues the viewer to the structure of the publication. Wherever heads are of equal importance, they should look similar.

There is always that nagging suspicion that *readers will be bored* unless we show them something new and different. Though the temptation of varying the look of the heads in order to "add interest" is hard to resist, refrain from introducing trendiness or variety for its own sake. The publication is in serious trouble if it has to depend on superficial tinkering like that to be "interesting."

STORY-TELLING

Potential readers are looking for information—and the headline is the first signal they seek. Pictures may attract them, but the head is what really informs them. The logical step from the head is to the deck (if there is one) and then into the text. To encourage reading, it is silly to position them in any sequence other than 1, 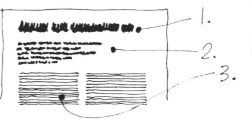 2, 3 down the page, unless there is a very good functional and overriding reason for some other variation.

Heads are serious persuaders. Yes, they are opportunities for playfulness "to attract attention," but overdoing it is dangerous. For instance, making the type enormous forces the reader to focus on the page twice: once at a distance (to read the big stuff) and then close up (to read the small stuff). The words the headline says had better be worth that bother. Imagine what you demand of the reader.

Headlines expose
their content (what they say)
by their form (how they look)

Mutual understanding of meaning and purpose helps the editor/designer team to handle "display" so that they increase the impact of their product. Nomenclature of the normal standards are shown here, tips on type on following pages.

Wall-to-wall head is written to fill out the available space from one side of the page to the other.

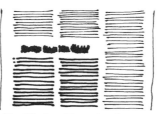

Straddle head is centered over more than one column. Leaves insignificant blanks at each end.

Centered head is equidistant from left and right; dignified, traditional, boring. *(See page 92)*

Staggered head places each successive line indented a step deeper and encourages eye flow.

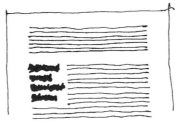

Stacked flush-left concentrates words into a strong black blob to contrast with text.

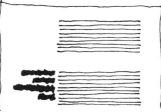

Stacked flush-right makes it "belong" to the text alongside which it is placed. Harder to read in bulk.

Hanging indent head pokes out into the left-hand margin for maximum noticeability.

Cut-in head is placed in white space chopped out of the text block which "runs around" it.

On its ear. Sideways or at an angle (reading upward always better than downward). A nuisance.

These heads are not strictly headlines, but their names refer to "heads," so they need to be defined and identified.

Standing head is a tag that identifies a regularly repeated section.

Running head repeats name of a section continued on several pages.

Jump head identifies story continuation by repeating key word from main head.

Stub head is title of farthest-left column in type tables (the "stub").

110 HEADS AND DECKS

Split heads. Allied segments can be shown to belong together by obvious continuation signals.

Tombstoning heads (aligning them across the page) works if they are separated by rules.

Key word in large size or color stands out by contrast. Ideal as **jump head** later*(see below).*

Patterned heads show that the elements have some affinity to each other. Three variants shown. Heads are valuable because they combine verbal meaning with visual form, so display them in enough white space to make them unskippable.

Jumping the gutter (crossing from one page to the other) is usually unsuccessful, unless the type is big enough to make it obvious. Works best in top quarter of the page. Never break a word in the gutter.

Bimodal heads written in two parts neatly solve the problem of jumping the gutter. The first part ends in a colon, dash, or ellipsis which leads into the second part, often a two-liner.

Kicker head is a word or two in small type leading into main part of headline with colon, dash, or ...

Hammer head is a topic word set in much larger type than the size used for the main headline itself.

Eyebrow head is a freestanding self-contained phrase or topic in contrasting size, color, character.

Type in headlines

So long as the meaning is lucid and accessible, there are no limits on creativity. However, never play with headline type just to show off inventiveness or for phony "variety."

Goudy Palatino Times Baskerville Garamond

Oldstyle: quiet, gentle, resembling pen drawing. So good that it is not noticeable. Moderate transition between thick and thin parts of strokes, slanted serifs, diagonal stress (if you draw a line between thin parts of the curved strokes).

Fenice Bodoni Walbaum

Modern: cold, elegant, mechanical, right angled, vertical stress. Marked contrast between thick and thin strokes creates a dazzling contrast especially in larger sizes. Serifs are thin and horizontal.

Clarendon Memphis Century Schoolbook

Slab serif: bold, dark, geometric, vertical. Little difference between thicks and thins. Serifs are heavy, horizontal, and squared off—hence "slabs". So highly readable that they are often used for children's reading primers.

Antique Olive Formata Gill Sans Franklin

Sans serif: also called gothic. All serifs chopped off. Strokes practically lack thick/thin variation. Vertical stress. Pick just one, because most fonts have wide variety of weights. Banal publication design combines sans serif heads with serif text type.

Reporter Shelley Volante Zapf Chancery Linoscript

Scripts: a wide variety of faces that look as if they had been written by hand. Use with great discretion (and never in all-caps!) but when you do, go for it boldly, because they can be very decorative, eye-catching, even poetic elements.

Addled SCARLETT FAJITA EXTRAVAGANZA

Decorative: immense variety of weird, startling, peculiar fonts available for specialized applications. Resist the temptation just to have fun. There has to be a meaningful reason for using any of these distinctive faces.

Which font? Display type must be legible, but it also has to attract attention, look interesting. Besides, it gives character to the product because it is so important, visible, and repetitive. There are literally thousands of "fonts" or "faces" to choose from. (There is a technical difference between these two terms, but for practical purposes they are interchangeable.) The six basic categories are *shown at left*. Use any face so long as it is stands out against the text by shape, darkness, color contrast, and is appropriate to the character of the product. The decision must be based on the understanding that any single headline doesn't matter all that much, but seen together in the package, they matter immensely.

Serif or sans serif? Choice depends on visual character of the product. Serifs or the lack of them is less important than avoidance of exaggeration. Both are fine if used with circumspection. Both are bad if the type is misused. (Too expanded, too condensed, too anything).

Different font for each story? If your publication carries no ads, you have no opposition to overwhelm or be seen against, and so you have more freedom. But don't make it a fancy-dress party. Using decorative type to symbolize the atmosphere of the story itself is a solution of last resort, if you have no photographs.

Same font throughout? People scan heads as a coordinated stream from page to page, when they flip pages. The interrelationship of the heads sideways (from impression to impression) is as important as their individual relationship to the individual story. If you can find one that has enough variations in weight and posture: sizes, boldnesses, italics etc., use it. It will make the editorial spaces stand out if you have to fight ads. Establish personality by restricting faces to the fewest possible. You (but nobody else!) will soon be bored with it but stay with it—it will come to represent you and your voice and will grow in value as a recognition symbol.

Big? The bigger the type is, the louder it shouts, so size is a language in itself. It is a visual pattern that communicates comparative value just by the way it looks: bigness equals importance. Never puff up heads just to fit them into a given space, because you'll mislead the viewer. Instead, establish a standardized schedule and stick with that.

Short? Yes, for eye-catching makeup. But they may need expanding with decks or intros to sell the value of the story. The more enlightening, the more irresistible they are. However, pithy shortness is less valuable than a promise of benefit, which might need a few more words, but bring in more readers.

Long? Yes, make them as long as they need to be to tickle curiosity. Smaller but bolder type in the same space draws the same attention but packs in a more meaty sales-pitch.

Italic
Thin
Light
Light Italic
Medium
Medium Italic
Bold
Bold Italic
Regular Condensed
Extra Compressed
Bold Condensed
Extended
Med. Outline
Bold Outline
Bold Condensed Outline
Shaded Center
Medium Shaded Right

Helvetica, one of the most versatile faces, comes in more than enough versions for a publication's need for "variety" within the stylistic unity that should dominate.

Sizes are infinitely variable, but the proven gradations are as workable today as ever. The steps look logically coordinated, yet are easily distinguishable.

1418243036424860**7284**

120-point "Impact" printed here in 25% grey, to prevent it from dominating the page. Imagine the impact of 100% black.

This headline is set in big Gill

This head in smaller, bolder, Gill tells more in same space

This is a headline in big type

This is a headline in big type

This is a headline in big type

Never squeeze or expand type, though the computer seems to encourage it. The type's designer worked out relationships of shape, rhythm, and spacing for optimal legibility. Cheating to squeeze in words by tampering with those relationships defeats their elegance. Use the discipline of headline writing when type was metal: establish maximum character-totals per type size and per column width. Write (and rewrite) headlines to fit. The extra effort is worth it.

For purposes of copyfitting, letters have varying widths. These are rules of thumb:

ABCDEFGHJKLNOPQRSTUVXYZ234567890 I1 MW

CAPS: all letters are a unit wide except **I** and **1** which are a half, and **M** and **W** which are two units.

abcdeghknopqrsuvxyz234567890 fijlt1 mw

Lowercase: all letters are a unit wide except **f i j l t 1**, which are a half, and **m** and **w** which are two units.

TRAIANUS AMAT ALL-CAPS

CAPITAL LETTERS MAY LOOK IMPORTANT AND DIGNIFIED BUT THEY EAT UP SPACE; BESIDES, THEY ARE HARDER TO DECIPHER THAN LOWERCASE. IS TRADITION A GOOD ENOUGH REASON TO MAKE READERS SUFFER?

Avoid all-caps in bulk because they are harder to decipher. Instead, use capital letters to pop out a couple of key words that are worthy of extra attention. Why are Caps harder to read? Because:

EACH WORD IN ALL-CAPS IS A RECTANGLE

but each lowercase word has its own outline shape

Ascenders and descenders give each word its own individual characteristic shape. Furthermore, it is not the bottoms of the letters that are important. It is the wiggly outlines of the tops of the letters that makes the words easily deciphered.

I bet that you can not read this headline easily:

But I'm sure that this is very easily deciphered

AND THIS IS EVEN MORE DIFFICULT TO FIGURE OUT

Avoid the up-and-down-style. It Is Harder To Read, Even Though We Are Used To It And Believe It Is Standard, Correct, Traditional Headline Handling. Why Do It? (See how much effort it took you to decipher this simple sentence?) After all, heads stand out because they are bigger and bolder than text anyway, so why do this as well? Lower-case reads smoother, faster. What is more, the Up-and-Down-Style robs you of the capacity to show off proper names and acronyms, because the capital letters that identify them do not stand out well enough. When everything is capitalized, capitalization is devalued into a meaningless and destructive pattern.

Setting Type This Way Makes As Little Sense aS dOES tHIS iDIOCY, wHICH iS mERELY iTS rEVERSE, But We Are So Used To The Up And Down Style That We Believe All Heads Are S'posed To Look This Way. Jan White Says This Looks Like Visual Hiccups. OK, Where In This Mess Is The Proper Name Or The Acronym? Can You Find Them, Fast? (Immediacy Is The Essence Of Display!)

Is "OK" An Acronym?

Use ragged-right setting in short lines for large type. That way you avoid irregular wordspacing (or even worse: letterspacing), which impedes smooth rhythmic reading. Headlines shouldn't be obstacle courses for the eye.

B A D T Y P E SPACING

Never justify big type in narrow columns because that leads to bad spacing.

Never justify big type in narrow columns because that leads to bad spacing.

Avoid letterspacing: the larger the type size, the tighter the tracking should be, to allow words to be perceived fast. Opening up between letters to make words fit into a given space is cheating.

We recognize (i. e., read) words as letter-groups and disintegrating them artificially this way just slows reading speed even if it looks cool.

Avoid centering heads vertically. The headline introduces and belongs to the text beneath it, so the space below needs to be tighter than that separating the head from the text above. Not an unimportant detail, adding up an issue's heads.

this type represents the last three lines of the text in the story above, that precedes the following headline.

This headline floats

This shows the first line of the text in the next story. The headline floats halfway between them, belongs to neither.

this type represents the last three lines of the text in the story above, that precedes the following headline.

Anchored headline

This shows the first line of the text in the next story. The head placed closer to it belongs to it visually and logically.

This headline sits
centered
in its space

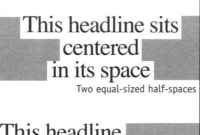

This headline sits
centered
in its space

Two equal-sized half-spaces

This headline
is ranged
flush-left

One massed empty space

**Four
reasons
not to
center
heads:**

1. Space. Centering creates mini-spaces on the left and the right (shown in grey). They are not as effective in adding dramatic white-space for contrast as is yielded by quad-lefting (i.e., flush-left or ranged-left setting). That bigger block of space is not merely a good contrast to the blackness of the headline type, but it also lightens the look of the page by bringing in some useful 'air.'

2. Disintegration. Placing lines on top of each other like a stack of pancakes makes each line a self-contained element and that slows eye motion.

3. Pompousness. Artificial and self-conscious shape exaggerates the self-importance of the headline. It makes it into a self-contained object, whereas it ought only to be an introduction into the text. Besides, who wants to turn flowing thoughts into objects in the shape of butterflies or Rorschach tests?

4. Phrasing. Breaking lines by phrase, as they would be heard when spoken out loud makes the clearest sense. Setting the phrases flush left, encourages the reader to continue reading, because the eye does not have to search for the start of the next line.

We hold these truths
to be self-evident, that all men
are created equal,
that they are endowed
by their creator
with certain
unalienable rights,
that among these are life,
liberty and the pursuit
of happiness.

This text is not written as a "headline;" it is also too long. It is used here deliberately in order to exaggerate and make the points obvious.

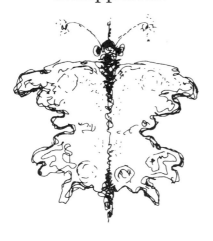

We hold these truths
to be self-evident, that all men
are created equal,
that they are endowed
by their creator
with certain
unalienable rights,
that among these are life,
liberty and the pursuit
of happiness.

We hold these truths
to be self-evident,
that all men are created equal,
that they are endowed
by their creator
with certain unalienable rights,
that among these are
life, liberty and
the pursuit of happiness.

Which version is clearer, faster?

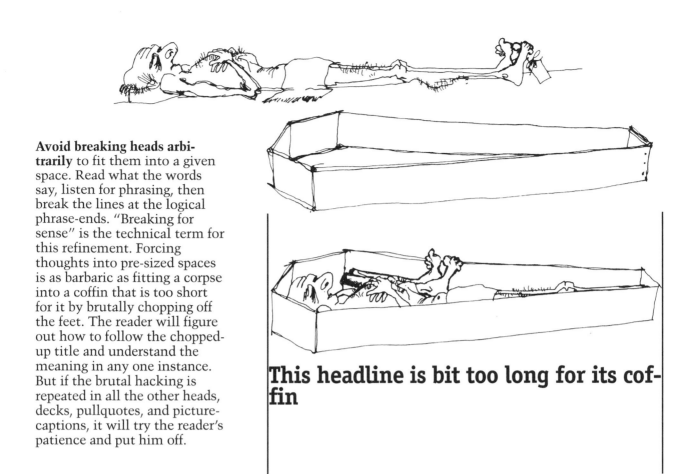

Avoid breaking heads arbitrarily to fit them into a given space. Read what the words say, listen for phrasing, then break the lines at the logical phrase-ends. "Breaking for sense" is the technical term for this refinement. Forcing thoughts into pre-sized spaces is as barbaric as fitting a corpse into a coffin that is too short for it by brutally chopping off the feet. The reader will figure out how to follow the chopped-up title and understand the meaning in any one instance. But if the brutal hacking is repeated in all the other heads, decks, pullquotes, and picture-captions, it will try the reader's patience and put him off.

This headline is bit too long for its coffin

Type is speech made visible:so just open your eyes and listen

Word size variation affects the meaning of the words. Read it out loud, following the sizes as clues to loudness. Do the variations explain and enhance sense?

Type is speech made visible: so open your eyes and listen

Typography can crystallize a tone of voice: it can be RAISED or LOWERED; it can appear to *shout*—or it can appear to *whisper*

Typography can crystallize a tone of voice: it can be raised or lowered; it can appear to **SHOUT**—or it can appear to whisper

Typography can crystallize a tone of voice: it can be raised or lowered; **it can appear to shout—or it can appear to** whisper

The buck stops here.

Avoid periods at the ends of heads. They act as stops, which is what you don't want. And avoid exclamation points **"bangs."** They are cheap shots.

!

Heads that focus attention on the photo and then promise a benefit need a minimum of 18 words

In advertisements, the photo attracts the viewer's first attention, but because everyone can interpret an image their own way, we must focus their attention on what it is that we want them to notice in the picture. Having done that, we then have to motivate them to read the text in the advertisement by promising them a benefit.

The text will then excite them enough to fill out the coupon and send for a free sample. So says advertising guru David Ogilvy in his "Confessions of an Advertising Man." In editorial work heads need to be as long as they need to be. (Perhaps you noticed how smoothly your eye moved down to the text?)

Make the second line shorter. That way the eye is closer to the start of the text beneath, encouraging continuation of reading.

<u>Lists are quick, good, and justly popular</u>
Lists are quick, good, and justly popular

Avoid underscoring. It interferes with the descenders (g, j, p, q, y) and makes the message a bit harder to decipher.

Où sont les neiges d'antan? Where are the snows of yesteryear?

Never set words vertically, even as a joke. The poor reader has to sound out the words like a kindergartener, because the familiar relationships of letter to neighboring letter and their intervening spaces are destroyed.

Best bet wet-pet set: fish

Avoid cuteness—unless puns are apt and enlightening, they devalue seriousness.

Basic headline arrangements
compared. Reading some of the
words may help convince you
of my personal preferences.
They are not prejudices, but
recommendations based on
observation, study, and empiri-
cal experience. Decisions
should never be only about
what something looks like; they
should always be about how
well a particular solution might
work within the given circumstances. All editing and designing is interpretive choice-
making.

Centering runs counter
to the fluidity
and phrasing of language
transformed into type.
The left-hand edge
of the column————————
is the edge
around which
everything revolves.
It is the edge to which
the reader's eye must
return to find
the start of
the next text line.
The left-hand edge
is the true
center of gravity
of the column.

THIS HEADLINE IS CENTERED
ON THE MATERIAL BENEATH.
TRADITIONAL, SELF-IMPORTANT, DIGNIFIED
BUT STATIC, A STACK OF PANCAKES
REPELLENT IN ALL-CAPS

mmmmmmmmmmmmmmmmmmmmmmmmmmmmmmmmmmmmmmm
mmmmmmmmmmmmmmmmmmmmmmmmmmmmmmmmmmmmmmm
mmmmmmmmmmmmmmmmmmmmmmmmmmmmmmmmmmmmmmm
mmmmmmmmmmmmmmmmmmmmmmmmmmmmmmmmmmmmmmm

This Headline Is Centered
on the Material Beneath;
Traditional, Self-Conscious, Formal, Dignified
but the Discredited Up-And-Down Style
Makes it Undecipherable

mmmmmmmmmmmmmmmmmmmmmmmmmmmmmmmmmmmmmmm
mmmmmmmmmmmmmmmmmmmmmmmmmmmmmmmmmmmmmmm
mmmmmmmmmmmmmmmmmmmmmmmmmmmmmmmmmmmmmmm
mmmmmmmmmmmmmmmmmmmmmmmmmmmmmmmmmmmmmmm

This headline is also centered
on the material beneath;
traditional, self-conscious, formal, dignified
but static, like a lump on a log;
all-lowercase is better—but still dead

mmmmmmmmmmmmmmmmmmmmmmmmmmmmmmmmmmmmmmm
mmmmmmmmmmmmmmmmmmmmmmmmmmmmmmmmmmmmmmm
mmmmmmmmmmmmmmmmmmmmmmmmmmmmmmmmmmmmmmm
mmmmmmmmmmmmmmmmmmmmmmmmmmmmmmmmmmmmmmm

This headline is set flush-left
with the type below;
it follows eye motion
since all type lines start at far left,
thus encouraging continuity of reading

mmmmmmmmmmmmmmmmmmmmmmmmmmmmmmmmmmmmmmm
mmmmmmmmmmmmmmmmmmmmmmmmmmmmmmmmmmmmmmm
mmmmmmmmmmmmmmmmmmmmmmmmmmmmmmmmmmmmmmm
mmmmmmmmmmmmmmmmmmmmmmmmmmmmmmmmmmmmmmm

Use an arrangement
that reflects
the phrasing of the words
so the way it is laid out
helps transmit the message fast and vividly

mmmmmmmmmmmmmmmmmmmmmmmmmmmmmmmmmmmmmmm
mmmmmmmmmmmmmmmmmmmmmmmmmmmmmmmmmmmmmmm
mmmmmmmmmmmmmmmmmmmmmmmmmmmmmmmmmmmmmmm
mmmmmmmmmmmmmmmmmmmmmmmmmmmmmmmmmmmmmmm

This is a headline that works
The topic attracts attention by size and dominating blackness.
This contrasting deck expands on it and explains its significance,
resulting in a one-two punch

mmmmmmmmmmmmmmmmmmmmmmmmmmmmmmmmmmmmmmm
mmmmmmmmmmmmmmmmmmmmmmmmmmmmmmmmmmmmmmm
mmmmmmmmmmmmmmmmmmmmmmmmmmmmmmmmmmmmmmm
mmmmmmmmmmmmmmmmmmmmmmmmmmmmmmmmmmmmmmm

Grey fog should be first words of headline, followed by some **What'sInItForMe**

mmmmmmmmmmmmmmmmmmmmmmmmmmmmmmmmmmm
mmmmmmmmmmmmmmmmmmmmmmmmmmmmmmmmmmm
mmmmmmmmmmmmmmmmmmmmmmmmmmmmmmmmmmm
mmmmmmmmmmmmmmmmmmmmmmmmmmmmmmmmmmm

Combination of image with headline is irresistible provided that 1) the picture is above the headline (so the head is, in effect, a caption for it), 2) the headline refers to the picture, and 3) the headline also promises a benefit.

Chief thief 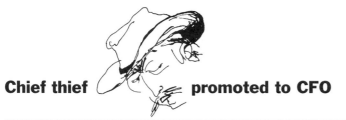 **promoted to CFO**

mmmmmmmmmmmmmmmmmmmmmmmmmmmmmmmmmmm
mmmmmmmmmmmmmmmmmmmmmmmmmmmmmmmmmmm
mmmmmmmmmmmmmmmmmmmmmmmmmmmmmmmmmmm
mmmmmmmmmmmmmmmmmmmmmmmmmmmmmmmmmmm

Small image inserted into the words, rebus-like, enlivens, personalizes, pinpoints meaning.

This story is about type in the headline

mmmmmmmmmmmmmmmmmmmmmmmmmmmmmmmmmmm
mmmmmmmmmmmmmmmmmmmmmmmmmmmmmmmmmmm
mmmmmmmmmmmmmmmmmmmmmmmmmmmmmmmmmmm
mmmmmmmmmmmmmmmmmmmmmmmmmmmmmmmmmmm

Blow up the key word so it dominates and provokes interest.

This story is about color type in headlines

mmmmmmmmmmmmmmmmmmmmmmmmmmmmmmmmmmm
mmmmmmmmmmmmmmmmmmmmmmmmmmmmmmmmmmm
mmmmmmmmmmmmmmmmmmmmmmmmmmmmmmmmmmm
mmmmmmmmmmmmmmmmmmmmmmmmmmmmmmmmmmm

This story is about color type in headlines

mmmmmmmmmmmmmmmmmmmmmmmmmmmmmmmmmmm
mmmmmmmmmmmmmmmmmmmmmmmmmmmmmmmmmmm
mmmmmmmmmmmmmmmmmmmmmmmmmmmmmmmmmmm

Run the key word in color, though it is better to run the key word in black and the rest of the headline in color. Black ink yields the strongest contrast against white paper and therefore it pops out more effectively than any color, even bright red, because any color is paler than black and therefore contrasts less powerfully. Even if it is a brilliant, pure, bright chroma.

Type in decks

Decks are the bridge in a three-step sequence:

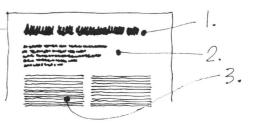

The headline (1) proposes a basic idea…

the deck (2) points out its significance…

the first paragraph (3) announces its usefulness.

Decks personalize the content, and thus persuade the potential reader to enter the text. *They sell.* But if they are too long, nobody bothers to read them.

Don't devalue the deck by blatant exaggeration and thus lose credibility. Never repeat words from the headline or preview them from the text that follows. It annoys readers who resent wasting time.

"This is unquestionably the greatest…"
Is it really?

"Tell'em whatcha gonna tell'em, then tell'em, then tell'em whadd'ya told'em"
The traditional journalistic cynicism that seldom works with today's breakneck pace.

Type font: should it match the headline (but smaller) or the text (but bigger)? Choice depends on the styling of the product and whether the wording is normally written to "belong" more to the head than to the text. In either case, it should be standardized throughout the publication as a personality characteristic.

Type size is obviously larger than the text, signalling its importance. Far more vital: when decks are scanned, the page is held at a greater distance from the eyes than when the text is slowly studied. Therefore it must be big and generously leaded enough to encourage fast reading—especially when lines are long.

Decks with short lines are best set ragged-right, to avoid the irregular gaps between words that result from forced justification. Regular rhythm is essential for smooth fast reading.

You want to have standardized word spacing between words specially in narrow columns

Break lines for sense, phrase by phrase for fastest comprehension, and flow them down the page informally.

Contrast scale, color, and texture of type on the page by stacking the deck in short lines and arraying them alongside the text block.

PRECEDES are decks written to lead into the headline. They can be self-contained (with an implicit pause before the title) or they can lead directly into the title's wording. The typographic arrangement responds to the difference. **Punctuation** (: colon, … ellipses) can be used to bridge the gap between the "precede" and the headline into which it leads.

SYNOPSES are self-contained compressed summaries of the article intended for quick reference. Information retrieval and keyword search are important factors. They must have clear, concise information without a trace of selling. A formal look is appropriate to their serious scholarly context. Center them for solemnity and set justified because ragged-right is deemed frivolous. Placed at the top of the page, they help signal the start of another article.

ABSTRACTS are primly conventional summaries normally restricted to some 120 words, citing PROBLEM/METHOD/TREND/ RESULT/CONCLUSIONS in research reports, THESIS/ARGUMENTS in reviews. Usually placed as first paragraph, in bold, a size larger than text. (Centered and isolated is better: readers can skip them more easily.)

A negative subhead "**breaks up the text**." The text is written as running copy, and when it is finished and placed on the page, interruptions are dropped in wherever they look good. Some significant word or phrase in the text is pulled out and repeated. Newspapers used to follow the "dollar-bill rule" that demanded subheads every 6″ whether they made sense there or not. Retrofitting—however traditionally accepted—is seldom as beguiling as more functional thinking.

A positive subhead is **a signpost to meaning**. That attitude responds to today's need for doing as much work for the rushed readers as possible: simplifying, segmenting, categorizing... and making it shout obviously at first glance.

STORY-TELLING

One level of readership (the fast one) is interested in the big ideas; the other level (the slow one) wants the details. The story is usually constructed of a series of sequential segments—each signalled by a headline. The point of each paragraph within those segments is made in the first sentence.

The purpose is to allow the looker to scan the boldfaced elements and **gather the gist of the story from a fast overview**. Readers are enabled to skip whatever may interest them less. The hope is that putting the most interesting sentence first may lure them into wanting to read on. The subheads should be those fascinating points worded succinctly and displayed in order to be noticed.

PRODUCT-MAKING

The difficulty in this style of thinking and writing is that writers need to know what they want to say before they say it, so they can structure the story in sequential, logical segments. Clearly, this can't apply across the board, but the majority of today's articles are not literary think-pieces and so deserve this treatment. Such helpfulness comes across as reader friendliness.

Type in subheads

Contrast makes the subhead stand out. It is made to look different from its surrounding text by:

Boldness
If the bold is bold enough to create sufficient color differential as it does here (using Trump Mediaeval), then this is probably the best technique. It is advisable to use the same font for both text and display in order to give the product a distinctive, recognizable personality, while keeping it simple.

Size
This is a bit exaggerated: a 14-point letter size in a 10-point text is a bit overwhelming, but it certainly does stand out. It would be much too big if the subhead were longer than just a short word like this one. 12-point type might do the job just as well, if not better.

TEXTURE
though it is not a good idea to use too many all-caps, since they are harder to read. Any single subhead is not a problem, but imagine how many of them you have to accommodate. Then it becomes a cumulative problem.

Italics
which are often used because they look different from the roman. The trouble is that some italics are paler than the roman, and as a result the contrast is hardly noticeable. In most sans-serif faces, the italics are deliberately made the same color and they just slant. In that case, compensate by writing two-liners so they stand out more, or set them a size or two larger, or place them in more space.

Typeface
such as a sans-serif in the context of serif text type, like this Helvetica in surrounding Trump Mediæval. Or vice versa: insert serifed face subheads in sans-serif text.

`Reverse type`
but watch it, this can be bit overwhelming, especially if the panel is black, not a deliberately weakened grey.

**Doubling up
the lines**
which makes a stronger contrasting visual spot, while saying more—a valuable capacity to help draw the potential reader into the text. If you do double-liners, don't mix them with single-liners in the same story. That looks untidy.

Develop a style and stick to it. Too many signal changes confuse the reader. On the other hand, you need to have enough variety to express different tonalities of emphasis. And, perhaps, to add some visual variety though, disappointingly, readers are less aware of such finesse than the editors and the designers. It's good that the readers don't notice. They should be so fascinated by the content that they couldn't care less about the manner of presentation.

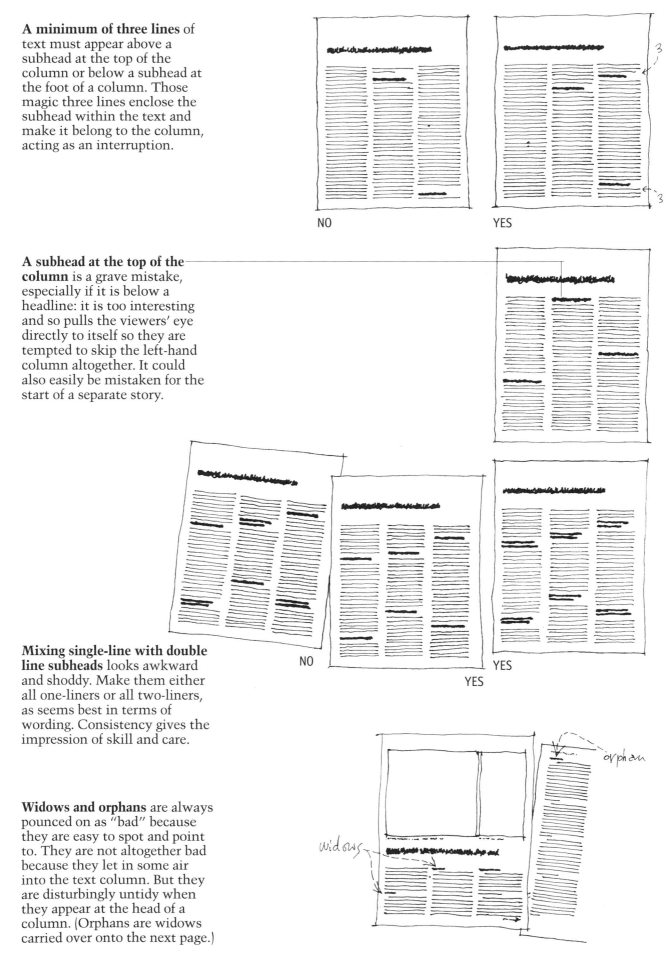

A minimum of three lines of text must appear above a subhead at the top of the column or below a subhead at the foot of a column. Those magic three lines enclose the subhead within the text and make it belong to the column, acting as an interruption.

NO   YES

A subhead at the top of the column is a grave mistake, especially if it is below a headline: it is too interesting and so pulls the viewers' eye directly to itself so they are tempted to skip the left-hand column altogether. It could also easily be mistaken for the start of a separate story.

Mixing single-line with double line subheads looks awkward and shoddy. Make them either all one-liners or all two-liners, as seems best in terms of wording. Consistency gives the impression of skill and care.

NO   YES   YES

Widows and orphans are always pounced on as "bad" because they are easy to spot and point to. They are not altogether bad because they let in some air into the text column. But they are disturbingly untidy when they appear at the head of a column. (Orphans are widows carried over onto the next page.)

orphan

widows

The placement of the subhead in relation to the text is an important detail. Never put the subhead closer to the end of the paragraph, like this

This subhead is in the wrong place

because it seems to belong to the wrong thing — the end of the previous text. If you float it halfway between the paragraph that precedes it and the paragraph that follows it, it may look nice and neat, and it may be the simplest thing to produce while setting the text on the keyboard, but it is neutral:

This subhead floats halfway between

The functional purpose of a subhead is to introduce the material that follows beneath it, so the reader is subtly drawn into it, like this:

This subhead is in the right place

So much for the up-and-down relationship within the text column. Now as to the side-to-side placement.

Where would you think is the best possible place to hide a subhead? Plumb in the middle of the text, so it drowns in the grey quicksand of the surrounding type. Despite the fact that the Junior High School teacher decreed that the center is the correct place to put headings and you have probably continued believing it ever since, it is time to reconsider. It is static, artificial, and moreover it hides that

Centered subhead

But reading is a lineal continuum that flows from left to right, each line starting at far left. To encourage the process of eye movement in a rhythmic way, it is far wiser not to break that motion as centering also does, because every such break makes the reader aware of the act of reading (and helps them to stop).

Flush left subhead

continues the smooth and consistent reading motion, while contrasting the dark type against a single large white area to its right which makes it more dramatic and visible. (Centering splits the white space into two insignificant bits.) For maximal noticeability use a

Hanging indent subhead

which pokes out into the white space to the left of the column. It pulls the reader into the text through curiosity (if the subhead promises

something interesting.) Sometimes you can play tricks, like placing the subhead flush right to the right-hand edge of the column.

Flush-right subhead

Why? To be different — which can be a perfectly cogent reason, given circumstances where you have nothing more functional to depend on.

Deep indent subhead

Align the subhead on the indent, if your indents are unusually deep. The normal indent is one-em (i.e., the square of the type size: if you are using 12 pt type, the indent is 12 points.) For a less visible break, consider using a

Run-in subhead, which reads directly into the sentence that it is a part of. It shouts more gently than freestanding subheads, but those bold-faced words had better be written to be worthy of bolding. A variation on this is to use words as a self-contained phrase ending in a period:

Sɪᴅᴇʜᴇᴀᴅ. It is doubtful, however, whether such single words can be provocative and informative enough to pull people into the text. In any case, sideheads (like other subheads) should be preceded by a sliver of space, and should not be indented, if they are to do their job of attracting attention.

You can add a rule to a subhead to give it more power, visibility, color. But

---

The rule should overscore

the subhead. The ruled line is a wall that separates one element from another. You want to separate the subhead from the text above it, not from the text that follows it, because that is the text it is meant to belong to.

The rule should not underscore

---

the subhead, because it splits text and head from each other visually.

You can also get a lot of power from taking the subhead and stacking its words in a vertical block which is then inserted in a space indented in the left-hand edge of the column:

This is a small subhead stacked in an indent There is some danger in doing this because the "runaround" can make the width of the text that is left over in the column so narrow, that it results in bad word- and even letterspacing. Therefore only do this in columns that are wide enough to accommodate such invasions.

Initials

Initials are widely used instead of subheads because they add color and graphic personality. They also grab attention, add some visual strength to the page and can help personalize the product. They are especially useful because they don't actually say anything, so they can be inserted wherever they are needed visually. However that is dangerous, because they also imply that "something new starts here"—so it had better be so, or the reader feels cheated.

They are called **"upstanding"** if they appear to stand in the first line, as the I above. They are "cut in" as **"dropcaps"** if they are inserted into the text, as the T below.

The space in which they fit must be tailored carefully to accommodate the various widths of the characters of the alphabet. (The I is narrower than the M.)

They must also align vertically so they fit into the text precisely. Nothing is more amateurish than initials that float around unanchored to the text to which they belong.
But visual subtleties should also come into play: notice how the top stroke of this T aligns with the body of the text in the first line. (The ascenders poke up into space.) Also how it overlaps into space at left, allowing the serif to sit on the left-hand edge of the text. These are refinements that vary with each letter's shape. They are advisable if the initials are very large and command much attention.

The biggest bang for the buck: freestanding or **"hanging initials"** placed outside the column like this.

NO L etters have shapes that need to be handled specially, if the initials are large and therefore command much attention. As in this case, where the first line of the text doesn't tuck into the space left in the inside of the L.

NO P ush the letters of the text into the space left under the overhang of the P, F, and T, so that the letters create a word as naturally as possible. In the following example, the edge of the text deosn't align with the slanting edge of the letter A. Does it matter? Yes.

NO A lways go to the extra effort of perfecting the typographic detailing. It is worth it, because it makes the product appear carefully crafted; and if it looks that way, chances are that its intellectual content will be perceived as just as dependable and credible. The A requires text to be corbelled, whereas V and W require pyramiding.

L etters have shapes that need to be handled specially, if the initials are large and therefore command much attention. As in this case, where the first line of the text tucks into the space left in the inside of the L.

P ush the letters of the text into the space left under the overhang of the P, F, and T, so that the letters create a word as naturally as possible. In the following example, the edge of the text aligns with the slanting edge of the letter A. Does it matter? Yes.

A lways go to the extra effort of perfecting the typographic detailing. It is worth it, because it makes the product appear carefully crafted; and if it looks that way, chances are that its intellectual content will be perceived as just as dependable and credible. The A requires text to be corbelled, whereas V and W require pyramiding.

Good and bad: Look how much easier it is to read all the versions at right. Yes, it takes more effort than just cutting a standard five-line indent in the text as in the ones at left.

Initials are dangerous traps. Take care that they don't spell an unintended word; it goes without saying that embarrassing foolishnesses happen in the most visible areas of the page. Also avoid unintended alignment ("tombstoning") across the page.

Sidescoring: This is just another technique of bringing attention to a part of the text, usually indicating changed or new material in a technical document. It is not used much in magazines because editors and designers seldom think to use it. If it is hand-drawn rather than a mechanical vertical rule like the one at right, it implies immediacy and personal linkage with the editors, like handwritten comments in the margin.

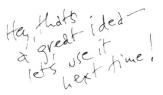

Hey, that's a great idea — let's use it next time!

PRODUCT-MAKING

They are usually used as snares when there is no picture to arouse that essential first-impression interest, but they are always better than a second-rate image.

Pullquotes use intellectual bribery to pull the reader into the story. Imaginative, provocative statements arouse attention, and if they are actual quotes from real people, they become a form of irresistible intellectual voyeurism.

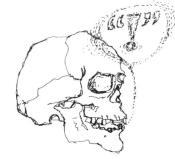

As a visual element they are an inexpensive substitute for artwork, and, if they are inserted in a consistent pattern, their visual style becomes one of the recognition marks of the publication or site. Moreover, they break up the daunting and unappealing greyness of cliffs of text.

STORY-TELLING

Not only are they useful as snare elements, but they also make the value-to-the-reader more obvious: they make information visible at the fast scanning level, and as a result they increase the velocity of communication.

The effectiveness of pullquotes depends on their "meatiness." They are words to think about and not just to glance at, so they must carry rich, challenging thoughts. Make them as long or as short as they need to be, because their success lies more in what they say than in how they look on the page.

Since they must be displayed prominently enough to do their job, they must be dressed in type to make them noticed. Their size, color (whether hue or degree of blackness) and texture must differ enough from their surroundings.

Avoid repeating the same words in the text: it annoys. But if repetition is unavoidable, place the pullquote far away from the text where it occurs.

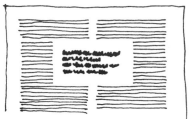

Isolate the pullquote from the surrounding text by a moat of white space. It doesn't need to be very wide, if its outer edges clearly define a simple geometric shape.

Imprison the pullquote in its own defined area: tintblock, color area, or box. (SEE BOXES AND RULES).

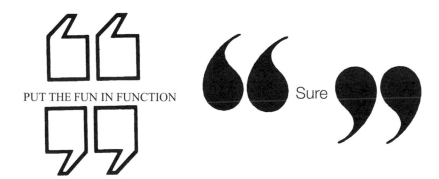

Insert horizontal barriers, and make them as simple or as embroidered as the character of the publication demands.

PUT THE FUN IN FUNCTION   Sure

Exaggerate the quotemarks; they are both fun and functional. Start the quote with 66, and end it with 99.

This line is set in fourteen point Trump

This line is set in fourteen point Trump italic

This line is set in fourteen point Helvetica

This line is set in fourteen point Helvetica italic

This line is set in fourteen point Centaur

This line is set in fourteen point Centaur italic

This line is set in fourteen point Centaur bold italic

This line is set in fourteen point Times Roman

This line is set in fourteen point Times Roman italic

Create strong contrast by setting the words in a font and size large enough to signal its own importance. The minimal size is usually 14-point, but there is no reason why a larger size would not make it more dramatic. For quotes spanning more than two-thirds of the page, 18-point is probably minimal. However, some fonts look bigger than others despite the point size. Go by the way it looks.

Interrupt flowing text with a sentence set differently from its surroundings. Here: bold type, indented at left, ragged-right by contrast to normal pale text set justified.

Use an incomplete thought (but an interesting phrase) that is part of the running text and emphasize it by larger type size, color, and perhaps even overlap it beyond the edges of the column. Incomplete thoughts pull people into the text even more effectively than self-contained sentences.

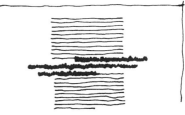

Break a paragraph by inserting the pullquote arbitrarily within it. Don't place it between paragraphs, where it could be mistaken for a headline and the start of another article.

Stagger the placement on the page, to avoid horizontal alignment ("tombstoning").

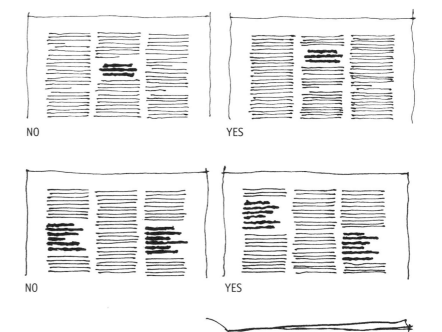

NO   YES

NO   YES

Place quotes at the right on the outside of the page. Not only are they more visible there, but they also probably compete less with headlines that are usually placed towards the left.

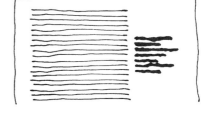

Cut the quote into the column by a little bit if the margin is too narrow to let the quotes float free. This is best restricted to the right-hand side, though the left is acceptable if there are no competing headlines around.

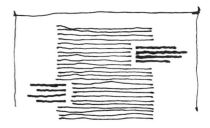

Make the quote lighter than its surroundings. Reversing the usual can work if the pullquote is cut in in a tight space within the columns of text.

Place a straddling pullquote near the top of the page, so the text beneath it isn't skipped by mistake.

A quote in the top margin is maximally visible, but it doesn't break up the text below or embellish it with a change of "color."

Stacking a pullquote at the top of the page takes advantage of the top margin's high visibility, but it could be mistaken for a headline to a new story.

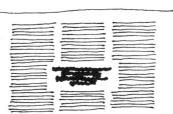

A quote between neighboring columns has a downside to avoid: the runarounds may result in such narrowing of the columns that legibility is jeopardized. Make such interrupting runarounds tall and thin rather than squat and wide.

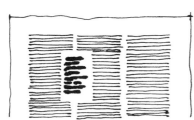

A tall, thin pullquote inserted between narrow columns is visually striking, especially if the color contrast is strong. Avoid making the narrow parts of the columns so narrow that word- and letter-spacing need noticeable variation.

LEGENDS, CUTLINES

Picture-captions are the most important words on the page. They get the highest readership, because people first look at the pictures when they reveal the next page. Then they look for an explanation, since images are fast, fun, and arouse *curiosity.* Thus the image fused to its explanation is a tempting twosome used to hook the uninvolved scanner into reading.

PRODUCT-MAKING

Much of the perception of the product as "interesting" or "boring" has to do with atmospherics and expectations. If it is packed with images and explanations that are irresistible and fascinating to its audience, it cannot help but succeed in the competitive marketplace. This is not superficial Public Relations but canny editing—and designing!—based on knowing the audience's interests and serving them efficiently.

If caption placement and handling are standardized, the pattern helps to build the product's positive image. Consistency unifies. But don't be rigid about it: if you must break the pattern to clarify a point, then do it, but be aware that you pay a price for it.

STORY-TELLING

Don't put off writing captions as the traditional last-minute nuisance chore, but write them *before* you begin the text. (That's right; you read it correctly). They should contain the very best, most startling, newest, most fascinating, most valuable nuggets of information, written so the reader will be avid for more details... reasons... background—all motivation for digging into the text itself. What they'll say and how you'll be showing it should be planned together from the moment you start working on the story.

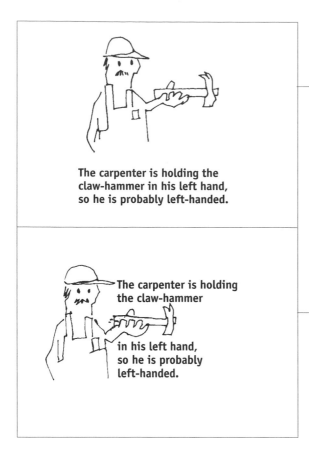

The carpenter is holding the claw-hammer in his left hand, so he is probably left-handed.

Think of the picture/caption as a single intellectual info-unit. Here the caption is tucked under the image, as you would expect. Nonetheless, it stands alone: it describes the image as if it were observing it from the outside. As a result, to link the words with the picture, we have to study, analyze, look, and think in order to understand the implication.

The carpenter is holding the claw-hammer in his left hand, so he is probably left-handed.

Here the identical words and image are interwoven into an integrated entity just by the way the words are placed. Their blended message is easier to grasp faster, because it has been made more obvious. Such speed and clarity are of service to the reader.

Ecological disaster threatens Africa

Elephants will be extinct by 2050

The opening picture must work together with dominant words. Be sure the headline and the opener reinforce each other, so that *the title doubles as caption for the image.* Examine them as one entity: do 1 + 1 = 3?

(Skip the normal caption for the opening mood-shot altogether, if possible, or push it out of the way so it doesn't interrupt the smooth flow of thought from picture... to the headline... to the deck (if any)... and then down into the text.)

Theoretical, uninvolving:
Here, the image of the elephant represents some vague symbolic African-ness, but it has little obvious relationship with the title's wording. Of course it can be figured out. And a photo of an elephant is always intriguing. But why not link the idea to the image so their interrelationship can't be missed? Hone the ideas in the words so they make sense together.

Direct, irresistible:
Here, the picture is also the subject of the words, so the message of the image and the words is clear and direct. The what's-in-it-for-me implications are that since elephants will be extinct in the near future, our grandkids won't have the privilege and fun of seeing any in the flesh, let alone in the wild. That vital aspect of the story can be brought out in the deck or the first sentence of the text.

Make captions as long as they need to be (but no longer). Ignore rules about three lines maximum or similar nonsense. If a lot needs saying in such a prime place, say it. If there is little, don't puff it out to some prescribed length. This will be seen as trustworthy forthrightness. *Allow caption lengths to vary,* because neatness is less important than the subject.

Pretend that the first phrase of a caption is a title setting the theme of a standalone mini-story. That forces you to point out the significance of the picture and lead into the what's-in-it-for-me value of the story.

BILL JONES has decided to expand his field of activity because of increased income. His prize cow Bessie has been producing so much more than expected, that he is...

NO

CASH COW BESSIE will bring Farmer Jones double the expected profits because she produces twice the milk one might expect. So he is investing in.....

YES

Start with a provocative quote from the person pictured and then name the person at the very end of the quote. The words that lie at the beginning and the end of a block of text get highest noticeability.

"When angry, count ten before you speak; if very angry, an hundred," from *A Decalogue of Canons for Observation in Practical Life*, by Thomas Jefferson.

Don't insult the reader's intelligence by describing the obvious. Avoid saying "ABOVE" "BELOW" "LEFT" "RIGHT" "OPPOSITE" even though *"We've always done it that way, aren't you s'posed to?"* If such crutches are necessary, then you know that the caption is in the wrong place. Rework the layout so each picture with its caption is perceptibly a single info-unit. Also avoid saying "LEFT TO RIGHT." Everybody assumes that, unless the image is so complicated that directions for identification are essential.

Left to right, Muriel DePrest, her husband Joe, (a.k.a. Hirsute or Suity for short), with their progeny Little Pimple, Joe Jr., and Mareeya.

Ask a provocative question to trigger curiosity or intrigue the reader. Get people mad: blandness doesn't raise hackles.

Who needs guns? Satisfy your macho rifle dreams just as bloodily with a good old-fashioned bow and arrow that kills more neatly than bullets. Besides, you have the unrivalled thrill of creeping up on your target before you fire and then can watch the blood spurt from close up.

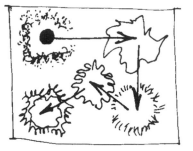

Refer to elements in their expected sequence: left to right, clockwise from top left. If it is complicated, give the reader clues to follow, but they are more tantalizing if you refer to "the guy with the bow tie" instead of "third from left."

Photo by Joe Doakes

WHEN YOU HAVE enough feed on the ground, the chickens are likely to come home to roost.

Don't cite the name of the photographer as the last words of the caption. That interrupts the flow of excitement. Put the name in small type alongside the photo or somewhere in a standard place on the page.

"WHEN YOU HAVE"
means nothing by itself, so its bold-cap eye-catching importance is wasted and the reader is cheated. A more magnetic caption might start with:

"CHICKENS ARE HAPPY
with lots of feed to peck, so they are likely to come home to roost."

Be sure the words make sense when you use a boldface lead-in. The purpose of boldface is to attract attention and entice the skimmer by something irresistible. It is wasted if what it says is unworthy. Test the words by reading them out loud. If they make no sense, rewrite them.

Evoke the mood of the picture by the style of the writing. Atmospherics and nostalgia expand the impact of the image increasing its appeal and its power to convince them to read.

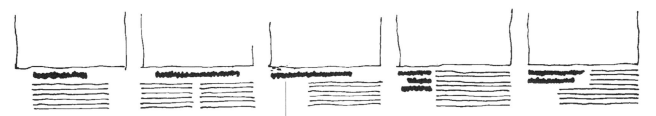

Use a catchline (or heading) when the picture and its caption are a self-contained mini-story. The clearest and most effective relationship is when the words are beneath the picture. Avoid separating the catchline from the caption unless the catchline is visually very powerful.

Every picture deserves its own explanation even if it looks messy and adds more elements. Avoid bunching the captions into a single unit somewhere else on the page—despite the neatness or improvement in the looks. The extra work searching for explanations is a nuisance that the fast-glancer resents. In the long run, what is more valuable: the design of the page or the satisfaction of the reader? Think it through and then make the decision.

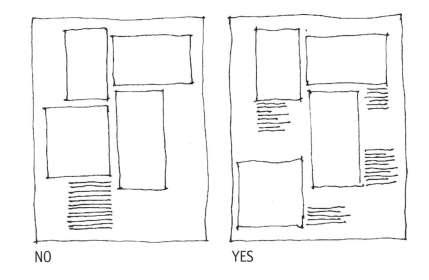

NO   YES

Use a font that will contrast with the text so the caption is easy to find. There is no "right" or "wrong" but only appropriate to the character of the particular publication: dark sans-serif balances colorful images; pale italics suit upscale elegance. In either case, it must be smooth and easy to read.

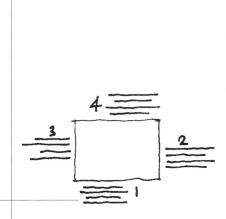

1. Best place for a caption (because we look at the image first and then search for its explanation under it).

2. Second best place for a caption (because we scan left-to-right if we don't find what we are looking for under the image).

3. Third place for an explanation (though only out of necessity, if there's no room below or at right).

4. Captions above images are too often skipped. Why risk it?

Put the caption where people look for it: beneath the picture. It is helpful to make the words immediately findable. Put them elsewhere only when there is a strong functional reason for it.

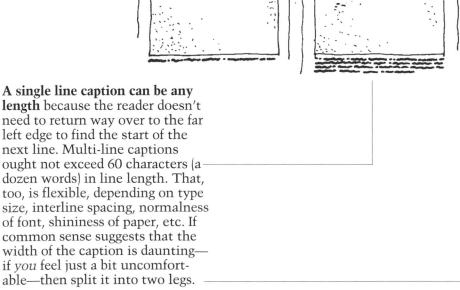

A single line caption can be any length because the reader doesn't need to return way over to the far left edge to find the start of the next line. Multi-line captions ought not exceed 60 characters (a dozen words) in line length. That, too, is flexible, depending on type size, interline spacing, normalness of font, shininess of paper, etc. If common sense suggests that the width of the caption is daunting— if *you* feel just a bit uncomfortable—then split it into two legs.

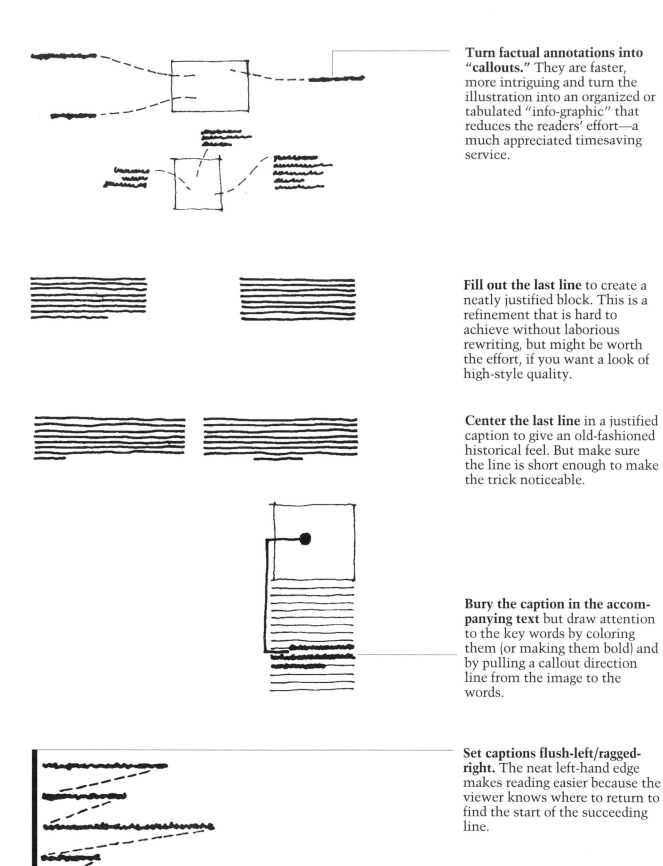

Turn factual annotations into "callouts." They are faster, more intriguing and turn the illustration into an organized or tabulated "info-graphic" that reduces the readers' effort—a much appreciated timesaving service.

Fill out the last line to create a neatly justified block. This is a refinement that is hard to achieve without laborious rewriting, but might be worth the effort, if you want a look of high-style quality.

Center the last line in a justified caption to give an old-fashioned historical feel. But make sure the line is short enough to make the trick noticeable.

Bury the caption in the accompanying text but draw attention to the key words by coloring them (or making them bold) and by pulling a callout direction line from the image to the words.

Set captions flush-left/ragged-right. The neat left-hand edge makes reading easier because the viewer knows where to return to find the start of the succeeding line.

Contrast the featheredged texture of unjustified captions with the more rigid geometry of the text columns. That brings in air, variety, lightness.

We hold these truths to be self-evident; that all men are created equal; that they are endowed by their creator with certain unalienable rights; that among these are life, liberty and the pursuit of happiness;

Justified x 10 pi
(artificial, unnatural, forced word spacing)

We hold these truths to be self-evident; that all men are created equal; that they are endowed by their creator with certain unalienable rights; that among these are life, liberty and the pursuit of happiness;

FL/RR —Flush Left/RaggedRight— max x10 pi (still forced, but steady word spacing and no artificial letterspacing)

We hold these truths to be self-evident; that all men are created equal; that they are endowed by their creator with certain unalienable rights; that among these are life, liberty and the pursuit of happiness;

FL/RR —Flush Left/RaggedRight— lines broken for sense, by phrase reflects language as spoken.

Break lines for sense. Don't force language into an artificial predetermined space, but make the space fit the language. Mirroring the structure of the language makes the information faster and easier to understand. Does it matter—it's just a caption? Multiply this subtle improvement by the number of captions in the issue and this becomes an obvious aid to readers' speed and comprehension.

Place words close to the picture so they obviously belong to each other as a single info-unit.

Split the caption from the text beneath it by an ample moat of white space. The purpose is to emphasize the picture/caption info-unit by contrasting it with the running text that usually surrounds it.

Exploit unjustified's secret advantage: flexibility of caption length. You can vary the number of words, yet have the same number of lines by setting some captions with longer lines and others with shorter lines as required. It is easy to do and makes a potential mess look neater and controlled.

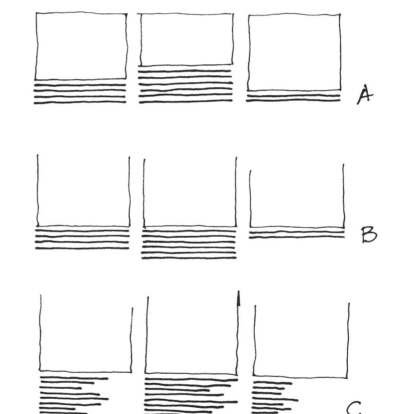

A Degrades the dignity of the pictures by arbitrary cropping just to align the captions across the bottom.

B Leaves an untidy edge beneath the captions (which looks even worse on a page with other elements).

C Camouflages the differences in caption-length by breaking the text into the same number of lines, while varying the line-length to accommodate the wording.

Set captions ragged-LEFT/flush-right, despite the common-sense rule that it is harder to read than ragged-right. Tying the caption to its picture by alignment is worth the risk if the lines are few (about eight) and short (about three words). Use the acid test: would you read it?

Flush-left is easiest to follow, because the eye knows where to return to at far left (even if the lines look fairly wordy, so long as there aren't too many). It is true that **ragged-left** is daunting if the lines are long, there are too many of them, and the variegation of the indents is deep. What you are reading now isn't what you really want to read, is it?

A caption that looks small like this, set in short lines with reasonably shallow indents is no problem.

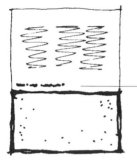

Never put the caption above the picture because people will miss it. Risk it only if there is no other place to put it because the picture bleeds down below. (See a note about this on page 137. It is repeated here because it is so important.)

Put the caption on the right, if not under the picture. We first look at the picture, glance down to search for explanation, then move to the right because we are used to the left-to-right sequence. If it isn't there either, we search over to the far left. If it isn't there, we give up. Most people miss captions above pictures.

Break captions into segments and place them around the illustration, so each segment is as close as possible to whatever the words refer to.

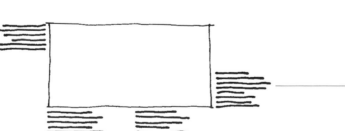

Center the caption below the picture even if it results in a dull blob. It does create an axis that ties them together. It should either be the same width as the picture, or much narrower; because the empty spaces at each end can look pathetic if they are narrow and unimportant.

Squared-off edges and corners (**1**) manifest skill and precision which translate into credibility and dependability. If you want it narrower, make it significantly narrower (**2**). The puny spaces in (**3**) look like a mouse had gnawed the ends.

Centering the caption alongside the picture north-south is likely to look even more untidy than centering it beneath it, because of those unsatisfactory leftover spaces. Best lift the caption up or drop it down to align it with the top or the bottom edge of the illustration. Alignment helps to make them "belong to each other."

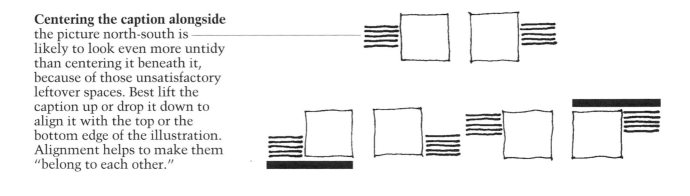

Always use the "sticky edge" to attach the caption to its picture. If you put the ragged edge next to the picture, a wide and messy space separates them, so they don't belong together nearly as obviously as when you put the flush edges next to each other.

The flush edge of the caption is close to the picture, so they adhere to each other. That is better than when...

...the ragged edge of the caption flanks the picture, and the untidy space between separates them from each other.

Align one edge of the caption with one of the vertical edges of the illustration. You want to anchor the words to the image as clearly as possible. This works whether the lines are set justified or ragged, but it is most dramatic when ragged. (And it is always better when the captions are placed below rather than above the picture.)

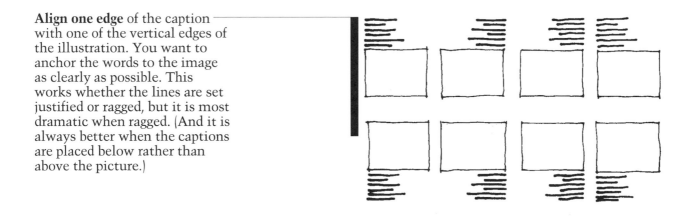

Align the top line or the bottom line of the caption with the top edge or the bottom edge of the picture to emphasize their interdependence. Do this in addition to using the "sticky edge."

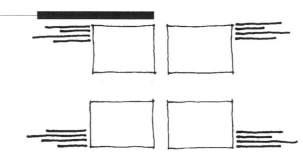

Enlarge the effect of the image/ explanation info-unit by capturing and exploiting its surrounding space. Tint blocks, color, shadows, outriggers, overlaps, framing… anything goes. (But should it?)

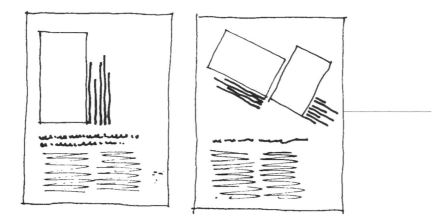

Tip the words parallel with the edge of the image if the photo is placed on the page sideways or at an angle. The words belong to the picture, not to the page. By orienting them in the same direction, you fuse the image and its accompanying words into one entity. But restrict tricks like these to unavoidable occasions.

This caption is surprinted on top of a pale background. It reads reasonably well despite the smallness and thinness of the type. But when it is over a dark area, it is impossible. In that case it must be reversed or dropped out of the background in white.

Surprint captions on pictures with greatest care. Type exists to be read. There is no excuse for illegibility. Place words only on a smooth background, never a mottled one. (Nomenclature: you "surprint" type in black on a pale background, and "drop out" type in white from a dark background. Color-on-color has no special name because it isn't ancient traditional technology.)

Rx:	increase type size	increase type size
	make the type bolder	**make the type bolder**
	add more linespacing	add more linespacing
	set the lines shorter	shorter lines
	switch to a sans-serif face	**use a sans-serif face**

Compensate for the increased difficulty of reading as well as the risk of poor printing (i.e., when letters "fill up") whenever type appears against a background that is not smooth plain white.

Pictures are as different from words as smells from sounds. Words go mostly to the intelligence, pictures go to feelings. What are the best pictures of a plane crash? A stocking hanging from a tree or a doll with a broken face. They tell you more than words—more, even, than pictures of bodybags being carried down the hill. ""—LINDA ELLERBEE, journalist

PRODUCT-MAKING | Pictures are the first thing anybody looks at on the page. They are fast, emotional, instinctive, and they arouse curiosity. Thus they open the viewer up to information. They must be used deliberately strategically, not just to break up the text or to make the page less boring. They are not subordinate elements, so don't treat them as such. Publications are a blend—a partnership—of the visual with the verbal.

STORY-TELLING | There are three kinds of photos and illustrations:

Mood shots are the exciting conceptual photographs or illustrations. Their purpose is to startle, intrigue, beguile, and thus bring in the customers, so anything goes. Perhaps a better term for them might be *shills*.

Informers are documentary, factual, realistic. Play them straight to retain credibility.

By-the-ways are the mediocre images we are all stuck with. They may be the best available, but are not worthy of playing up. Make them small.

Each kind is legitimate in its own way, and needs to be recognized for what it is, so it can be treated appropriately.

Beautiful
but
irrelevant

Ugly
but
interesting

Pick pictures for their significance, not for their prettiness. Obviously it is better to have good-looking subjects, but beauty is often a secondary consideration. Does the image advance the cause of the report, the story, the article, the message? If it also happens to be beautiful, then great!

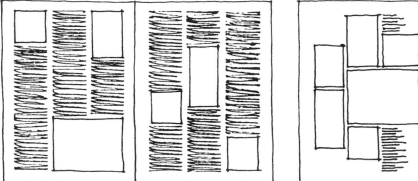

Make the significant picture dominant in both size and placement. Use the other images and ideas in the group to support it. (This is sometimes called "the hen and chickens principle"). Build the layout around this focal point. Obviously: this must be the result of editor/designer understanding.

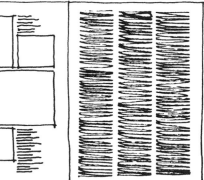

Cluster little images into an impressive group in order to make the most of their combined impact, instead of peppering the page with them individually. Potential readers look at everything nonverbal first, so if it impresses at first glance, it will register and make the magazine more "interesting."

AUTHOR

Anything unexpected in its context is startling and therefore beguiling. An elephant appearing among pages of statistical charts and tables is bound to titillate the most dedicated, jaded statistician. Dare to use the dangerous pic.

Use words to direct viewers to what you want them to notice. Everyone interprets an image his or her own way. Therefore explain every picture with words—individually. The purpose of these two images is to illustrate the effectiveness of cropping: horizontal landscape, vertical ballplayer. Yet all sorts of other interpretations are possible and one such hypothetical set is in the stream-of-consciousness italics.

"What a pretty landscape... reminds me of the rolling Downs in Sussex... they're made of chalk... lots of sheep... and if you don't like the weather, wait five minutes... that's when we had that delightful picnic with... must've been in '97... how time flies... "

"Tall kid, must be 14, I guess... wonder what made him grow so fast? Excess hormones... wonder why just him... maybe it's his sneakers... wait till he's 40, boy, that'll change..."

Place pictures above the type referring to them. Images arouse curiosity and emotion, so use them as hooks to pull readers into the story. People first look at the image, then normally search for the explanation underneath it. (See page 137 and the rest of the CAPTIONS chapter.)

Pterodactyl chick hatched 11 million years late.

Jump the gutter with a large element. It will enlarge the scale of the impression and change the shape of the spread into one impressive horizontal out of two puny verticals. The strength overwhelms the interruption the gutter creates, so ignore printing misalignment because nobody notices it. But watch out: the gutter can ruin the important part of the image, as it does the Salzburg castle here.

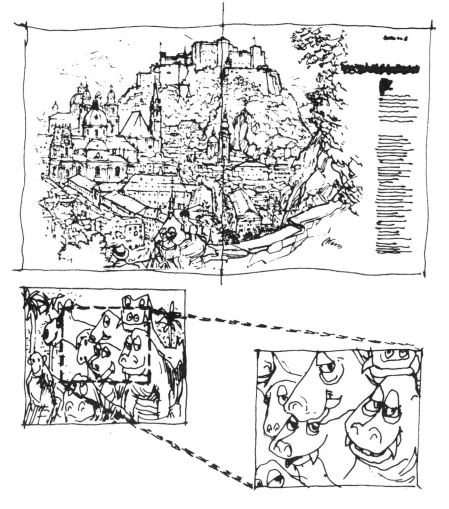

Crop till it hurts. Get rid of distractions and irrelevancies by making only the significant part visible. Sacrifice the image ruthlessly for the sake of the meaning. Start at the focal point of the picture, then move outwards until the suitable cropping point is reached. Then stop. Fit the picture's shape to the message, not the area into which it is going to be inserted.

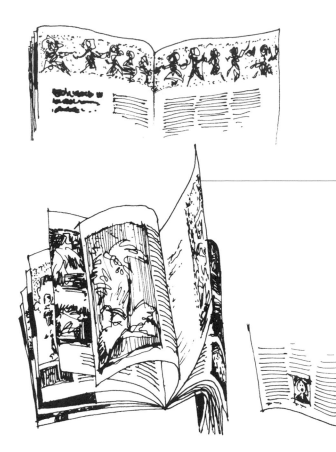

Place pictures across the top, because that is where page-scanners look when looking at the issue the first time. Make the most of the images' magnetic quality to draw people in.

Place pictures down the outsides of the pages to show them off as pages are flipped and riffled by the unconvinced investor who must be persuaded by them to become a buyer... and then be turned into a reader.

Hide unimportant pictures at the foot of the page, because that's where nobody looks. Put those boring but inescapable grip-and-grins, people shaking hands or getting an award there.

Relate the innate direction of the picture with its placement on the page: looking downward belongs at the foot of the page, looking upward is best on top. That logic expands the impact and illusion of each image as well as building a more powerful spread.

Emphasize left-to-right and overleaf flow by deliberately directing the look *off* the page. Forget the hidebound dictums that "people must look into the spread." It is comfortable to have people looking into the spread, but comfort is not the main criterion. Vivid communication is, and that demands using every technique available, even if it breaks the rules.

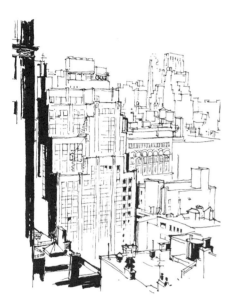

Frames around pictures are useful but dangerous. Bold ones or those in color call attention to themselves; but they can add character if they are used throughout. Light ones define edges of light areas. Clean and simple is usually best, but it all depends on the circumstances.

Bleed for maximum impact. Bleeds continue the image in the imagination outward and beyond the trim. Bleed big, don't bleed small. Small-scale bleeds are hardly noticeable, specially if the margin is narrow. (*See MARGINS*)

Good   Better   Best   Gatefold

Make big pictures look bigger by contrasting them to tiny ones, (SEE BIGNESS). The lone afghan looks bigger next to the chihuahua. Avoid gussying up their surroundings or background. Such visual static denigrates the importance of the pictures themselves and often reduces the intellectual impact of the whole—while possibly increasing its visual interest. Again: content overrides form.

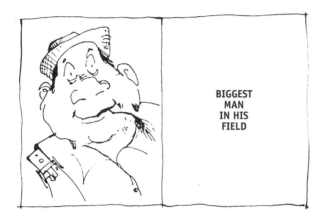

BIGGEST
MAN
IN HIS
FIELD

Give a picture the size its importance deserves, but never bloat a picture just to fill the available space. Big equals important, small equals unimportant. Be sure to size pictures large enough to discern details clearly, when their purpose is to inform.

Dead-center composition in pictures just sits there like a bump on a log. Move the horizon: if the sky is important, horizon must be lower. If the ground is important, horizon must be up towards the top. Unexpected viewpoints enliven the ordinary subject: worm's-eye, bird's-eye, inside-out...

NO   YES

People pictures should be spontaneous, natural, candid. They shouldn't be pictures of self-conscious people having their picture taken. Nor is a magazine a place for photo IDs. Credibility and realism depend on emotional content as well as an explanation of why the subject is interesting. The mugshot should bring that out.

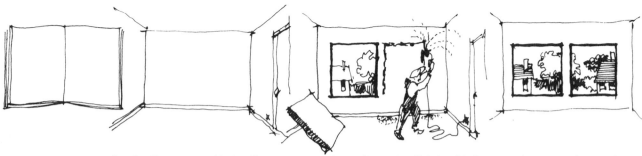

Imagine the paper as a blank wall... ...a workman who cuts two "windows" in it... ...and you see a view out there.

Exploit the relationships of adjacent "windows." What is a printed picture but an illusion—a miniaturized version—of the reality viewed through a window?

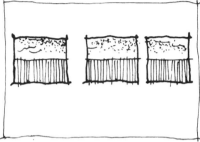

Nothing unifies these three window-views... ...here the horizon line dictates placement... ...alignment creates a picture-window effect.

Align the horizons in adjacent pictures. And take the shape of the pictures into account, too.

Align peoples' eye-levels, because that is the equivalent of a horizon-line when there is no real horizon line visible. If they don't align, then you have the nagging suspicion that perhaps some of them must be standing in a hole or propped up on boxes?

Relate the scale of the subjects in neighboring pictures so they make sense together. They should relate internally, in size, as well as externally, as rectangles on the page.

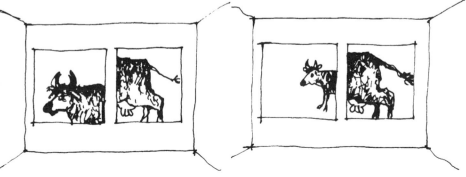

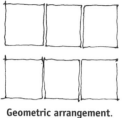 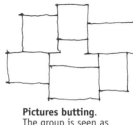 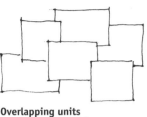

Geometric arrangement.
Regular and boring. Not
very inspiring, but perhaps
it makes ideal sense for a
sequence?

Pictures butting.
The group is seen as
a unified object,
a statement, a thing
in itself.

Overlapping units
from center outward
like a bunch of grapes
adds motion and
congeals the images.

The group is a focal point, a
nexus of meaning. A tight
cluster is an editorial ploy that
is potentially much more
useful in focusing the story for
concentrated impact than just
bunching a few images together
because they look nicer and
stronger together. *Editorial
purpose and reason* commands
how pictures should be combined. For instance, mugshots:

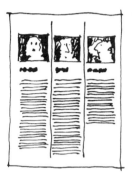    

Mugshots arrayed in rigid
geometric alignment
camouflages variety of
text lengths.

Mugshots overlapped
(watch out, the largest is
assumed as the most
important).

Mugshots silhouetted,
overlapped, and composed
at varied scale to create
naturalistic grouping.

Mugshots skewered on
ruled lines. Vertical
shish-kebabs for the
year-book look.

Mugshots pushed down to
foot of page in order to
emphasize their quotes
that float above them.

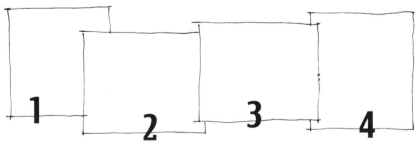

Clues for logical arrangements:

…natural affinity of subject.
Relationships, ages, common
interests…

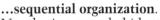

…sequential organization.
Numbering or verbal identification; symbols of linkage,
such as ampersands, brackets,
parentheses or even math-
ematical symbols such as
$x + x + x - y = <z$ …

  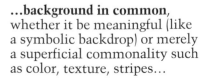

…background in common,
whether it be meaningful (like
a symbolic backdrop) or merely
a superficial commonality such
as color, texture, stripes…

...common shape. Tall and thin, short and squat, circular, or all cropped at an angle. Or taken a step further and combined with the direction in which the pictures are shot: all as bird's-eye views or worm's-eye views...

...visual themes such as postage stamps, pictures in album, film-strips with numbers, photos in frames or with sprocket holes...

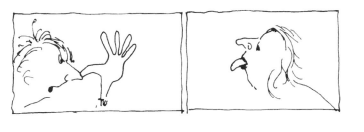

...people reacting to each other in friendly or unfriendly fashion in neighboring images...

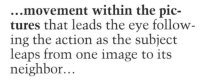

...movement within the pictures that leads the eye following the action as the subject leaps from one image to its neighbor...

...an element poking out and overlapping into the neighboring image, to emphasize and dramatize the motion and direction...

...mechanical joining. Sheaf of papers held by paper clips, a hand, mechanical binding...

...fitting into matrix. Surface become the shape into which pictures are inserted. Boxes, honeycomb, tiles, etc.

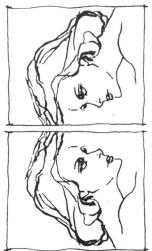

Mirror image: flopping the original creates the illusion of duplication, opposition. Mirror image sideways and upside down: reflection in a pool? Watch out for buttons on wrong side... and words SDRAWKCAB.

Warning: Tricks used once may work, but used twice, they work only half as well. Used more than twice they probably don't work at all because readers become aware of the trick as trickery and that turns them off.

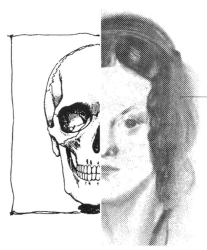

Butting half-images: as long as they are related in shape as well as meaning (pro/con, fat/thin, pretty/ugly, young/old, empty/full, before/after, inside/outside).

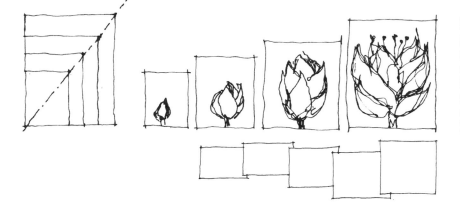

Increasing size emphasizes growth. Decreasing makes shrinkage obvious. Taking it a step further by **overlapping** implies a much more intimate relationship. Besides flow, it can be interpreted as from/to, before/after, cause/effect.

Inserting a small image inside another large one implies a relationship within a surrounding context. The cat is follwing the mouse, but the shadows make the scene eerie.

1: A seven-headed hydra in the distance. Not threatening: we're safe on this side of a wall, watching him through a picture-window.

2: He waddles closer, grows bigger, so our comfort-level is decreasing, specially since he seems headed directly towards us.

3: Now he sidled up to our window, his heads staring in, checking whether there might be something edible inside— on our side of the wall.

4: Oops! One of his heads broke the glass and has penetrated to our side of the wall and is inside the room with us! He may be smiling—but his breath!

Key element erupts out of the confines of the photo. Partial silhouetting plays tricks with the imaginary space that separates the viewer from the subject in the image.

Edges of picture dissolve into soft outline: dreamlike, fugitive. Opposite of the "window" trick, above. Added advantage on the page: a non-rectangular shape within the geometric patterns.

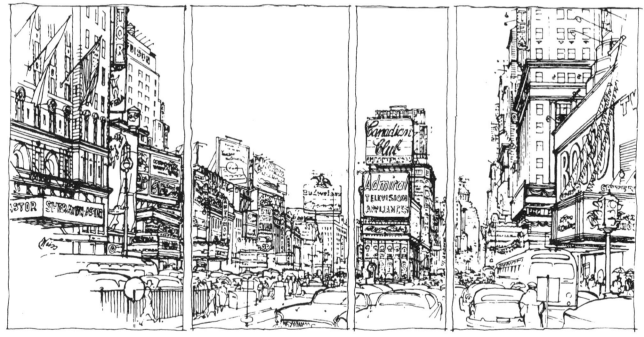

One image split into segments to emphasize the multiplicity of elements as well as their complexity, while retaining the evident interdependence of the subject-matter.

Negative version is strange, ghostly, threatening, unreal. Not as easy to read as the positive version, but more moody.

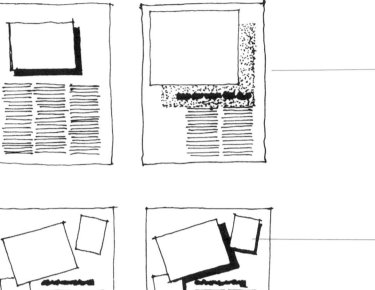

Pictures as pictures of pictures.
See pictures not merely as images, but as realistic objects made of paper on which images have been printed. Then handle the substrate—the paper—as the "object" to be reproduced.

Floating above the background because of the shadow it casts. There is more to this than just adding a black edge on two sides of a picture, so *see Shadows* to get it realistically persuasive.

Dropped on the page like autumn leaves. Just placing pictures at random angles and overlapping them here and there can do it, but the illusion is improved by coupling it with shadows.

Dog-eared corners work as an illusion if they are correct: the angle of the turned corner must be 90° and the line AB must be straight. It is often curved and looks wrong because that is a physical impossibility. Try folding a piece of paper.

Torn edge of the paper on which the original photo appears to have been printed gives a feeling of immediacy, violence, realism (or divorce?)

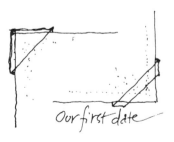

Our first date

Photo corners and handwritten notes and sepia color or brownish spots seen on old photos in albums.

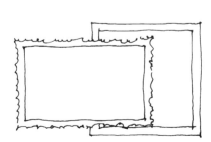

White paper frame useful for old-fashioned photos that used such wiggly shapes.

Drawings are not just pictures drawn by hand. They have editorial advantages that make them invaluable as communication media, if they are used functionally. Their capacity is subtly different, and a separate part of the rich and complex editorial mix of communication techniques. *"Through the picture we see reality and through the word we understand it. Through the drawing we understand the photo and through the photo we believe the drawing,"* says Sven Lidman, president of the Swedish Word and Picture Academy.

Selectivity: interpreting by removing (i.e., "editing out") extraneous matter, to bring out what is important. Why does the house at right have no front door? Ask the editor.

Visualization of internal structure and anatomy that can't be demonstrated any other way. CUTAWAYS and EXPLODED VIEWS break such complexity down into bite-size chunks to make those relationships accessible. Here we see where the closet is, what it contains and how it functions.

Explanation of how something works and how things relate to each other as in this BLOBOGRAM. Charts and graphs turn statistics into pictures *(see DIAGRAMS)*.

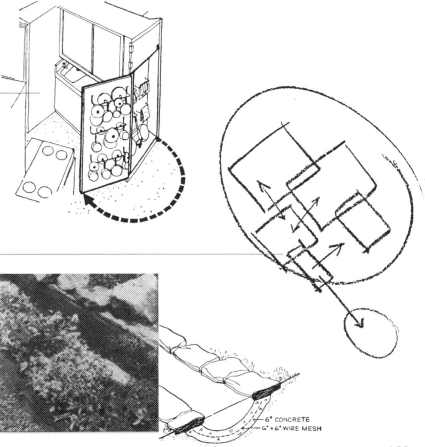

Combining the real "what" with the technical "how" in an EXTENSION DRAWING that expands the photo beyond its own edges and there explains how the object in the photo is constructed.

6" CONCRETE
6" × 6" WIRE MESH

*Fourscore and seven years ago our fathers
brought forth on this continent,
a new nation,
conceived in Liberty,
and dedicated
to the proposition that
all men are created equ*

Quotations attached to the picture of the speaker combine words with images to create vivid understanding and editorial commentary.

Word-pictures are easy to make up if the words describe position or direction, because all you need is an established datum and then work the word around it.

dea□ MIS ING P*I*SA 6ix

Visual puns play with letters, their shapes, positions, and even absences.

Rubber stamps have an aura of immediacy—even if their technology is reminiscent of old-fashioned snailmail.

Words interwoven with pictures add a touch of whimsy and can lighten the character of the story a bit.

All visualizations—from word-tables to pictorial representations—are *interpretations* of ideas or data. The "purest" way is to present the facts elegantly, simply, cleanly, neutrally and let viewers draw their own conclusions. The "impure" way is to explain and *use visual emphasis to draw attention to the nub or conclusion*. In the context of publication-making, the editor and designer must decide what the point is and present it so the meaning is laid bare. That isn't falsification, pandering, or dressing-up but integral with the service that a publication is intended to give: transmitting knowledge fast and vividly. There is always danger of exaggeration and misinterpretation. "There are lies, damned lies, and statistics,"said Benjamin Disraeli, Queen Victoria's Prime Minister.

OBJECTIVITY   **DISTORTION**

BALANCE
depends on your integrity and judgment.
You determine what and how you
highlight,
emphasize,
downplay.

PRODUCT-MAKING

Diagrams are useful because people like visuals, especially functional ones. They increase readership and add perceived value. They enrich the product and so help add stature. Furthermore, since they are under our visual control, they can be manipulated to enhance visual character.

STORY-TELLING

Diagrams increase velocity of communication by displaying statistical relationships faster and clearer than words do. While showing the context, they focus on the vital aspects of the message. They reveal connections, illustrate nonvisual concepts, invent a metaphor or symbolic icons for the subject. Because they are visual, they can be used as hooks to pull potential readers into the text and, of course, they can persuade and sway opinion (as Disraeli implied).

In the context of a publication, a good diagram is
> **functional** if it contains facts,
> **persuasive** if it conveys an opinion,
> **effective** if its opinion is clear and fast,
> **useful** if it focuses on comparisons such as:

> *What is most important?*
> *How did it change?*
> *What is likely to happen?*
> *How important will the change be?*
> *How does that affect the reader's interests?*

If you are talking about plastic coffee cups, don't insist they are cheap, made of common chemicals, easy to manufacture, simple to stack, efficient to pack, biodegradable, light... and all those technicalities that are fascinating to engineers and manufacturers but nobody else. Instead, talk about what the cups do for you—*keep coffee hotter longer without burning your fingers*. That's the reason consumers probably care about them. Then dig into the technicalities, if they still matter.

What you say and how you say it should be so valuable, so clear, and so fascinating that it needs no dressing up. If it is boring, then the content is boring, and it'll stay boring no matter what visual fireworks you gussy it up with.

Edit out gratuitous embellishment that takes attention away from the point. Use backgrounds only where they add to understanding. Less is more.

Have a point of view—and say it strongly. A label is not enough of an inducement to study statistics. Give each visual an active headline with a verb in it. The title makes a provocative claim, the diagram is credible proof, the caption a cogent explanation.

Concentrate on the significance of the data to the viewer and show it as simply as you can. The goal is clarity.

Identify the major comparison and expose it visually. Point out the conclusion readers should reach. Do their work for them.

Choose the format that fits the data's purpose. There is an infinity of permutations and combinations of the basic ones.

Standardize handling of recurrent elements like figure numbers, sources, scales, north points, keys, frames, etc., so searchers can always find them quickly the same way in the same place.

Pie charts show the relationship of parts to the whole. The circle represents the total, the wedges are its segments. Start at "noon" and continue clockwise from largest to smallest.

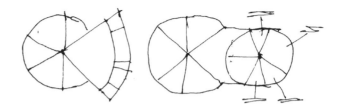

If there are more than six segments, break one out and subdivide it or add subsidiary pies. Pinpoint the message by using an icon instead of a plain circle. Put labels as callouts outside the figure.

Horizontal bars show independent amounts compared to each other, but unrelated to a total or to a time sequence.

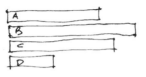

Stacked horizontally, they can be arranged in random order, in alphabetical sequence, ranked in ascending or descending length... any way that makes sense.

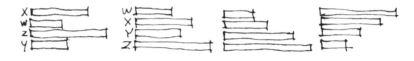

The bars can be made of countable units, or visualize the subject of the statistics. If they are too long, they can be folded or split. Label inside.

Vertical columns compare amounts to each other and can also imply trend over time, with "from" at left, "to" at right. If this is not intended, use horizontal bars instead.

Arrange columns by meaning, randomly, or by ascending or descending order, or whatever helps communicate.

Substitute pictures for bars (pencils, smokestacks, giraffes...) and place labels reading upwards.

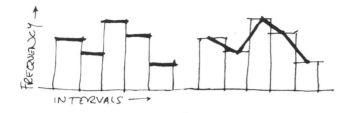

Histograms or step charts compare amounts with abrupt periodic changes. Placing columns so they touch emphasizes the left-to-right flow, strengthening the "historical" aspect. Joining the apexes emphasizes the trend rather than the periodic changes.

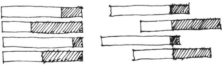

Population pyramids or winged bars compare two variable sets of figures.

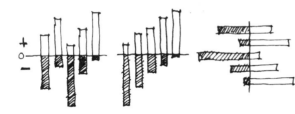

Columns with **benchmark line** compare variation of activity from standard.

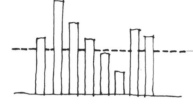

Sliding bars or **columns** compare variations within series to a given benchmark. Positive is thought to be above or to the right of the benchmark, negative below or to its left.

Comparing variations of segments within a total: the total dominates, making differences harder to discern; organizing the bars about the internal value line exposes their differences.

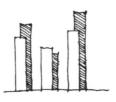

Floating range columns compare varied units against a common set of scales.

The length of bars represents one set of values, the thickness can represent a secondary one... and even growth.

Editorialize about importance by overlapping, allowing the important ones to dominate in the foreground.

Segmented columns or bars compare both the totals as well as their constituent components. More than four segments per bar can become incomprehensible.

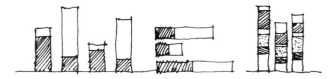

Graph (or fever, curve, line chart) emphasizes the trend of fluctuation over time because it is shown as a line joining data nodes. A sharp zigzag line implies sudden changes. A curved line represents gradual changes. The degree of steepness indicates the rate of change.

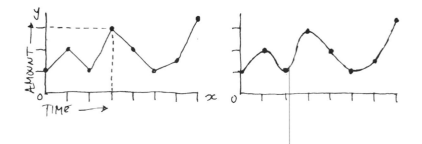

Surface chart emphasizes the amount of the fluctuation over time. Instead of forming a line, the data define the edge of an area. That throws the emphasis onto the accumulated amount below the edge (line).

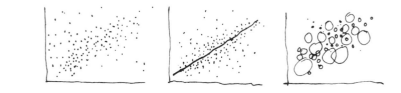

Scatter or dot charts plot multitudes of details before some ordered or averaged pattern can be deduced. In embellished charts, the dots show facts, the line describes the trend. Comparative values can be weighted by varied dot sizes.

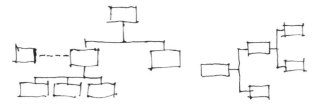

Organization chart or **tree diagram** (the org chart sideways) shows human hierarchy and lines of responsibility. It can be read in any direction, but traditionally the boss is at top or at left. To parade the names or titles, embellish the boxes; to stress the relationships, strengthen the links and play down the boxes.

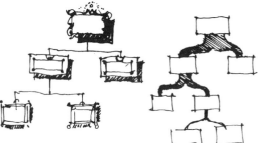

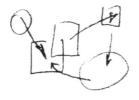
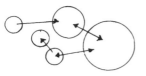
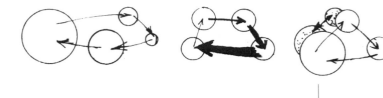

Blobograms, bubble diagrams, schematics, or activity network diagrams show relationships of theoretical concepts. Sketchiness denotes spontaneity, flexibility, idea-generation (drawing on the back of a napkin). Tightness connotes rigidity, decision.

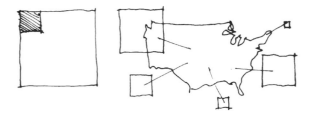

The sizes of blobs correspond to the importance of the elements they represent. Width of connecting lines reflects hierarchy of linking processes. Important elements can be placed in front, supporting ones behind.

Rectangular blobograms compare proportions of areas clearly. They do it much more accurately than pie segments or blobs.

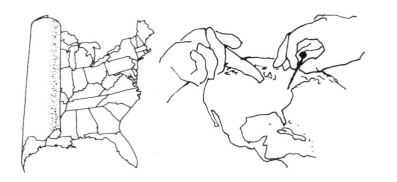

Maps locate places in space and show their relationships. They can be accurate for scientific reference, or reality can be twisted (even cartooned) to make a point—especially when the image is a well-known one, like the outline of the United States.

Plans locate physical objects in space and relate them to each other, showing what they look like from a bird's-eye view.

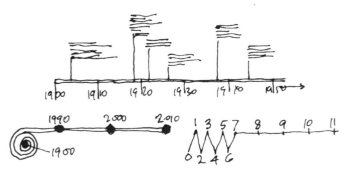

Timelines plot sequences over time, starting at left. The line itself can be rolled or folded to squeeze it. Milestones can be indicated by symbolic icons.

Flowcharts, process charts, or tapeworm charts plot lineal sequences of thought. When boxes touch and overlap, the flow is more emphasized.

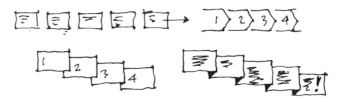

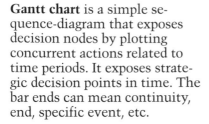

Gantt chart is a simple sequence-diagram that exposes decision nodes by plotting concurrent actions related to time periods. It exposes strategic decision points in time. The bar ends can mean continuity, end, specific event, etc.

Decision trees or prioritization matrix describe *yes/no* and *if so/then what* logic sequences.

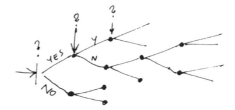

PERT (Project Evaluation Technique) and CPM (Critical Path method) charts are activity network diagrams. They plot complex relationships of processes over time and alert management to critical points where actions overlap. Line lengths represent time required to complete a step. The longest (the critical path) in bold controls all the others.

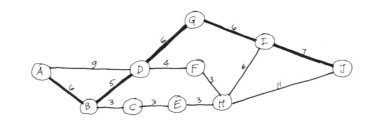

Prioritization matrix is a grid on which to plot items and preferences to help in decision-making.

Positioning diagrams plot comparative values or preferences on the Cartesian Coordinates (x and y axes). Zero is at center. Here, green is thought to be much better than pink— useful for decision making.

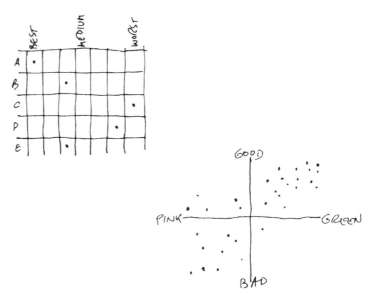

Tables

Their purpose is to compress a lot of information into a small space. If they are constructed intelligently, they make facts more easily graspable. There are two basic kinds: statistical (amounts, percentages, frequency, etc.) and verbal (*see page 166*). As in everything else in communication, the message and its analysis, as well as its intended interpretation by the recipient, dictates the intellectual organization and thus the resultant shape of the table. The variations of arrangements is infinite. However, even the most dauntingly complex are constructed of simple standard ingredients. Working within standardized patterns is vital, because the recipient of the message should not need to puzzle out the technique, but concentrate on its content.

Numbers are used in journals or reports for referring to the table in the text and cross-referencing. Tables should be placed so close to their referent that the numbers should not be needed.

Titles are of two styles: 1) terse concise label defining the topic (academic, scientific, technical publications), or 2) full sentence explaining both topic and implications (more didactic, journalistic contexts).

Subtitle (in smaller type) for elaborating description or the implications of the data.

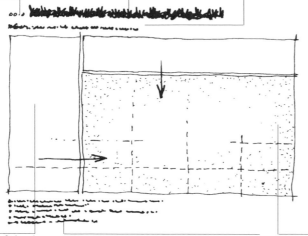

Stub is the left-hand column of the table listing the subjects or categories into which the information is divided.

Footnotes should be set in smaller type than the table itself, but retain clear legibility. Each item ought to be on a separate line, starting flush left. Where a, b, c are not used to identify the notes, the recognized sequence of symbols is this: * † ** ‡ § ¶. "Note" subjects are run first, "Source" last.

Field or body of the table contains the data called for by the stub and the headings.

Stub head defines topics below, but if the table title fufills that function clearly, the stubhead can be omitted.

Column headings define variable factors in column below. They are usually too long and dictate tale width, so they have to be concise and abbreviated.

Span head brackets two or more columns together by means of a ruled line or simple space.

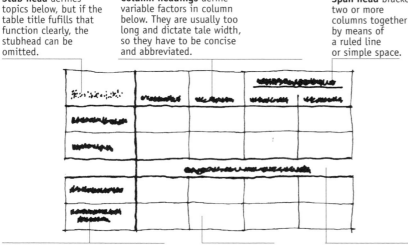

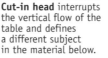

Stub topics should be long enough to define the subject intelligibly. The first line of each item should be flush left, turnovers indented for ease of scanning.

Cells are units of space where a horizontal item intersects with a vertical one.

Cut-in head interrupts the vertical flow of the table and defines a different subject in the material below.

Set tables wider or narrower than the columns. Aligning them with the columns make the page neater, but un-aligning breaks them out as "illustrations," making most of their contrasting texture and shape within the rigid grey structure.

	Factor 1	Factor 2	Factor 3
Topic A	mmmm	mmmm	mmm
Topic B	mmmmmm	mmm	mmmmm
Topic C	mm	m	mmmmm
Topic D	mmmm	mmmmm	mm

Chasms between columns much too wide

	Factor 1	Factor 2	Factor 3
Topic A	mmmm	mmmm	mmm
Topic B	mmmmmm	mmm	mmmmm
Topic C	mm	m	mmmmm
Topic D	mmmm	mmmmm	mm

Tighter: much easier to make comparisons

Don't set the tables too wide. Artifical gaps between columns impede reading and making comparison. Avoid sizing tables to fill pre-existing holes. Instead, give them the size the material needs.

	Factor 1	Factor 2	Factor 3
Topic A	mmmm	mmmm	mmm
Topic B	mmmmmm	mmm	mmmmm
Topic C	mm	m	mmmmm
Topic D	mmmm	mmmmm	mm

Easiest: items set flush-left instead of centered

	This ridiculously long heading eats up space	Long heading placed at an angle	Heading placed vertically	Please don't	Very long heading in short stacked lines
Topic A	mmmmm	mmmmm	mmmmm	mmmmm	mmmmm
Topic B	mmm	mmm	mmm	mmm	mmm
Topic C	mmmmm	mmmmm	mmmmm	mmmmm	mmmmm
Topic D	mmmmmm	mmmmmm	mmmmmm	mmmmmm	mmmmmm

Control the length of headings. They are often the reason for excess table width. Stack them instead.

Heads tucked under each other at an angle look cute

Run type sideways "on its ear" only out of desperation

Illegible: never, ever, under any circumstances

Short words or judicious abbreviations or set in condensed type

Define tables with boxes, horizontal rules or tint block backgrounds to give them a crisp rectangular shape. It fosters an impression of carefully crafted precision.

Improve horizontal tracking to help the eye travel west to east and back east to west again, improve legibility, and clarify relationships within the table.

	Factor 1	Factor 2	Factor 3
Topic A	mmmm	mmmm	mmm
Topic B	mmmmmm	mmm	mmmmm
Topic C	mm	m	mmmmm
Topic D	mmmm	mmmmm	mm

Generous line-spacing

	Factor 1	Factor 2	Factor 3
Topic A	mmmm	mmmm	mmm
Topic B	mmm	mmm	mmmmm
Topic C	mm	m	mmmmm
Topic D	mmmm	mmm	mm

Rules between entries or groups of entries, so long as these separators aren't confused with the ruled lines that bracket items functionally

Insert a sliver of extra space every three lines'-worth so the reader intuits they are reading the upper, middle, or lower line in each group of entries

	Factor 1	Factor 2	Factor 3	Factor 4
Topic A	mmmm	mmmm	mmmm	mmmm
Topic B	mmm	mmm	mmmmm	mmmmm
Topic C	mmmmmm	mmmmm	mmm	mm
Topic D	mmm	mmmm	mm	mmmmm
Topic E	mmmmm	mmm	mmmm	mmm
Topic F	mmmm	mmm	mmmmm	mmmmm
Topic G	mmmmm	mmmm	mmmmm	mmmmm
Topic H	mm	mmmm	mmmm	mmm
Topic I	mmmmm	mmmmm	mmmm	mmmmm
Topic J	mmm	mmmmm	mmmm	mmmm
Topic K	mmmm	mmmm	mmmm	mmm
Topic L	mmmmm	mmmmm	mmmm	mmmm

A very pale band of grey or color behind every other entry (or every other group). Type on color or grey reads less well than on white, so such harder-to-read lines may be skipped

	Factor 1	Factor 2	Factor 3
Topic A	mmmm	mmmm	mmmm
Topic B	mmm	mmm	mmmmm
Topic C	mmmmmm	mmmmm	mmm
Topic D	mmm	mmmmm	mm
Topic E	mmmmm	mmm	mmmm
Topic F	mmmm	mmm	mmmmm
Topic G	mmmmm	mmmmm	mmmmm
Topic H	mm	mmmm	mmmm
Topic I	mmmmm	mmmmm	mmmm

Management Proposals Opposed by Shareholders

- 10% profit increase in next six months deemed insufficient
- Extra 45¢ dividend per share thought unjustified
- 33% management salary increase believed outrageous
- Purchase of three executive limousines judged extravagant
- Lease of Lear Jet rejected as conspicuous consumption

Management Proposals Opposed by Shareholders

- 10% profit increase in next six months deemed insufficient
- Extra 45¢ dividend thought unjustified
- 33% management salary increase believed outrageous
- Purchase of three executive limousines judged extravagant
- Lease of Lear Jet rejected as conspicuous consumption

Management proposals opposed by shareholders

- 10% profit increase in next six months deemed insufficient
- Extra 45¢ dividend per share thought unjustified
- 33% management salary increase believed outrageous
- Purchase of three executive limousines judged extravagant
- Lease of Lear Jet rejected as conspicuous consumption

Management proposals **opposed by Shareholders**

- *Increasing 10% profit in next six months* **deemed insufficient**
- *Declaring extra 45¢ per share dividend* **thought unjustified**
- *Increasing management salary 33%* **believed outrageous**
- *Purchasing three executive limousines* **judged extravagant**
- *Leasing Lear Jet* **rejected as conspicuous consumption**

Management proposals opposed by Shareholders

10% profit increase next six months:	deemed insufficient
Extra 45¢ per share dividend:	thought unjustified
33% management salary increase:	believed outrageous
3 executive limousine purchase:	judged extravagant
Lease of Lear Jet:	conspicuous consumption

PRO: Management	**CON: Shareholders**
+10% profit next six months	Insufficient
Extra 45¢ per/share dividend	Unjustified
33% mgmt salary increase	Outrageous
3 executive limousines	Extravagant
Lear Jet lease	Conspicuous

Word charts

Made of words, they are a "diagram" because they are not running text. They present bits of information related to each other, but without comparing data. The usual way of identifying them is as a bulleted list. If the information were sequential, numbers would be used instead of bullets...

... never center the items because that way the bullets' capacity to identify the whole piece as a bulleted list is camouflaged. Always align the bullets flush left.

... don't rely on decorative gimmicks to dress it up. Avoid splashes, color... anything extraneous that doesn't help explain meaning.

... rewrite the message to expose the structure of the thoughts. Organize the ideas intellectually so that they can be displayed visually to make the message more vivid. Identify the protagonists by typeface, size, boldness, color.

... tabulate the information in side-to-side comparison for greater speed than as sentences to be read. Forget the bullets: let the visual structure do the organizing.

... and perhaps edit it all down to the irreducible minimum so it can be tabulated. *Now* it is a "picture of thoughts"—a set of ideas visually organized: **a diagram**.

Tips for making better charts

Avoid confusing complexities like these spaghetti. Edit material ruthlessly to get rid everything not germane to the issue. Compare only four lines in a graph (unless they are clearly separated.)

Make draftsmanship elegantly functional to rank the information: Use the boldest or brightest color line for the major subject, medium-wide line for the information the subject is compared to, and the lightest line for subsidiary information.

Steer attention to the main points with words. Annotate the nodes. Leave everything else off the chart but cover it in the caption.

Force the eye to notice direction with arrows. Or, if the data allows it, do it more subtly by poking the line out into space.

Express opinion graphically: a thin line is weak and diffident when indicating future projections, whereas a bold line shows confidence in the future.

Communicate instantly by substituting words for icons or icons for words. But do it with care, and replace clichés with fresh ideas.

Make understanding as fast as possible. Avoid keys and legends because they demand time and effort to decipher. Label the elements themselves for immediate comprehension.

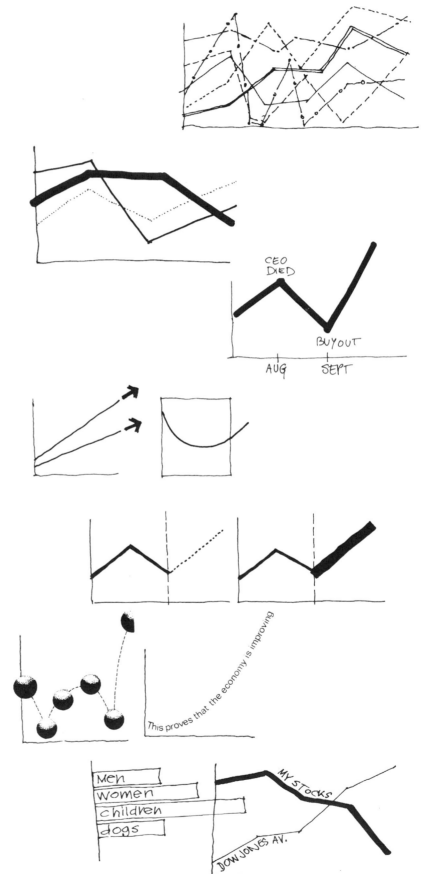

... but don't do this, it is cheating

We interpret what we see according to habit: Things are *supposed to be* a certain way because they have always been that way. When the line on a graph points down ⟍ we deduce that something bad is happening, but when it points up ⟋ we conclude that things are also looking up. A steady line ⎯⎯ indicates little change, but dramatic activity is shown by fluctuation ⋁⋀

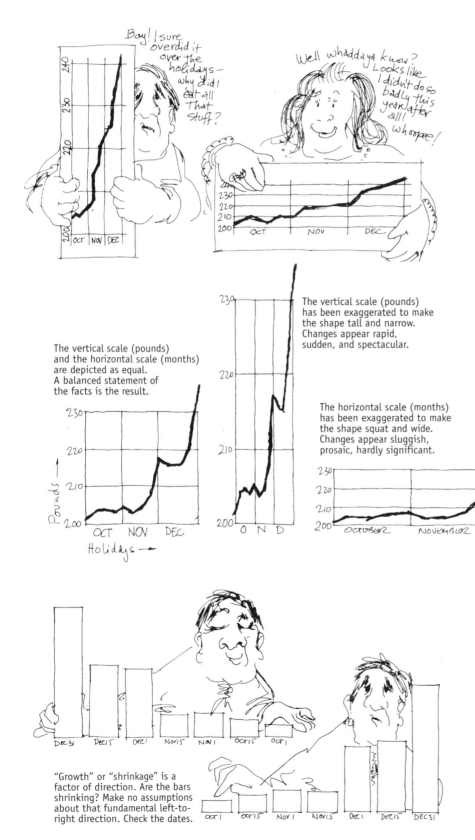

Distort to make a point more vivid. He feels badly because his line goes up so steeply. She feels happy because her line looks reasonably flat. Which is correct? Both. His rate of change is much more dramatic than her sluggish one, yet *the information is identical.* Only the scales are different. Would you call this clever communication or just plain cheating?

The vertical scale (pounds) and the horizontal scale (months) are depicted as equal. A balanced statement of the facts is the result.

The vertical scale (pounds) has been exaggerated to make the shape tall and narrow. Changes appear rapid, sudden, and spectacular.

The horizontal scale (months) has been exaggerated to make the shape squat and wide. Changes appear sluggish, prosaic, hardly significant.

We take left-to-right for granted. Things begin at the far-left and end at the far-right. Changes occurring in sequence are plotted in the same direction, of course. The connotation is so well established, that it is practically instinctive. Can there be any other way?

"Growth" or "shrinkage" is a factor of direction. Are the bars shrinking? Make no assumptions about that fundamental left-to-right direction. Check the dates.

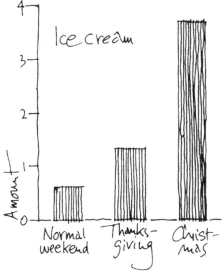

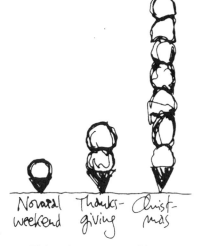

Ice cream

Each column is drawn to the same width and their height indicates variation.

If the columns are turned into countable pictorial units, but the overall proportions of the columns remain constant, the comparisons are clear—perhaps even clearer.

When the tall symbolic bar becomes a realistic picture, its tallness (which is what is supposed to be measured against the others) expands sideways and becomes overwhelming. Comparisons are skewed: tallness turns into hugeness.

The danger in pictorialization. The meaning of the diagram is skewed, because the size of the "tallest" ice cream cone is so overwhelming. We stop seeing *tallness* and see *bigness*.

The illusion of space and perspective. The imaginary place in space from which objects are viewed makes all the difference. It is all a question of closeness and angles. A carton of orange juice looks larger when it is standing close to you than at the far end of the counter. Perspective and direction can be exploited to misdirect interpretation.

The carton seen straight on. Imagine it to be made of transparent Plexiglas, so the level of orange juice inside is visible; three-quarters full.

Fly's-eye view of the same side of the carton. The top looks huge because it is closer, so it looks much emptier.

Cockroach-eye view. The carton appears much fuller, because the top looks so much smaller. The statistics in all three versions are accurate.

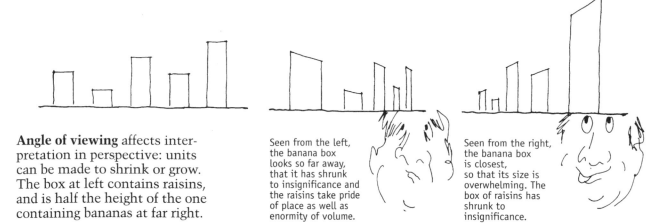

Angle of viewing affects interpretation in perspective: units can be made to shrink or grow. The box at left contains raisins, and is half the height of the one containing bananas at far right.

Seen from the left, the banana box looks so far away, that it has shrunk to insignificance and the raisins take pride of place as well as enormity of volume.

Seen from the right, the banana box is closest, so that its size is overwhelming. The box of raisins has shrunk to insignificance.

Looking straight down at a pizza: a neutral statement showing the pizza divided into a quarter and three-quarters, all equally far away.

Seeing it at an angle introduces the factor of relationship in space. The quarter slice is way over there, far away, so it belongs to your companion.

The quarter slice is in the front, closest to us as we look at the entire pizza, so you had better not touch it, it's mine!

If the quarter slice is separated from its circle and pushed closer towards us, there is no longer any question: grab it.

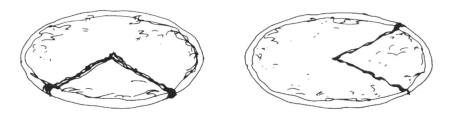

At first glance, which makes that quarter pizza look larger than the other? Both pizzas show a quarter slice cut and each is statistically and geometrically accurate. Do you see the opportunity for dishonesty?

Three-dimensionalizing has dangerous effects. We exist in 3D space, and instinctively interpret its built-in signals. Objects closer to us intrude on our consciousness more powerfully and have a greater urgency than those far away. If we see a pizza from the side, the way it is brought in on a tray, the slice nearest us becomes *ours*. The implication of closeness has altered our relationship to what we are looking at.

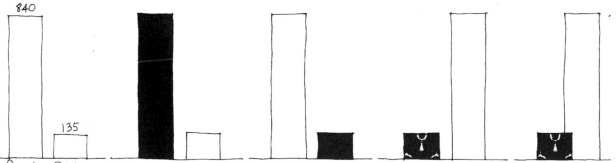

840

135

Peanuts   Potatoes

The calories in a cup of peanuts (840) and mashed potatoes (135) have been plotted as simple outline bars. No opinion is implied and just the dry facts are shown.

The tall Peanut bar has been blacked in. The power of blackness draws the eye to itself. As a consequence, the Peanut bar dominates the insignificant Potato bar.

The short Potato bar has been blacked in. Despite its diminutive size, it is more noticeable than it was in the previous version, diminishing Peanuts' importance.

The positions have been switched. Potato is seen before Peanut, and its flamboyant texture reduces the much bigger Peanut bar to a supportive role in the background.

A new trick has been added: overlapping. It leads us to deduce that Potatoes are "in front of" Peanuts. The one closest to the viewer has the advantage.

Graphic appearance of elements influences meaning. How the surface textures, tones, and patterns of the items are rendered and where they are placed can embellish and draw attention. They can be made to pop out or sink into the background.

THIS STUFF
MUST BE
IMPORTANT,
DISPLAYED
WITH SUCH
SWAGGER

THIS LOOKS SMALL, UNIMPORTANT, AND ISOLATED

What's in them for you?

They enliven and enrich: each box is
another opportunity for yet one more
arresting headline.

They clarify: they play up important points
when they are placed at the top of the page; they play down
unimportant ones at the foot of the page.

PRODUCT MAKING | They pull the product together and give it personality if their
format is standardized and consistently repeated.

STORY-TELLING | They simplify the story because sidebar matter that would be
a stumbling-block in the main flow of the story can be broken
out and pushed aside. Besides, the main part of the story also
looks shorter, so it appears less daunting.

They entice readers into the story, since people are attracted
to whatever looks short and effortless.

They layer the message by separating a subsidiary element
from the mainstream.

Boxes are make-believe dividers. How do we segregate things from each other in the three-dimensional world?

1. Imprison the object in a fenced area. The fence looks like a line from the air. ———————

2. Make the object hard to reach. Raise it on a plane floating above its surroundings.

On the page you create the illusion of planes by having the plane that is floating cast a shadow on the plane beneath.

Looking straight down at it, we expect traditionally to have it look something like this. (*See next chapter on Shadows*).———

3. Play up the object's value or specialness by placing it in a symbolic setting, such as a jewel on a cushion.

The cushion would look like a background of some sort in color, texture, shape...

4. Imprison the object in a coffin—OK, shoebox. Less depressing.

Here's what it looks like from that airplane at an angle ———— (looking straight down at it is simply a box just like the cow's fence, above).

Leave out the walls that define the "inside" and you have made a pedestal on which the object is displayed. (This trick might work well for the "ice" example, too).

Leave out the outside walls and you've carved the illusion of a niche in the surrounding surface. —————

Display the object in a fancy frame and hang it on the wall for everyone to admire to make it special.

...Or keep it simple:

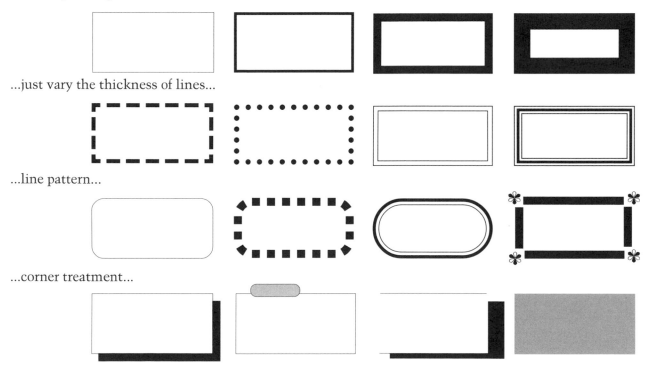

...just vary the thickness of lines...

...line pattern...

...corner treatment...

...or be inventive with shapes, colors, shadows, tints...

...or miniaturize a frame and reproduce it on the page. You don't have to design your own. It is easier to swipe one, if you can find one appropriate to the subject, the context, the vehicle, the readership.

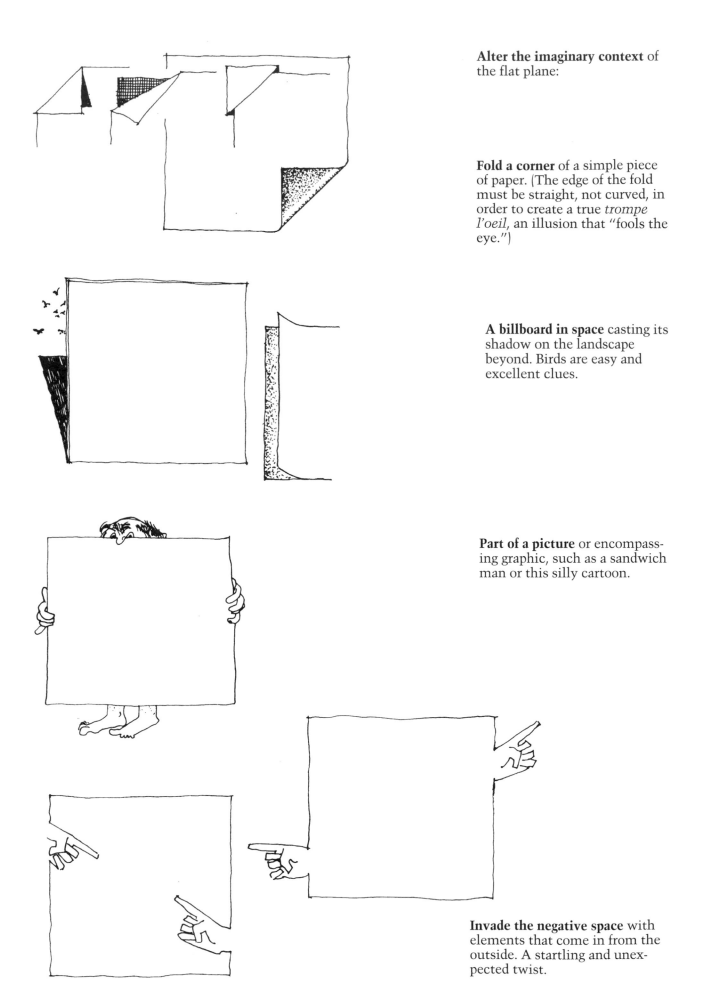

Alter the imaginary context of the flat plane:

Fold a corner of a simple piece of paper. (The edge of the fold must be straight, not curved, in order to create a true *trompe l'oeil*, an illusion that "fools the eye.")

A billboard in space casting its shadow on the landscape beyond. Birds are easy and excellent clues.

Part of a picture or encompassing graphic, such as a sandwich man or this silly cartoon.

Invade the negative space with elements that come in from the outside. A startling and unexpected twist.

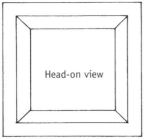 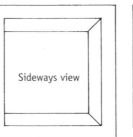 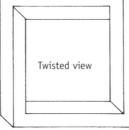 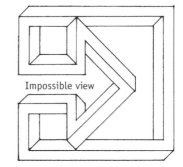

Head-on view   Sideways view   Twisted view   Impossible view

Play with "impossible figures." Draw three equidistant parallel lines that surround a shape. Join the corners. Some of them make visual sense, some look wrong. If you join the "wrong" ones on the inside and lop off the "wrong" ones on the outside of the figure, you end up with an impossible illusory shape.

A box too small for its contents. The material inside gains size, stature, and threat by breaching the perimeter and spreading out into the surrounding space.

For dramatic contrast place an area in the foreground against an unexpected background. The poster looks enormous because it is defined by a rhino, which we know to be enormous. (This is a 1515 woodcut by Albrecht Dürer.) Bleeding the words off into space beyond the box's edges creates the illusion of making whatever is inside the box bigger still.

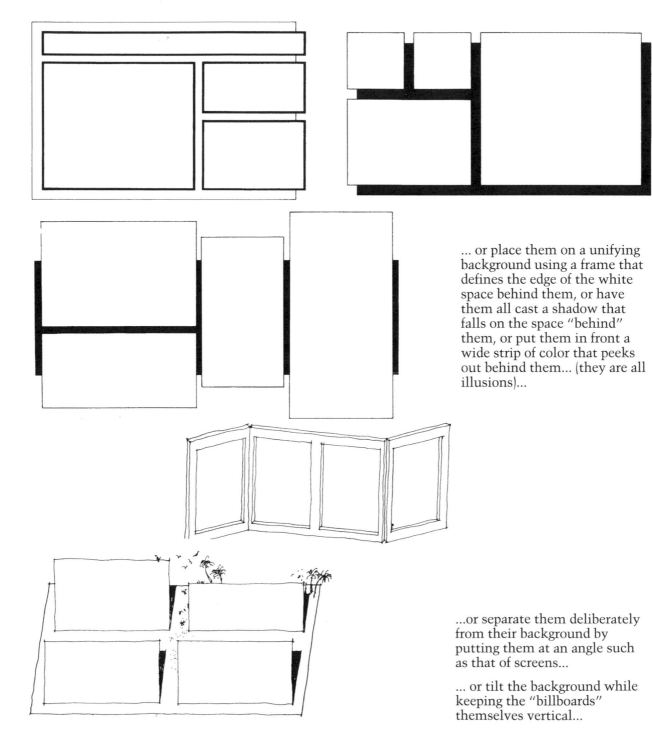

Cluster boxes in order to 1) combine disparate units into a visually more impressive mass, and 2) establish a relationship between them or with their surroundings. This way they can become an editorial tool whose value lies in its capacity to explain by arrangement.

Tie boxes together by means of some shared graphic characteristic such as rounded corners...

... or place them on a unifying background using a frame that defines the edge of the white space behind them, or have them all cast a shadow that falls on the space "behind" them, or put them in front a wide strip of color that peeks out behind them... (they are all illusions)...

...or separate them deliberately from their background by putting them at an angle such as that of screens...

... or tilt the background while keeping the "billboards" themselves vertical...

... or put them on a picture because the image is loaded with meaning and telegraphs the context at first glance...

...or embroider the pure graphics for the fun of it: see them as parts of three-dimensional illusions, like ends of beams advancing towards you, or panels of a stepped wall, or—anything!

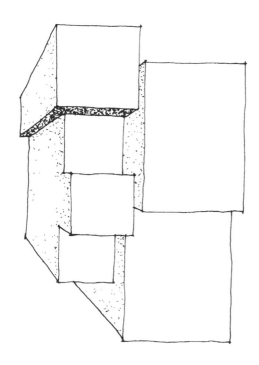

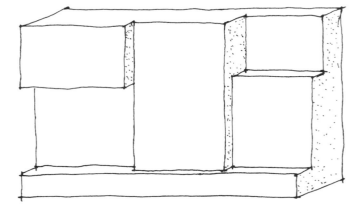

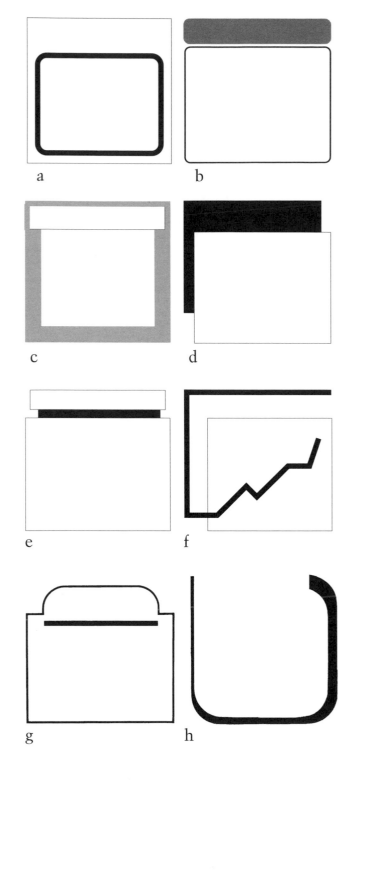

a

b

c

d

e

f

g

h

Merge titles with frames:
Recurring elements can and should be built into the structure of the design because that enriches the cumulative impression of all the diagrams. Editors know ahead of time what and how much to write... and production is easier: you don't have to reinvent the wheel every time. Here are some approaches to the infinite variety:

a. A TV-screen with rounded corners in its case...

b. A grey label stuck above the label on the medicine bottle...

c. A white label superimposed on a label with a grey outline...

d. A white label floating in front of a bigger, colored one...

e. Two stacked labels joined by a bar...

f. The label area defined by the end of the graph line pulled out from the box—a bit of hocus-pocus just to open the floodgates...

g. Tabs... filecards...

h. An open space ...

Let
the artwork
do
the talking?

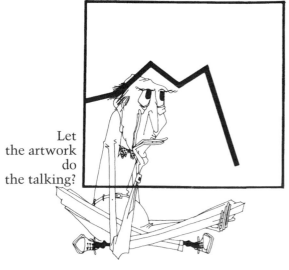

RULES

Ruled lines (rules, for short) are instantly available in infinite varieties of thicknesses and patterns. You don't need to search for them, because they are built into all typesetting softwares. See them as free artwork.

8–point	▬▬▬▬▬▬▬▬▬
4–point	▬▬▬▬▬▬▬▬▬
2–point	─────────
1–point	─────────
1/2–point	─────────
1/4–point (hairline)	─────────
double (equal thickness)	═════════
scotch (thick and thin)	═════════
coupon (dashes)	─ ─ ─ ─ ─ ─
leaders (dots or periods)	· · · · · · ·

Rules organize space, which is the most valuable material with which we "design" pages. They articulate edges and, like walls and fences, are marvelously useful as signals to the fast scanner. They help define elements on the page.

Rules add "color" to a page by simple contrast: imagine a page with nothing but pale grey type with a fat black rule dropped in it somewhere... or a delicate hairline rule contrasted to big black bold type. The combinations are limitless and add life, sparkle.

Rules can be used functionally to spotlight and thus emphasize significant words in display, either as overscoring or underscoring. The word they are attached to sounds "louder."

"Good fences make good neighbors"

Mending Wall, 1914, Robert Frost

This is fine-textured, light text type set in an easy-to-read, fairly narrow column of some forty characters per line. The face is CENTAUR and it was designed in 1912 as a fine book face by Bruce Rogers, 1870-1957. It is a noble face and should be reserved for situations where its grace and subtlety are appropriate to the subject of the story, the purpose in running it, as well as the publication's audience.

Regrettably and admittedly, it is misused here, reduced as it is to a mere typographic sample just to contrast its gentle, pale color to a brutally aggressive vertical 8–point rule sidescore flanking it a left.

Franklin Gothic is dark, heavy type
whose thick texture
can be further intensified
by contrasting it to the fine
hairline rules between the lines

This short statement contains absolutely vital information

This sentence does not contain an important word

This represents text set ragged-right and placed in narrow columns, perhaps four to a page. That means that there are few words per line. And to make typefitting matters worse, only a very deep hyphenation zone of three picas is specified to define the right-hand edge. As a result, the right-hand ragged edge is very ragged indeed, which is perfectly acceptable in a poem or a single column, but when you place several columns next to each other, the spaces between the columns (or so-called gutters) can look disturbingly untidy. To reestablish a modicum of tidiness, inserting a vertical hairline rule between them gives a geometric patterning that helps overcome the ugliness of that excessive raggedness. The two columns at far right in this example are separated by rules that are not centered between the columns but are placed deliberately closer to the left-hand edge of the columns. They seem to belong together better that way. • This represents text set ragged-right and placed in narrow columns, perhaps four to a page. That means that there are few words per line. And to make typefitting matters worse, only a very deep hyphenation zone of three picas is specified to define the right-hand edge. As a result, the right-hand ragged edge is very ragged indeed, which is perfectly acceptable in a poem or a single column, but when you place several columns next to each other, the spaces between the columns (or so-called gutters) can look disturbingly untidy. To re-establish a modicum of tidiness, inserting a vertical hairline rule between them

Rules make a page neat, when you are using ragged-right setting (which can look a bit too rough and untidy). The text explains more about that; read it, even though it is very small. It is shorter than it appears, because the text is repeated after the bullet, so don't bother reading it all over again. It is set in 6/7 Times Roman—much too small.

This is nine point Times Roman set solid, without additional linespacing, and using tight tracking, because this is intended to be an example of crowding a lot of words into a small space. It is just an example, and is not meant to be a recommendation, because it is false economy to crowd so much material into so small a space and expect to have it read. If something looks unacceptably thick and small and uninviting, it will be rejected. As a result, giving readers that much stuff is a failure, because packing it in is counterproductive. No money is saved, and all the money that has been invested in squeezing all this stuff is wasted, because the product does not fulfill its purpose. The one good thing that can be claimed for this travesty is that at least the horizontal scale of the Times Roman has not been tampered with, so its proper legibility remains unsullied. Just look how awful this type looks when its horizontal scale is reduced to 90%—"We can get away with it, nobody will notice." Yes they will.

Rules can be used as "column rules" to separate columns that are closer together than they should be in order to save space. (Yes, this type example might be worth reading, too.)

This is nice and legible text type, set in 10/12 Times Roman with normal tracking and at horizontal scale, as an example of text type run alongside an advertisement, represented by the grey rectangle, separated from it by an interestingly patterned column rule.

Rules can add personality to the product if they have a subtle pattern of their own, like the old *New Yorker* magazine's squiggles, or are made up of dots (leaders) run in color. Such special rules separate editorial matter from the neighboring ads not just physically but stylistically, to the advantage of both.

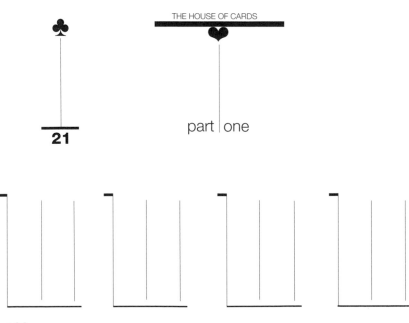

THE HOUSE OF CARDS

part | one

21

Rules can enrich the page by coupling structural definition with personalization if they end in interesting finials at the top and bottom. Topic titles, continued lines, page numbers, identification symbols... anything.

Rules can be patterning elements in the background to give successive pages a special character that acts as a recognition factor to tie segments of a publication together. They can be joined into shapes such as partial boxes.

PRODUCT-MAKING | If it is to be trusted—and succeed—in the marketplace, the publication must establish an aura of trustworthiness. Phoniness and pretense are risky. We undermine our own credibility if our readers feel funny about something (probably without realizing precisely what it is that makes them so uncomfortable).

One of the more obvious places to make ourselves look amateurish—second, perhaps, to bad spelling—is in our attempts at creating *realism* on the page and not getting it quite right. Shadows create an illusion of reality. Since they are a natural phenomenon, they follow natural laws. Therefore, if they are to work for the product, they had better be correct.

STORY-TELLING | Shadows are useful for two reasons.

First, they create the illusion of dimensionality, which enriches the images.

Second, they create the appearance of layers floating in front of each other in space. That layering is a technique that can help organize material for the reader and help rank ideas. Things that appear closer to you are more prominent than those far away, so they are probably more worthy of attention than the others. It is worthwhile getting the geometry and its look right, so the illusion really works.

If you haven't been trained in descriptive geometry like the artist who drew the column on page 184, the ideal way to figure out realistic lighting and shadows is to build a model and light it—a good investment of time and effort.

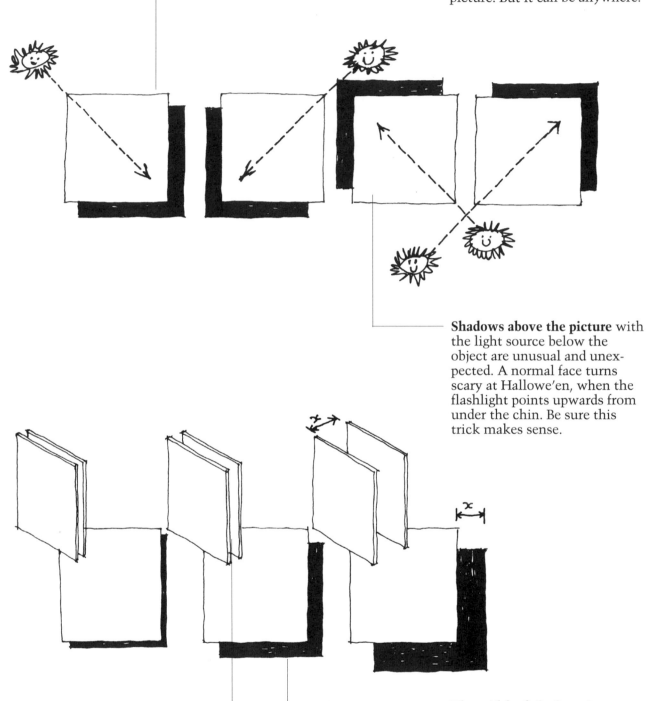

The light source is conventionally placed at 45° above the top-left corner of the figure, so the shadow appears beneath the picture. But it can be anywhere.

Shadows above the picture with the light source below the object are unusual and unexpected. A normal face turns scary at Hallowe'en, when the flashlight points upwards from under the chin. Be sure this trick makes sense.

The width of shadows is not arbitrary. It is significant. In nature, its width depends on the distance between the object and the surface on which the shadow is cast. Rule of thumb: the greater the distance, the wider the shadow. X = X. (The angle of lighting also affects it, but for practical purposes you can forget that).

Avoid the one-dimensional look where the shadows are all equally wide and fall arbitrarily over foreground and background planes. This is just a superficial effect that looks false.

To construct correct shadows, start with the background and build upward. The widths vary in proportion to the distance between the object and its background. It looks complex, but it is perfectly logical when you build it step-by-step.

A is closest to the background, so it casts a narrow shadow.

B overlaps **A**, so it must be closer to us and further away from the background. That's why its shadow is fatter (except where it overlaps the corner of picture **A**—which is the trick that makes it look realistic).

C is further away still since it overlaps **B**, so its shadow is commensurately wider (except where it is cast on the surface of picture **B**).

Therefore **D**, which is in front of **C**, must cast the widest shadow of all. (Where it overlaps **C**, though, the shadow is narrow). Make sense?

Darkness of shadows is also related to width. The narrower the shadow, the darker it is. The wider the shadow, the paler it is. (The wider the separation between object and background, the more light can sneak between them.)

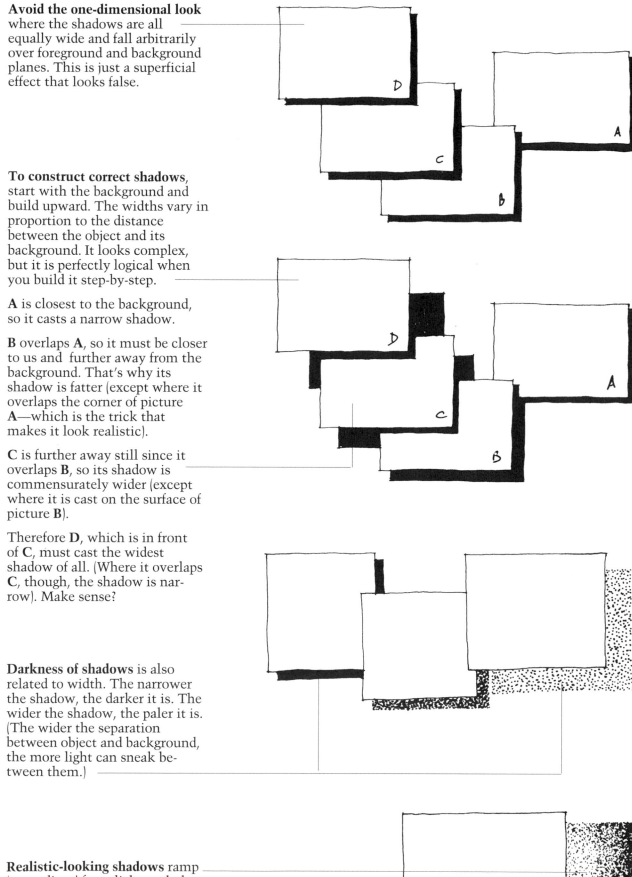

Realistic-looking shadows ramp (or gradient) from light to dark, with the darkest part lining the outermost edges. (Reflected light plays tricks.)

Drawings by William Wirt Turner

Just study this for a minute: all the shades and shadows are in a logical, correct place, so even such a hard-edged mechanical drawing as this looks realistic if you squint at it with half-closed eyes. (A *shade* is on a surface hidden from the light source; a *shadow* is cast onto a surface by something else). There are no flat tones in nature: the doughnut has all sorts of highlights—maybe it is glazed?

Cover-design is not an artistic process. In this rabidly competitive market, each publication must establish its brand and its cover embodies that character and shows off that sense of self. It is cold-blooded and commercial, first and foremost. Not only is it the most vital page because it is a showcase that represents "you," but because it has several other essential and interwoven functions. It must be:

Recognizeable from issue-to-issue (that's the brand)

Emotionally irresistible (by the appeal of the image)

Magnetic and curiosity-arousing (to pull the reader in)

Intellectually stimulating (promising benefits)

Efficient, fast, easy to scan (introducing your "service")

Logical (making sense as investment)

LOGO

PRODUCT-MAKING

The cover is a miniature poster, like a billboard delivering its message as you barrel past at 65 mph. Therefore you must think in bigger scale—the simpler, the better. Fussing with nuances and clever details doesn't succeed because everybody else does that. (Go and study a magazine rack and imagine swapping logos from one publication to another: it wouldn't make much difference, would it?)

Figure out *what makes your product special and play that up.* Use rational business thinking to define what is unique and thus deserving of emphasis. Be deliberate in ranking what is important. Every decision is a compromise and carries hidden costs, and the result probably has little to do with æsthetic "liking." Of course you want the cover—and you—to look good, but good looks are a secondary consideration.

Good designers know how to fulfill the business purpose while making it look good, at the same time.

Always examine designs in their context. Seeing them lying isolated on a conference room table is misleading because the temptation is to consider them as "art." They must be seen the way the potential investor will see them—fleetingly—competing for attention. Tuck the proposed cover among other current magazines in a typical magazine rack. Take the dummy to the newsstand and hide it on the shelf among all those others publications. Paste a life-size photomural of a newsstand on the wall and tack the new cover on it, to make its context as realistic as possible. If your product is not for sale on the newsstand, hide it in the in-box on a desk, or among the junk mail. Be realistic. Don't be misled by design competitions that reward superficial aesthetics unless you are fortunate enough to be working on a product whose æsthetics are part of its mission.

Full bleed makes the most of the poster-quality of the cover. The picture appears bigger because it continues beyond the confines of the page and all you see here is the nucleus of a larger scene. But seldom is it seen "unspoiled" by words!

Frames concentrate attention onto the enclosed area. They also separate this product from the surrounding competition on the newsstand, while helping give it its recognizeable personality. But they reduce the picture size.

Several pictures multiply the number of "appeals" to attract a broader range of targets to a product covering wide areas of interest. The more appeals, the smaller and more insignificant each becomes. Make one dominant, add several little ones.

The picture is the eye-catcher to arouse viewer's curiosity and attention. It must be different from the last issue (to show this is a new one) yet remain stylistically the same (to identify the product, and separate it from others). However, it is the words that really draw the potential reader into the issue because they tout the what's-in-it-for-me appeal.

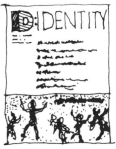

Logo and coverlines dominate the cover, with the picture an incidental element to help identify the issue and add visual interest. Sensitive color choice is imperative.

Learnèd journals avoid such light-hearted frippery as pictures. Intellecual variety of content is paramount; visual variety, other than background color, perhaps, is deemed unserious.

Compromise: put in everything to please everybody. It may look like a mess, but that may well be the right image for the product. What's the competition doing?

Should the image be dominant? "Of course!" say designers. Journalists say, "No, that's window-dressing, it's the words that matter." Circulation people don't know, but they run tests and ask focus groups. Ad sales people cite the competition's latest gimmick and insist we outdo them. Obviously, it all depends on the characteristics of the product, its audience, its market niche.

The format should be standardized, because quick recognition is a vital factor in competitive success—and easier to produce. Paradoxically, the more rigid the framework, the greater the freedom in the artwork inside it. That said, the format must not be allowed to become a straitjacket—allowing departure when it makes sense.

The logo is the symbol, the unique design whose image must come to mind immediately the name is mentioned. It is not just the name set in type—it must be personalized from word into monogram. It is also the first in a series of signals that ought to have a consistent look to tie the product together: not just department headings, but also in headlines.

LOGO Plain type

L O G O Type embellished, personalized

LO OG Embellished type turned into "picture"

Rich graphic character of the logo is important when the subject of the magazine is not easily illustratable. If the images can be depended on, then the logo can be reduced to a simple identifier. In both cases, **display the logo in its own clean, uncluttered space** with pride and dignity. Surrounding it with slogans, skyboxes, appeals, dates, volume numbers, overlapping corner tags, and whatnot is disturbing visual static that denigrates the logo's stature.

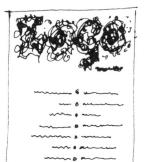

The logo is in the top-left corner so the first few letters are visible when the copies are overlapped on newsstand racks. If single-copy sales are unimportant because subscribers receive the magazine by mail, then the logo can go anywhere, and its placement is unrestricted. It can even vary from issue to issue as the image or coverlines demand.

REALISTIC COVERLINE OPINIONS

No! They spoil the picture! protests the designer

Who cares—they sell the issue... insists the publisher

(They had better say something our readers care about) mutters the editor

Cute type better not distract the viewer from the thought! adds the circulation director

Short-and-snappy or sentences with verbs? " Yes," opines the consultant

What is the ideal number? that varies, as many as necessary, asserts the guru

Does anybody know anything definitive? no, they all agree for the first time

This is why the phrase *"flying by the seat of your pants"* was invented.

Coverlines sell the issue. They exist to be read—fast. Keep them simple; playing clever self-serving type-games doesn't attract readers who care only about what the words *say*, not in how cute they *look*. To be persuasive, lines need to be long enough to say what they need to say. Use lowercase because it reads faster and takes less space, so you can make it bigger in the same space as all-caps. CAPS are big and impressive but hard to decipher in bulk. In Any Case Never Ever Use This Outmoded Up And Down Style.

Coverline type size must respond to the distance at which the product is to be seen: newsstand distance demands a larger scale from the intimate one appropriate to the closeness when the magazine is taken out of its mailer. Best compromise: scream the main story big, but reduce the rest to no bigger than 14–point. Their smallness will force potential buyers to pick the magazine up and once they've done that, you've probably made a sale.

The ideal cover color is monochromatic. It makes the product look larger and more elegant. A single color also separates it from its gaudy competitors. The more colorful and exciting it looks on your conference table, the more it disappears among the others. Everyone uses process yellow for its high visibility. Avoid it, unless you really want to blend in with the opposition on the newsstand. Coverlines should not compete but contrast with the picture so they mutually show each other off. In this respect, the obvious black or white are best because they are neutral.

PRODUCT-MAKING

The TOC is seen as a special problem because it is a multi-tasked receptacle fraught with so many expectations. But, though we consider it in isolation, it is not a standalone. It follows the cover as second in a one/two punch sequence. The two must be transparently linked because the hoped-for reader checks it to find those promises made on the cover

—NOW.

It is also the place to display other goodies to the unconvinced, so it has to sell, sell, sell. They need to be shown so the target can understand the menu and easily choose bits from it and

—FAST.

Therefore it must be organized for the target's use. The traditional FEATURE/DEPARTMENT/COLUMN breakup creates complications that are neither essential nor useful.* A sequential listing exposes the issue's structure best. All the readers want to know is: 1) what else is there, 2) by whom, and 3) where

—IMMEDIATELY.

There are two other target audiences:

1) Those who are looking up something specific in a past issue. They want a checklist laid out by topic, subject, author, date, page number. Tabulation is a verbal diagram. What matters is the way it is written, how it is organized, and the way the items are disposed in space in relation to each other. Its purpose—INTUITIVE SCANNING.

2) Those advertisers and their agencies who are non-readers but intimately involved with what the issue consists of. They want to invest in an

---

* In the good old days—before around 1980—there used to be a distinct split between the Front of the Book (FOB), the Middle of the Book (MOB) or "Editorial Well," and the Back of the Book (BOB). That well (or "hole") was a sacrosanct section devoted to feature stories, and ads were kept out of it. Glamorous ads were up front and the rest were sent to Siberia in back. "Editorial support" (in the form of small-scale stuff like letters, departments, columns, new products, etc.) was slotted between the ads in the FOB and MOB. The differences between the sections were clear in terms of content and scale, so it made sense to list them that way on the TOC. Now, with "flow-through makeup," ads invade editorial and columns or departments are dropped in arbitrarily. Distinctions are unclear and readers get lost, yet the old mindset in structuring the TOC remains. *Why?*

environment that is perfect for their product or services. Few of them appreciate the excellent details of your product. They just need to know the topics and areas of coverage. The TOC is where they look for clues and QUICK LISTING.

In addition, the TOC reveals the relative value of articles by the way they are emphasized or played down in type size, color, isolation, spacing, and possibly capsule summaries.

Furthermore, conventional wisdom decrees that you have to gussy up the page with pictures to tickle curiosity and act as shills to hook the casual page-flipper. But by devoting space to visual blandishments, you may not be able to do the organizing properly, because there's not enough space left. Are those visuals really essential? What is more valuable?

And somewhere you have to shoehorn in all that stuff shown

No TOC can do it all. Each publication's TOC must reflect its own particular character and needs. Invest in fifty magazines of various kinds. Tear out their TOCs, hang them on a wall for easy comparison, then analyze them. Figure out their targets and how they reach their objectives. Only then start work on your own. Define your problem first. Writing the program is the most difficult step of all, but when you have it, the physical arrangement becomes easy. The "design" grows out of the needs, because each problem carries within itself the seeds of its own solution.

Is one shape "better" than another? No! The only criterion: does the arrangement fulfill the needs of *your* publication? (You are not abdicating editorial freedom if you seek and welcome the participation of the business-side in planning this page.)

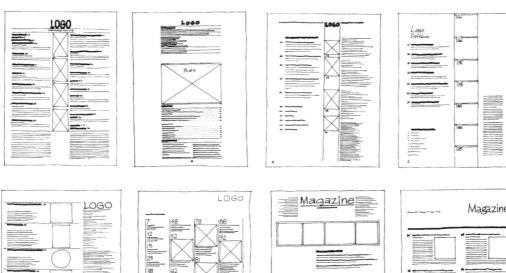

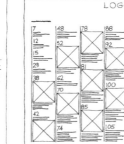

The TOC can not and should not be a catchall. The list of articles should be as clear and helpful as possible. Everything else is ancillary. All the extras must remain subservient, never outshout the listing. Tabulation must be efficient—that is why the page was invented: the ultimate in user-friendliness. Avoid making the page too full and visually confusing. Don't drop in elements without apparent logic. Instead, group things, tighten space within the group, separate groups with more space. And always consider whether the table's shape is easy and fast to scan.

Date, Vol., No. Don't make them too big because on this page they are for reference only. They can be quite small, yet remain noticeable, if they are in their own little bubble of space. (On the cover they are for quick finding.)

Cover miniature, its explanation and credits. Often utilized in lieu of the logo as a heading above the masthead.

The masthead listing editorial staff in descending order with function and e-mail address. In many listings the job title outweighs the name in blackness and importance. The list should include names of professional advisors, association directors, publication committee members etc. Business and advertising staffs are usually listed with the Ad index, where they logically belong.

The indicia that gives essential publishing information, address, frequency of publishing, and all that technical stuff should be placed elsewhere if possible. (Post Office demands it in the first five pages.) It is grudgingly inserted as an undignified space-eating footnote on the TOC set so small that it looks like an illegible smudge.

The word **Contents** usually blown up huge for design impact eats up a huge area of prime real estate at the top of the page. What for, if the page looks like what it is? Wasted effort and space. Why paint the lily?

Slogan or mission statement is often accommodated on the TOC because it is part of the publication's registered name. Normally it is run near the logo on the cover, but in order to clear the area around the logo to make it dramatically visible, this ancillary wording can be moved here.

www. home page is a miniature house ad and self-promotion in the guise of "service." Doesn't belong on the TOC.

How to get in touch with the editors. Usualy a chatty invitation. A cleaner solution: put the e-mail addresses on the masthead next to the names. Or have that information as part of a direct-to-the-reader column of instructions... coming next month... other stuff... and incorporating the indicia.

Logo ought to set the visual style for the chain of succeeding department logos but seldom does, because the logo was designed years ago and the inside has been tinkered with since. Make it small here. Or, if you use a miniature of the cover, rely, on that for identification.

Notes like *Founded 1863, incorporating Cement-Pourer* to establish trust, snob-value, or retain ancient names and trademarks legally. Make them small, light, and insignificant.

Page numbers often overwhelm everything else, becasue they are pretty, easy to align, and look like fun. And they say "list". Their purpose is not to decorate the page. The reason for their existence is as references to where the wonders touted in the headlines are to be found. They are the last (and least important) element in a thinking-sequence: What is the topic?... What is the subject?... What is it about?... Who is responsible for it?... Aha! Sounds interesting—so Where is it to be found?

Coming next issue ought not to be squeezed in here. It just confuses and devalues this issue's value by promising even better in the next issue. It should be shown off elsewhere.

Repeat the coverlines using *identical wording on the* TOC *(as well as the headline on the story itself).* Avoid puzzling the curious reader with cute verbal variety because "it is more interesting that way." Is such confusion worth it? You want immediate, obvious recognition so they can find it *now.*

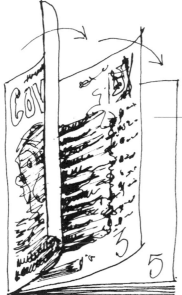

Place the TOC on page 3 or 5, the strategic position where the reader is most likely to look for it. But wherever it is placed, establish that as a sacred position. To force readers to search for this guide page fails to win friends or influence people.

A spread is impressive and useful, because it has so much room for display. Two singles are not nearly as helpful. In fact they are confusing, unless they are twinned rights or lefts that follow sequentially and are deliberately clearly designed to act together. Their only advantage: you can sell two preferred positions opposite them.

Forget features/departments/ columns as an organizing base, even if "it's always been done that way." It serves the editors' organizational purposes more than the readers' needs. But if these categories are imperative, define them typographically, while displaying items sequentially. Since Features are most important, they can be in big fat type and in color. Columns are special so they can be in caps-and-small-caps. Departments are smaller, quieter. That way you get two-for-the-price-of-one and everybody is better served.

The TOC is a roadmap first, and only incidentally is it a sales-tool showing off how wonderful you are. The ideal and most helpful roadmap presents the product in miniature, listing the items one after the other, the way they appear in the issue.

Use topic names to display content and show off the various franchises covered. List them so they are the dominant and easily-scanned element. Ranking the information visually makes information-retrieval most efficient.

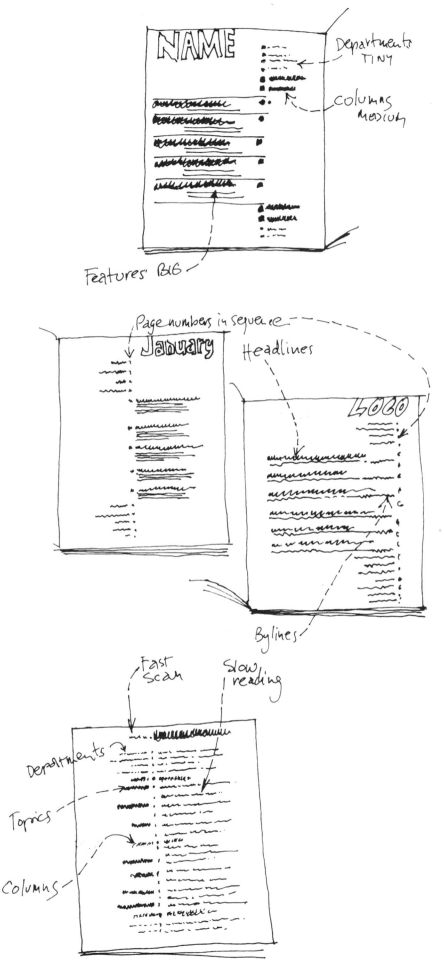

Pictures are believed to add interest and magnetism. Images are fun, immediate, and raise curiosity, whereas words have to be thought about. A good TOC can do both: accommodate pictures *and* act as an efficient roadmap. But don't let the tail wag the dog. Make the pictures tiny, because they don't need to be studied—they'll fulfill that function in the story itself. If they are small, crop in on symbolic details to make them act best as teasers. Think how small postage stamps are, yet what a wallop they carry.

NO

YES

In this issue...

NO (Good page but pictures are in gutter because it is a right-hand page.)

P.S. Don't forget to change the design when the page is switched from a left to a right in the last minute to accommodate a late-closing ad.

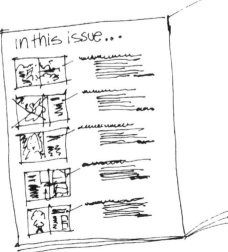

In this issue...

YES (Identical layout as the one at left, but pictures are on the outside because this is a left-hand page.)

Design TOCs either as a left- or as a right-hand page, because their physical characteristics are not the same. If you use pictures, don't bury them in the gutter, but use them to pull the page-flipper into the text. Put them where they'll do the most good—on the outside, where they'll be seen first. When pages are flipped, the outside half of the page is exposed. Seeing text there is slow and ponderous. Exposing the pictures on the outsides makes the TOC (and the issue) look more lively. On the other hand, the listing of stories is really what the page is for, so perhaps that ought to go on the outside to be seen first. The choice depends on the kind of impression you consider right for your product.

Signals and labels are all the elements that speak directly to the viewers and tell them what they are looking at as well as where in the publication they happen to be: logos, department "slugs" (standing artwork logos), page numbers, direction indicators, etc.

Examine all your signalling devices as an interrelated group. Look at them separately, just by themselves. Hang them up on the wall so you can see them all together as a group. Look for ease of recognition, use, as well as consistency, so they can fulfill their three functions:

PRODUCT-MAKING | *1. Recognition definers.* By definition, all labels and signals must be noticeable. That essential visibility simultaneously makes them important links in the chain that add up to create a visual personality for the product, whether it is printed or electronic. As such, they help to make the whole greater than the sum of its parts.

STORY-TELLING | *2. Locators.* They act as street signs that help the viewer/readers orient themselves in the issue, whether it is a printed object or electronic sequence.

3. Navigation aids. They are signposts to guide the viewer/readers to whatever it is they are looking for. Immediate findability is the key to service when readers are in a hurry (as they always are).

All the signals are components of *a deliberate system of clues* built in throughout our processional product, that goes beyond just a nice-looking Table of Contents decorated with pictures to act as shills. It encompasses service-oriented details such as making the page numbers large enough so they can be discerned while the product is held far enough from the eyes for quick page-flipping.

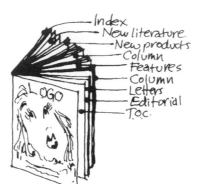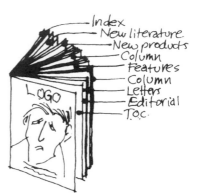

Put repeated elements in the same place in every issue or on every Web page. Subscribers feel comfortable when they find their favorites where they're supposed to be. Consistent placement fosters habits and familiarity, so they perceive their product as being their own. Besides, they are easy to locate.

Place signals where they'll be seen because their purpose is to be noticed. They belong in the top-left corner on lefts, top-right on rights.

Don't bury labels in the gutter (the top-left corner of a right-hand page). They aren't visible unless the page-flipper looks for them. Expose them to view.

Left-hand-pages are not interchangeable with rights. Establish a system that alerts you whenever a left-hand page has moved to a right-hand page because of a last-minute ad insertion. Fix it. Move the label to the outside. Always.

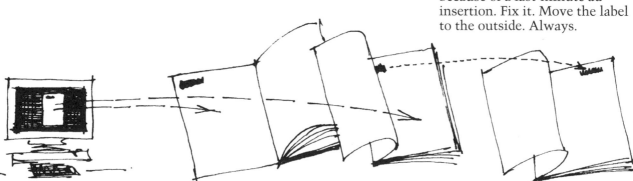

Remember to shift logos to the outside when lefts become rights.

This page
is all about
pigs…

This page
is all about
sheep…

This page
is all about
hippopotami…

… and they are all parts
of the zoo story.

Signals are topic labels for the material on the page while, at the same time serving as links in a chain that defines the group as a whole. Each is a different animal, but they are all animals. Their individual graphics must be both clear (to explain the page) and consistent (to assemble the group).

Reflect the graphic character of the cover logo in the full panoply of department labels. Each represents a segment of the entity that the logo stands for. The importance and individuality of the product as a whole grows by this controlled series of consistently recognizable impressions.

Make labels conspicuous to make them maximally useful. The audience are not as familiar with the product as you are, so don't assume that its structure is as obvious to them as it is to you. It's part of your life, whereas they only see it for a short while. They need and appreciate help. Signals may need to be more intrusive than you might prefer, but they have a job to perform.

White space makes the signal visible. Without it, you have to scream to get attention. With it, you can make the labels smaller, tighter, more elegant. This little detail affects the character of the product, and is an integral feature of its styling.

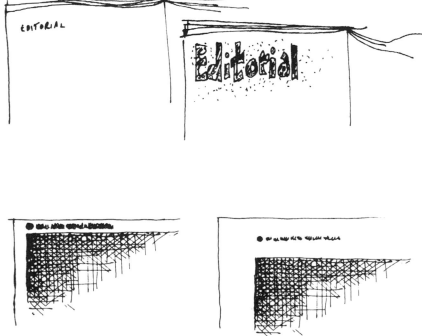

Small logo in squeezed space is undistinguished   … but it commands attention in ample space.

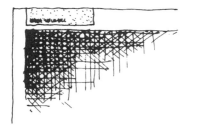
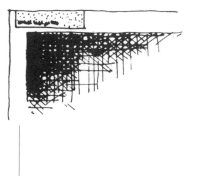
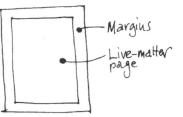

Margins

Live-matter page

Pull the label out of alignment with the edges of the "live-matter page." It may not look as clean, but it separates them from each other and isolates the signal, and that way highlights it as a link in a chain of signals.

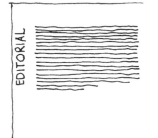
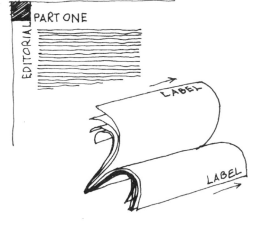

EDITORIAL

EDITORIAL   PART ONE

LABEL

LABEL

Sideways placement, reading upwards, (with "type on its ear") removes the signals from the text and emphasizes their separateness. It also encourages the reader to hold the book sideways, flip the pages and scan them fast like a catalog. (That's why it makes sense to have the wording read upward on both left- and right-hand pages.) A label reading around the corner can break information into two levels.

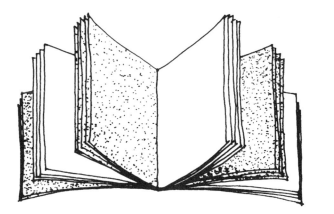

Stock of different colors is the ideal way of distinguishing parts of the product. Probably impractical, but wouldn't it be nice? How about printing the color? Or imagine all the editorial spaces with a pale yellow background: that would tie them together, split them from the small-space ads, and signal editorialness wordlessly.

Thumbtabs, file dividers, or other such indexing devices may well be the ultimate icons for organizing and filing the stories by sections. If the material breaks down into such clear-cut segments, why not make it a noticeable feature and show off the ease-of-use as a unique service?

Confusing alternate wordings: **Renovations of High School take center stage**

Arguments about High School renovation

Headlines. Use identical words for the cover lines, table of contents, and the headline on the story. Some editors believe they add "interest" and "variety" to the issue by varying them but they pay a heavy price: readers who are in a hurry —i.e., everybody—can't find anything and that's frustrating. No, it is infuriating. Repeating the same words is clearest and fastest. They can be made to look different by typographic handling in size and posture.

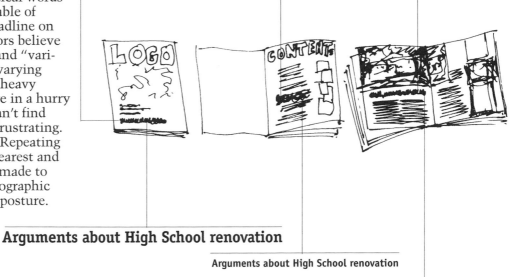

Arguments about High School renovation

Arguments about High School renovation

Identical wording made to look different by type variation: *Arguments about High School renovation*

Jump lines. Use key words for ease of recognition—fast. Avoid intellectual puzzles that demand reading, analyzing, thinking, even if writing clever follow-up heads shows skill. Signals should be obvious immediately and repeated key words are the simplest and most direct forms of identification.

Main head: **Renovations of High School take center stage**

Idiotic jump: **Center stage** *ctd from p. 27*

Center stage is idiotic because it is just a figure of speech and the metaphor by itself is misleading. The story has nothing to do with acting.

Mediocre jump: **High School** *ctd from p. 27* — **High School** is mediocre, because what it says is uninteresting. However, it is easily recognizable, especially because the first letters are capitalized.

Good jump: **Renovations** *ctd from p. 27*

Renovations is good because it not only encapsulates the story in terms of meaning, but it also repeats the first (and thus the most noticeable) word of the headline.

Continued lines. The graphic styling must be consistent with all the other labeling and signaling devices. "CONTINUED ON P.00" and "CONTINUED FROM P.00" are services vital to the user. As long as they do their job clearly, they can be in words or as symbols like arrows. (There is no need for continued lines where the continuation is obvious; don't use them when the story flows opposite or even overleaf onto the next page.)

continued on page 135   >135   ☞135

continued from p.27   <27   ←27

The traditional arrangement
of page number and name on
the left-hand page and date and page
number on the right-hand page has
now often shrunk to

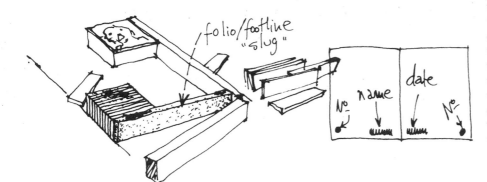

00 NAME DATE   DATE NAME 00

and is often personalized with
doodads, dots and dividers like

| ● ❑ — ✳

Folios/footlines (page numbers/
name of the magazine and date
of issue) are not nuisances that
mess up the page but vital
character-yielding signals. Place
them in the lower corners
where readers expect to find
them. (Why are they normaly
placed there? Habit: Printers
used to make a page-wide metal
"slug" with the folio on the
outside and the name or date on
the inside. The slug identified
the page while acting as founda-
tion for building the pages from
the bottom upward. Each line
of text was a piece of metal, as
were the "cuts" or pictures and
the spaces between them.)

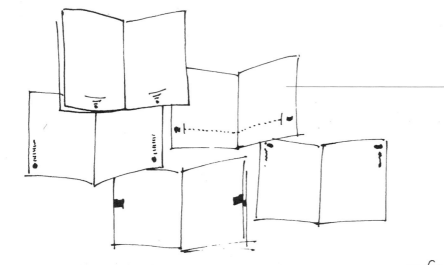

**Reject habit and put folio
footlines elsewhere**—where you
want to. Be as different as you
wish—so long as the pagination
and identification are obvious
enough to work.

Footlines must be designed as
an integral part of the string of
symbols that identify/instruct/
signal. The magazine's name
should echo the logo in style.

**Page numbers must be large
enough** to be easily discernible
when they are most needed, at
page-flipping distance. (They
can be elegantly tiny at read-
ing-distance but that presup-
poses that people will indeed
read, which may be somewhat
arrogant.)

Color—as color—is just a neutral raw material, just like space, type, and pictures. Using it cleverly demands more than just "running a title in blue" or that the page could use some "dressing-up." Undoubtedly, color may well improve the images and be *pleasing to the eye*, but that is hardly enough. It must also be *revealing to the mind*. It must have broader significance that grows out of the meaning and is integral with that meaning. Such practical utility is far more valuable to the reader than color's prettiness, however exciting that may be.

PRODUCT-MAKING | In working print, color is not primarily an æsthetic medium, but a rational technique to be applied for functional purposes: recognition… emphasis… linkage… organization… persuasion… and, sometimes, the deliberate creation of beauty, but usually only as by-product.

STORY-TELLING | "First-glance value" is not just a professional catch phrase, but the very kernel of functional communication in print. It emphasizes the valuable ideas in the words, while simultaneously exposing them to view in the layout. Therefore it demands that writing/editing and design be blended into a single process. To use color as a functional material:

1. Define the thrust of your message.

2. Decide what is most valuable to your readers.

3. Expose it by blending words, images, and space in a lucidly laid-out arrangement, using verbal/visual language they'll understand and exploiting color to *make the ideas clear, vivid, memorable*.

Don't pick colors because you _like_ them. Plan deliberate effects with purpose. Peaceful harmony is usually more successful than clashing variety. Choose colors that are related. Play it safe and pick colors related by one or more of the following:

1) *hue* (i.e., the kind of color it is—e.g., redness)

2) *saturation* (i.e., its intensity, brightness, chroma)

3) *value* (i.e., its shade, darkness, paleness)

Value is the most critical factor in print because it affects contrast, and contrast is what makes things stand out—and making things stand out is one of the effects you use color for.

Colors play tricks. The same color looks different depending on its background and surroundings.

It looks darker on a light background, lighter on a dark background…

warmer on a cool background, cooler on a warm background.

It also appears different on a textured surface from a smooth, shiny one, and you have no idea what it will look like printed on colored stock. (Test it!) Colors also vary on-screen depending on calibration.

There are other tricks color is capable of, but forget them, if precise color matching—or fine art—are not critical factors. In functional communication, **what the color is used for is far more vital than what it may look like.**

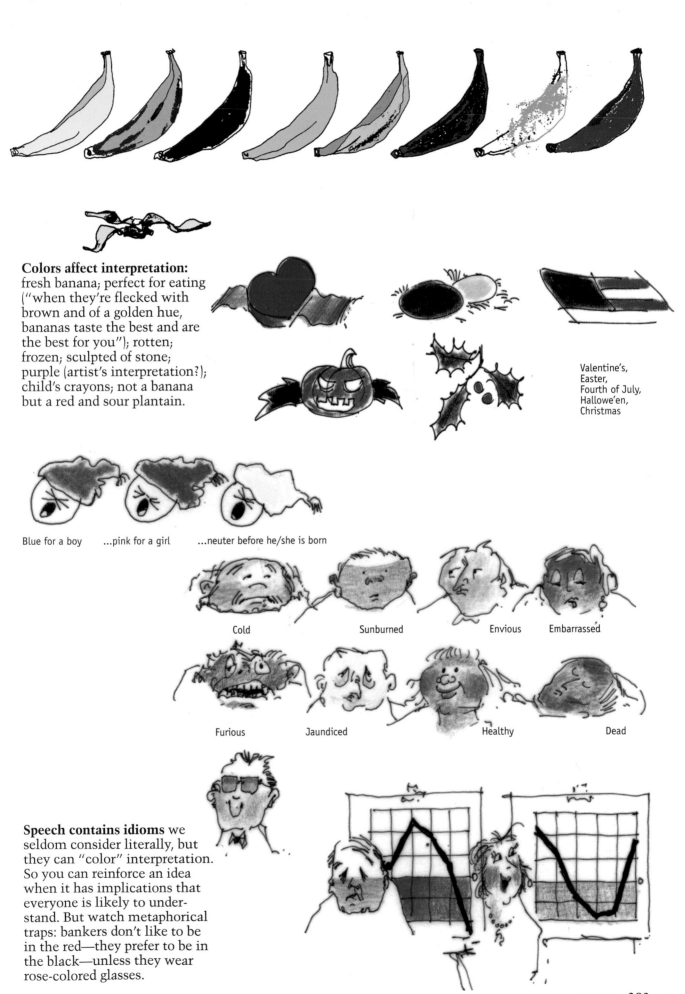

Colors affect interpretation:
fresh banana; perfect for eating ("when they're flecked with brown and of a golden hue, bananas taste the best and are the best for you"); rotten; frozen; sculpted of stone; purple (artist's interpretation?); child's crayons; not a banana but a red and sour plantain.

Valentine's,
Easter,
Fourth of July,
Hallowe'en,
Christmas

Blue for a boy   ...pink for a girl   ...neuter before he/she is born

Cold   Sunburned   Envious   Embarrassed

Furious   Jaundiced   Healthy   Dead

Speech contains idioms we seldom consider literally, but they can "color" interpretation. So you can reinforce an idea when it has implications that everyone is likely to understand. But watch metaphorical traps: bankers don't like to be in the red—they prefer to be in the black—unless they wear rose-colored glasses.

RED
Hot, passionate, bloody, horrifying, burning, revolution-
ary, dangerous, active, aggressive, loving, vigorous,
impulsive, crude, broke, stop!

PINK
Fleshy, sensuous, girlish

ORANGE
Warm, autumnal, gentle, informal, affordable, ripe,
wise

GREEN
Natural, fertile, restful, calm, refreshing, financial,
prosperous, youthful, abundant, healthy, envious,
diseased, decaying, go!

KHAKI
Military, drab, warlike

BLUE
Serene, calm, loyal, clear, cool, peaceful, tranquil,
excellent, just, watery, hygienic, distant, conservative,
deliberate, spiritual, relaxing, trustworthy

DARK BLUE
Romantic, moonlit, discouraging, stormy

BROWN
Earthy, mature, ready to harvest, obstinate, reliable,
conscientious, stolid, parsimonious

SEPIA
Old-fashioned, faded, old

PURPLE
Royal, powerful, luxurious, churchly, pompous, cer-
emonial, vain, nostalgic, mourning, funereal

WHITE
Cool, pure, true, innocent, clean, trustworthy, simple,
honest

GREY
Neutral, secure, stable, mature, successful, affluent,
safe, restrospective, discreet, wintery, old

BLACK
Authoritative, respectful, powerful, strong, present,
practical, solemn, dark, morbid, despairing, evil,
empty, dead

Gold
Sunny, majestic, rich, wise, honored

Use common sense in picking colors, despite the fact that colors are said to have psychological implications, like the ones listed here. They may or may not be valid, because nationality, age, environment, social, and economic class, and even mood all affect how people react. Besides, many professions and groups have developed specific color palette vocabularies. To complicate matters, **colors are affected by their surroundings.** The proportions of one to the other changes their effect (*see page 202*). Even light makes a difference: in a dark office, bright colors and big type will be more effective than if the publication is seen in bright sunlight, when subtler colors and smaller type are appropriate. There are no rules.

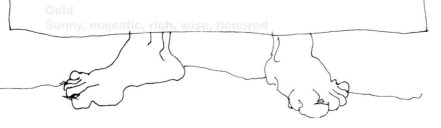

See page 240 for technical terms.

Rainbow sequence *(red… orange… yellow… green… blue… indigo… violet).* (Remember it by a mnemonic: "Richard Of York Gains Battles In Vain")

Pastel colors *(pale blues, pinks, yellows, pale greys).* Femininity. They are seen to be gentle, loving, caring, soft, misty, sentimental, springlike.

Fresh, clean colors *(yellow, bright blue, bright green).* Health. Remind viewers of cool water, dewy lawns at sunrise, scent of lemon and lime, fresh-picked fruit, outdoors.

Natural colors *(earth colors, browns, oranges, dark greens, reds, golds).* Security, dependability. They denote foods traditionally grown in organic soil: healthy and good for you, the way grandma made things. Hence nostalgia by combining them with old-fashioned type and images.

Loud colors *(Primary: red, yellow, blue. Secondary: orange, green, purple).* Dominating. Their vibrant presence jumps out at you. They shout for attention, so can be interpreted as aggressive.

Clashing colors *(any unexpected combinations).* Exciting. Seen as contemporary when gaudiness is in fashion; therefore they speak to youth. Dynamic. Innovative.

Quiet colors *(any colors that are muted and subdued).* Relaxing. They are seen as passive, friendly, peaceful, unassuming. They tend to sink into the background and are preferred by older, more affluent sectors of society.

Dark colors *(black, grey, silver, purple, brown).* Masculine and sophisticated when used with restraint and in a minimal way. Reminiscent of dinner jackets or the grey cutaways and top hats worn in the Royal Enclosure at Ascot. High-tech in the 1990s.

Elegant colors *(silver, gold, brown, grey, maroon, dark blue, black).* High style, upmarket; quality and expense.

Use common sense when talking about color preferences. All sorts of tests and surveys show that by and large, women prefer warm and light colors, whereas men prefer darker, cooler ones. Women prefer red over blue, whereas men prefer blue over red. Children prefer yellow, white, pink, red, orange, blue, green, purple—in that order. Adults prefer blue, red, green, white, pink, purple, orange, yellow—in that order. Does that help? Not much. It is far too vague. What precisely is "red" or "orange"—there is an infinite range of subtle shades. These generalizations exist to make the choice less frightening. Relax. **What you use color FOR is more important than the hue you pick to do it with.**

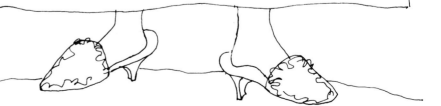

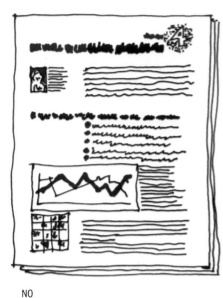

NO   YES

Color's most obvious difference is its most valuable asset: *it is not black*. That's what helps you lead the viewer's eye to what you deem to be important. Don't waste it. Color is only noticed if it is bright enough, large enough, conspicuous enough, and *rare enough*. Less is more.

Use color boldly, decisively, strongly when you are using it, because you know it adds value to the communication technique. Little spots are hardly noticeable, so they are hardly worth the effort. The element that is run in color should be worthy of being in color and therefore should be worthy of popping off the page and into the viewers' eyes powerfully.

Place color where it will be seen so it does you the most good. Don't bury it in the gutter where it will be hidden. It will help to invite the potential reader into the product when it is noticed on the outsides of the pages. The publication is an object that is held in the hand and its pages are flipped, so it is only common sense to make the most of its physical characteristics and capabilities.

Rank information by brightness and amount of color: the more important, the more colorful. The lowly soldier is identified by a little red scarf and hat. The lieutenant has a jacket. The general is resplendent with eye-dazzling redness.

Make important things notice-able by strong, saturated, dominant, aggressive colors. "Warm" colors appear close and jump out at the viewer. **Play things down** using shy, reces-sive, pale colors. "Cool" colors appear to recede far from the viewer.

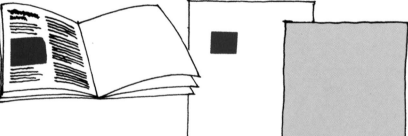

Consider tonal values: The larger the area, the lighter and more unobtrusive the color should be. The smaller the area, the more vivid and bright the color can be. Think in terms of proportions and their relationships more than in terms of hues.

Choose the background color first, then conform the color accents to it. Consider color relationships: no color exists by itself, so always take its sur-roundings into account. The effect also changes as the propor-tions of the colors to each other vary. The only rule is trial and error and experience. Make an album of annotated tearsheets to keep a visual record.

Assign color deliberately to fulfill specific functions. Plan for it from the start. It can be retrofitted as an afterthought but adding it after-the-thinking-has-been-done seldom does justice to color's capacity as functional, rational, intellectual material. This is an obvious instance where that editor/designer understanding and cooperation are essential. However attractive and decorative color can be, it is more valuable when it also helps to tell the story.

Emphasize the main points in the text: run the key paragraphs in color to highlight benefits... flag the advantages. Make the reason for bothering to read stand out.

Pull viewers' attention to what you want them to notice:
the special offer...
the telephone number...
policy expiration date...
warning about safety...
profit (or loss)...
data that exceed the norm...
values that exceed tolerances...
changes in procedures...
whatever concerns them most
(like their own names)...
Editing the material to make optimal use of color that way helps to sharpen the message, make it easier to assimilate and to remember.

Compare two sets of data.
Distinguish new information from old… current situation versus projected… this year's soccer team's results vs. last year's… revisions in specifications… etc. Whether the material in color is more important than the black depends on the proportions and typographic emphasis. In either case, presentation can be organized on two levels, and readily understood by the viewer at first glance.

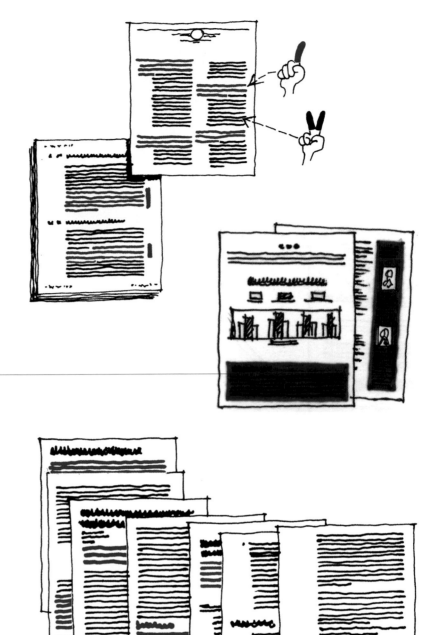

Organize, classify, codify, categorize information.
Separate and shut subsidiary information in boxes. Fence off sidebars in their own areas. The things in colored boxes are understood to be a secondary category—skippable, but available if and as needed.

Make text look shorter by using color to identify and thus separate abstracts… conclusions… biographies… summaries… instructions… self-tests. The article still takes the same total amount of space, but it looks as if there were less text to read, because the ancillary elements have been broken away and made to look different by color.

Split the message from the publication's "housekeeping" signals such as page numbers, headers, footers, logos, etc. Run those repetitive elements in color. The pages will look simpler, less full, and it becomes easier to concentrate on the story.

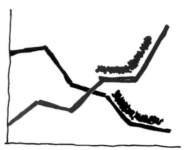

Link related elements to each other. The purple title intuitively belongs to its purple line on the graph, just as the lady in the purple dress immediately notices her rival in the same color dress at the party. Be wary of this relationship, because unwitting use of it can mislead the viewer into linking elements on the page that are not meant to be related to each other.

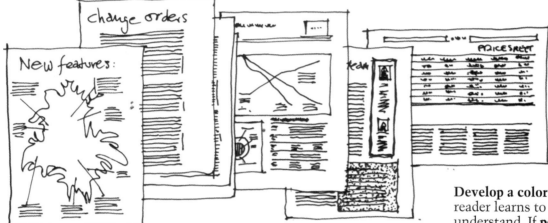

Develop a color language the reader learns to recognize and understand. If **positive attributes** are first identified in brownish, then every time **brownish** is seen, whatever it refers to will be interpreted as **positive**.

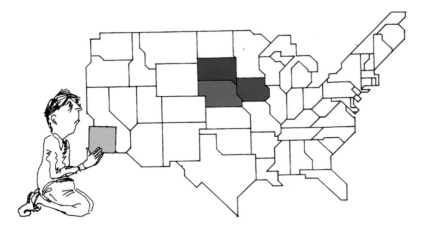

Keep color coding simple. Use no more than four colors plus black, otherwise you have to have a color key explaining the coding every time. (And you want to avoid color keys which take time and energy to study). Black plus three distinctive colors are easily remembered.

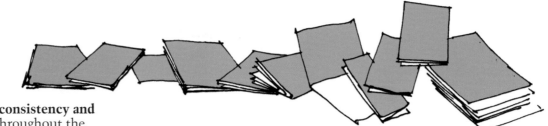

Color code for consistency and predictability throughout the issue or a range of related publications, including those on the Web. Establish personality.

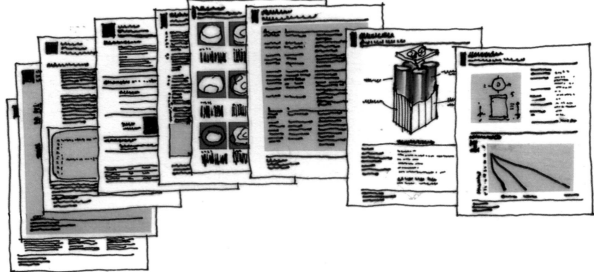

Provide color continuity because a coherent look strengthens, variety disintegrates the product. Use just one color for backgrounds. Repetition helps segments look familiar, as the viewer expects them to be. "Belonging" is advantageous to the page, the story, the series, the image of the periodical.

Interrupt long flows with break pages. A big publication such as a directory so segmented seems smaller, more accessible, and the whole more user-friendly. Color can identify recurring pages such as chapter openers… thematic illustrations or statements… process diagrams… locator maps… subsidiary tables of contents… self-tests… summaries.

Identify special sections by colored stock, but stick to the typographic styling. The color makes it different, everything else helps it "belong."

This text is deliberately set too small and too tight. When it is printed in black on a white background, it can be deciphered fairly easily. The words stand out best because black on white creates the maximal tonal contrast and we are used to it, find it natural, easy, and so prefer it. This is just an illustration and not a recommendation.

When the same text (deliberately set too small and too tight) is printed in black on a colored background, it is more difficult to decipher, but if the color is light, you can get away with it. The paler the color of the background, the greater the tonal contrast, and therefore the less disturbing it is to habit and normal expectations.

When that same text (deliberately set too small and too tight) is printed in black on a colored background, it is much more difficult to decipher if the color is dark, like this. Who will ever bother to dig their way through this disaster?

This is an illustration of what not to do.

This text is set bigger, less tight (i.e., wider tracking), larger size, with more leading (interline spacing) in shorter lines. In black on a white background it can look a bit clunky.

This text is set bigger, less tight, larger size, with more leading and shorter lines. Printed in black on light colored background, it is easy to see, so it is easy to read and therefore it is acceptable.

Printed in black on a darkly colored background, it is less unpleasant than the example above. It is still not ideal, but you can get away with it if you absolutely must.

Black type on colored background. The darkness of the background color affects legibility of black type.

This text is deliberately set too small and too tight. That makes it harder to read when it is printed in white on a black background. There is too much tonal contrast and we are not used to it. It hurts the eye. Besides, the tiny, thin letters fill up with ink and we are forced to work hard in order to decipher them.

This text is deliberately set too small and too tight—and it is hard to read when it is printed in white on a dark-colored background. Not only is there too much tonal contrast we are not used to, but the tiny, thin strokes of the letters fill up with the layers of inks unless the printing is in perfect register. This sort of thing should never be inflicted on the reader.

This text is set sans serif, less tight (wider tracking), larger size, with more leading (interline spacing) in shorter lines, bolder.

This text is the same as at left. It is simple, the strokes are of an even thickness, and it is set unjustified, in order to keep wordspacing rhythmically even.

White type on colored background reads best on a contrasting dark color. White on black is too stark. Use sans-serif, to prevent serifs from filling up, and avoid ultrabold faces whose counters can also drown in ink.

This black-on-color type looks less important than

this black-on-white type, which pops out at you more strongly

because of the stronger contrast of black on white.

This black-on-a-pale-color type reads as clearly

as does this line, although the hues are different,

because the tone values of the colors are balanced.

Equalize the tone values of the background. Since black is easier to read on white than on a color, an immediate priority is established: the easier-to-read lines are noticed first and so their content gets unintended priority. Balancing the tonal values of the background colors overcomes such unintended and misleading inequality.

When it is printed in cyan, it is deciphered much more easily, because cyan's black equivalent is 67%. A 67% screen of black is a dark grey. The contrast with the white background is greater, so the words are decipherable.

When it is printed in cyan, it is deciphered much more easily, because cyan's black equivalent is 67%. A 67% screen of black is a dark grey. The contrast with the white background is greater, so the words are decipherable.

To compensate for color's paleness: increase boldness, increase type size, increase interline spacing, decrease lines length, set ragged-right.

Keep typography simple.
Use sans serif,
avoid weird,
exaggerated,
ultra-expanded,
ultra-condensed,
ultra-oblique faces,
pale italics,
too many all-cap words.

Allow the color to do the shouting.

Colored type on white background
suffers from reduced contrast,
since color is paler than black.
Compensate with dark color and
simple typography.

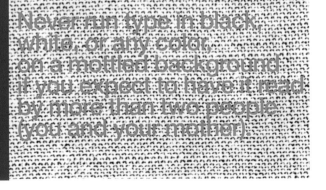

If it hasn't been done before, there's probably a damn good reason why.

Never run type in black,
white, or any color,
on a mottled background
if you expect to have it read
by more than two people
(you and your mother).

Colored type on colored back-ground is dangerous. Pick the colors for contrast, not pretty hues or brilliance. Avoid tiring the eye with bright colors on bright backgrounds. Run tests.

Never run type in black,
white, or any color,
on a mottled background
if you expect to have it read
by more than two people
(you and your mother).

Ramped color is kinetic. It appears to move. A gradient fill creates the illusion of change (from/to, out of/into, before/after). The natural sequence starts at the left and moves towards the right, but that can be altered by the color itself: the eye is likely to be attracted towards the bright color first, then move towards the duller or paler one, no matter where it happens to be placed.

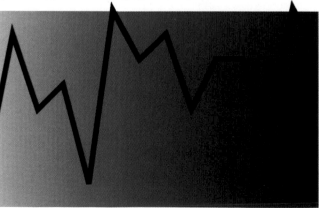

A change in the colors from one part of the ramp towards the other increases the drama of motion, especially if the colors are meaningful. The cold end of the arrow at the frying pan end becomes heated as it flies from the frying pan into the fire.

The end of the line (the "latest information") at top-right is emphasized because it is a white line seen against dark violet. The start at far left (the "old part") is de-emphasized because it looks pale on a pale background. The exact opposite happens when the graph line is black.

The more tonal contrast, the greater the noticeability. Guide the viewer to notice what is important by placing it on a pale background if it is in a dark color... and a dark background if it is in a pale color. This has nothing to do with the color's hue or brightness but its darkness/lightness. This technique can be used to make a point vivid and clear—or to cheat the viewer.

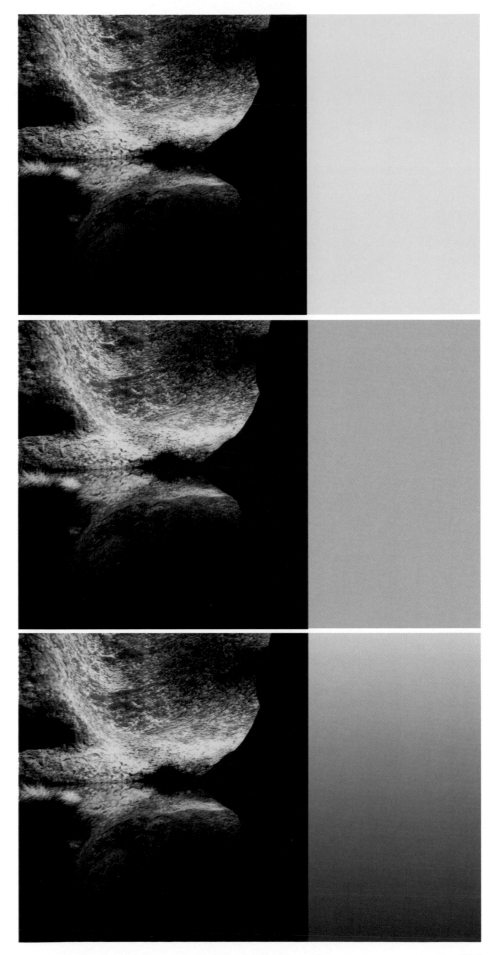

Handle color panels with care. Unless your publication uses a standardized color for all panels as an element of its graphic styling, the panels near color photographs should be considered with those images as part of an overall effect. Here, The blue panel clashes with the tan photo. Is there a reason why you want it to? If so, then fine. If not...

...match a color of the photo in order to expand the power of the picture. The color you pick will emphasize that aspect of the photo that you wish to draw attention to. Here it is merely the color of the rock (which happens to be Ayer's Rock or Uluru, in Australia)...

...better: use ramped color panels in the vicinity of full-color photos. Ramping (or gradient fill) looks more naturalistic than flat panels, because there are no flat colors in nature. Flat color exists only in artificial situations like print. The sky's blue changes in tone value from top to bottom. The wall may be painted a flat color but its appearance varies according to the way it is lit. Notice around you. Use color panels with care.

Call attention to an element in a color picture by manipulating the color. Think of this as another form of "editing." Obviously, we should leave good pictures alone and protect them from corrosion or "improvement." On the other hand, perhaps the speed and clarity of the message might benefit from some manipulation of the image.

A simple example, the blue feet of the blue-footed booby from the Galápagos Islands. Is one of the "improved" versions below better than the original? Is either of them necessary? Is tampering with the purity of the original image worth this result? The problem is a philosophical one and its solution is not purely aesthetic but editorial: what are we trying to do, who are we, what do our customers need and want? How do we tell them most vividly, forthrightly?

Option A.

Tampering with the color of the rest of the picture. Here, by making it just black-and-white, leaving the booby's blue feet in full color.

Option B.

Leaving the picture alone, but surrounding it with a matching-blue frame.

PRODUCT-MAKING

A good publication does not need to be "different" if it is at least one or two of these: topical, provocative, opinionated, riveting, controversial, fascinating, enlightening, illuminating, instructive, and has integrity.

A publication that is alive reflects its editor's courage. Some can get away with being more daring, inventive, and original than others. But publication-making should never degenerate into a desperate search for creativity, innovation, or flamboyant fashionable design. Its look should never be exaggerated, but fit its purpose and its audience. We are making the product for them (not us). Never let the band get too far ahead of the parade.

Expectability is what readers want, because they are familiar and comfortable with it. If you have managed to devise a format that makes sense and is right for your purposes, which is no easy task, and it is servicing the subscribers rather than your own vanity, then use it and stick with it. Knowing why you are who you are is an invaluable attribute.

Originality that works is a result of the balance between fresh approaches and expectability. Expectability only becomes *boring* when both the form and the content are unoriginal. The trick is to separate the permanent form from the temporary content. (This runs counter to everything this book is about, where form and content are blended; but in this context and just for now, please separate them in your mind.)

The *normal form* yields expectability and recognition. Fresh handling of the *journalistic content* gives life, surprise, excitement. But if it is packaged in a radically different format, it endangers the expectability of the issue as a whole. You have to balance originality against expectability.

STORY-TELLING

Of course you want to shine, and want the product to be "exciting." But we all work too hard: we think that if we add a layer of visual fireworks to the piece, we'll attract attention and glean higher readership. Yes, it'll be noticed, but for the wrong reason. Instead of depending on embellishments, we should trust the excellence and interest of the subject itself. Decide what its most valuable aspect is, expose it, display it so that *it* is what pesuades investors to buy and readers to read.

You don't need to be "original" if you:

1. **Do not overfill the pages.** They'll be skipped if they look stuffed too full, even if the material they contain is profitable. If something is worth publishing, it must be 1) notice-able and 2) appear valuable. It deserves to be shown off—persuade management to invest in more paper.

2. **Split information into its component parts ("info-units").** Many people remember information by visual clues: where they saw it on the page... what it was next to... what color it was... how big it was. Build pages out of segments. Display info-units as independent elements on the pages.

3. **Organize space on the page into well-defined zones.** Separate the zones by "moats" of white space or "walls" of rules. Define the areas by color background or a variety of type fonts. Vary them by texture or scale. Break them away from each other by taking them out of alignment with each other. It may look less tidy, but that is what works better for the recipient. Which is more important to the well-being of the product?

4. **Devise shapes appropriate to the material.** Instead of unthinkingly pouring text and pictures into the rigid standard two- or three- or four-column vertical tubes of space, develop frameworks that make sense for the material and the way it has been structured in the writing. If that structure shapes the material on the page, the look will be a clue to what it is—it will be a device for visual orientation as well as a source of variety.

5. **Vary the visual texture with the way the text is written.** Running text should look different from bulleted lists… numbered sequences… fast-to-scan display type… abstracts… summaries… bylines… pullquotes… That way ideas become easier to distinguish from each other and recognized for what they are. That visual difference also makes them easier to remember.

6. **Don't mix information types within the info-unit.** Make the most of their potential visual differences:
Abstract (fast overview introducing purpose and scope)
Review (summary at end of chapters)
Concept (defining what something is)
Structure (how something is assembled or organized)
Procedure (what to do and how to do it)
Process (how something operates)
Classification (catalog of elements)
Comparison (pro/con, before/after, good/bad)
Explanation (footnote)
Cross-reference (exegesis, parallel information elsewhere)
Exercise (self-test, review, practice, simulations)
Index (lists of contents, bibliographies, glossaries, etc.)

7. **Use contrast to help searchers find what they are looking for.** Show off what is important by making it big and bold, and place it up near the top of the page. Let it poke out into white space. Give it air. Bury less significant stuff down below and make it smaller and paler.

8. **Use the same visual techniques throughout.** Repeat them from page to page, issue to issue, publication to publication. If they fit the material, they will not become boring. Instead, they will develop into a language that aids speed and comprehension. Furthermore, such a unique language will help to distinguish your products from the competition's— not because they are visually weird, but because they makes sense and so add value to the product.

9. **Use verbo/visual means appropriate to the material.** Substitute charts, graphs, maps, photos, diagrams, icons, etc. for text wherever possible. Turn statistics into visual form and then cut the verbal description from the text, to avoid duplicating the information. The text will be shorter, the statistics more easily graspable.

Few ideas come as brilliant flashes of inspiration. Most of them come from hard thought and concentration. "Genius is one percent inspiration and ninety-nine percent perspiration," said Thomas Alva Edison—and he ought to have known. To encourage ideas to come:

Yes, but what if you are stuck for ideas?

Work at it: be aware and ready to catch those unexpected ideas. Capture them before they evaporate and make notes on 3x5 cards, constantly. Then sleep on it.

Develop and keep up a file: cull ideas or inspirations from wherever... and annotate them, so you remember what it was about them that you thought was applicable to your needs. And flip through that file of tearsheets. Resurrect old ideas that were rejected but now might work. That is neither plagiarism nor research. It is searching for inspiration.

Loosen thinking: consider the problem as fun and stop taking it so seriously. Keep an open mind, be ready to take risks. It's just one issue and there'll be a next one much too soon—and nobody will remember your mistake. Nobody knows that it didn't work out the way you hoped it would, so they aren't as disappointed as you are.

Forgive yourself if something goes wrong and doesn't work. Reduce risk by constructing a network of trusted friends with whom to check out ideas.

Eliminate the negative: don't reject anything because *"We've never done it before," "They'll never buy this."* Who says that *"They'll never understand this"*? Reassess all assumptions. Challenge old preconceptions. Don't hold back on anything. Stop being your own negative judge.

Generating visual ideas is not easy for anybody, but there are a few techniques that have proven useful. Their chief utility lies in the fact that they relax that tightness caused by fear... they loosen your capacity to think by giving you some tools (tricks?) to use:

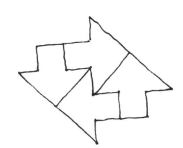

Use your hands to describe action... direction... enclosure... motion... Then illustrate the hands. Hands are as expressive as arrows.

Describe the subject in words, then think of visuals to illustrate *those words*. But watch out not to mislead: a "mammoth parade" isn't a parade of mammoths.

Look for patterns in order to create order out of apparent chaos. Maybe what they have in common can be visualized.

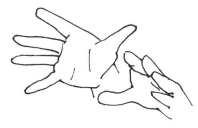

Substitute a pictorial metaphor for the subject. The ideal one is the arrow—yes, the obvious, hackneyed arrow. It can be twisted into an infinity of meanings and interpretations.

Use a detail as a symbol if you can find a segment to represent the whole.

Transform the familiar and obvious into the strange and startling by exaggeration. Look at it from someone else's viewpoint. How might another profession react to the same problem?

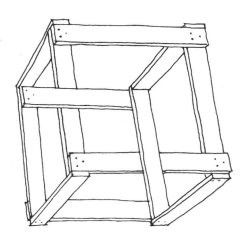

Look for a new angle on the subject by asking factual questions like: What is the cause? What direction does it come from? How is it delivered? What is its scale, bulk, and density? Where in the world is it happening? Where can it be viewed from? When did it happen in history? What is the time of day and the weather?

When print was black-and-white and anything else was luxurious and rare, pictures in color were startling. Nowadays nothing much is rare (unless it be pictures in black-and-white). You need more than inks. The surprise cannot be just visual. It has to carry meaning. That's where editing by design comes in.

If you do want to create graphic surprise:

Powerful mood in emotional images created by their angle, color, lighting.

Violent action and motion using blurred photos.

Unusual color combinations in photos or artwork.

Personal intimacy by looking directly into viewer's eyes.

Larger-than-life-size images printed on the page.

Unexpected scale combinations (like this tiny man painting Mona Lisa).

Enormous words blown up (but only if they are indeed significant).

Vantage points from anywhere but the normal eye level.

Combining several versions of the same subject in one image.

Butting images in irregular, intermixed shapes.

Sequences showing change in strip form like timelines.

People turned into animals for wry (dangerous) comments.

Exaggerated size, color, proportions of anything abnormal.

Incongruous combinations of things that don't normally belong together.

Naturalistic photos mixed with two-dimensional cartoons.

Anything goes.

What you see on-screen is virtual. It isn't the real thing (unless you are actually doing Web pages). The reader who eventually receives your product doesn't get screen dumps but a floppy object made of paper. Therefore think constantly in physical terms: paper.

PRODUCT-MAKING

Printing out hard copy of each page in miniature is a reminder of the reality of *paper* and is more effective than displaying the publication on-screen in miniature. Moreover, seeing the pages displayed on paper in sequence forces your thinking into the three-dimensional flow mode.

Paper miniatures come as close as possible to what the buyers will see: the big-scale patterns is what they are subliminally conscious of when they first flip or scroll through the pages; only later, when they concentrate on reading, do they become conscious of details. Paper miniatures allow you to check the patterning without getting lost in detail. It is a visual process that must be done visually; it cannot be done by imagining it in memory. Seeing it on-screen is also removed by a whole generation. Paper reality is worth the extra effort, because looking for consistency and sequencing improve the issue.

STORY-TELLING

And then check some other things right before closing. Read the headlines for spelling as well as for sense because that's where the most embarrassing typos always happen. Concentrate attention to root out other silly things like bad spacing that somehow seem to sneak in:

SKIP ANTS

SKI PANTS

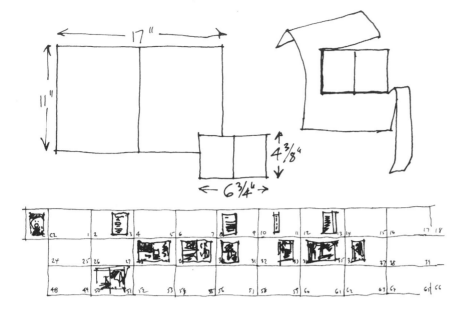

Make hardcopy printouts reduced to about 40% of final size of all pages. That is large enough to discern patterning (which is what you want), but small enough to lose detail (which is what you don't want to get lost in). Trim away all excess paper. Hang them on the wall. When the issue is nearly complete, check for flow… contrast… surprise… liveliness… repetition… slow versus fast stories… Compare story-to-story contrasts. Think of relationships over space and time.

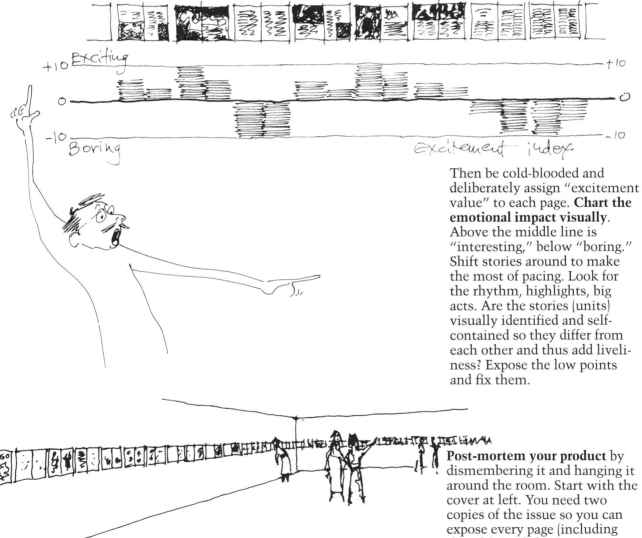

Then be cold-blooded and deliberately assign "excitement value" to each page. **Chart the emotional impact visually.** Above the middle line is "interesting," below "boring." Shift stories around to make the most of pacing. Look for the rhythm, highlights, big acts. Are the stories (units) visually identified and self-contained so they differ from each other and thus add liveliness? Expose the low points and fix them.

Post-mortem your product by dismembering it and hanging it around the room. Start with the cover at left. You need two copies of the issue so you can expose every page (including the ads). Look for patterns: repeats where they should be, anomalies where they should not. Do this periodically, whenever you have a staff hair-shirt session.

When you are judging page designs, you normally pin them on a wall. That disembodies them, and makes them unreal: you see them flat, but they will never be flat in real life. It also changes their scale, because seeing them at a distance only shows up big elements and plays down details that are visible at the normal viewing distance (twelve inches from the tip of your nose). **Therefore, insert the printout in its context** to force you to see what your reader will see.

Fold the paper to check alignment from one side of the sheet to the other. Don't take it for granted that just because you expect it to be a certain way, it will in fact appear that way in the finished piece. Accidents are inevitable. The problem is that they are perceived as shoddy, careless craftsmanship by the reader, so the stature of the product suffers. That is why it is essential to be on the lookout for inconsistencies and misalignments.

Spread out hardcopy pages in a line to check accuracy of alignment of edges. Fanning them out or quick-flipping doesn't work nearly as clearly or dependably.

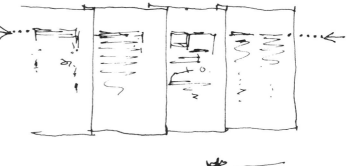

"Showthrough" of the image from one side of the paper to the other happens when the paper is too flimsy. It is regrettable, because it spoils both the "recto" (front) and the "verso" (back). But it can be helpful for checking the precision of alignment and relationships such as the edges of pictures that back up on both sides of the paper. Put the paper printout on a lightbox or hold it up against the light coming through the window.

Turn the layout upside down to force yourself to see it as an abstract object. The images turn into rectangles instead of images and so the composition stands out clearly as arrangement. The upside-down trick also exposes typographic anomalies most vividly. Look how the rivers of white between the words are highlighted when the text is rotated 180°.

In particularly narrow columns like this exaggerated example, justification forces disturbingly artificial word spacing which results in "rivers" of white space flowing inside the column. Gaps inhibit smooth reading.

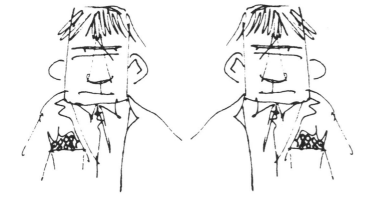

Pictures flopped left to right by mistake not only make the personage look peculiar (because all faces are unequal), but the breastpocket is on the wrong side, or the roadsign in back there reads POTS instead of STOP.

Look for unwanted words spelled out by the drop-caps. It is amazing how often such unintended disasters sneak their way onto the page, especially in the display type.

Ask *"So what"* out loud after reading each headline, so you can hear yourself. If the answer is *"Well, not much,"* then it is an empty, vapid, uninvolving headline. Rewrite it; add an ACTIVE VERB; insert YOU in the meaning. It doesn't need to be short, if a few more words would make it fascinating and irresistible.

This is a headline set *normal*, as designed to be ideally comfortable

A headline expanded to the same line length

And this is a headline that is too long for that same space, therefore it had to be be condensed so that it becomes almost illegible

Don't allow type to be stretched or squeezed to fit into pre-specified width. Brutal artificiality destroys the very character of the type on which so much of the product's personality depends. Just because it can be done technically doesn't mean it should.

These are all set in 18–point Oficina Book, tight tracking, with horizontal scale for the top line at normal, the middle line at 154%, lowest at 49%.

Her cheek was as soft as a camellia's petal

Ridiculous line breaks in headlines. Meanings are distorted by bad phrasing. Think of the words as language represented on the page visually, rather than just a bunch of little black marks on paper. Don't let display be mechanically fitted into a given space. Read the heads out loud, checking for line breaks to make intellectual sense.

Soviet virgin lands short of goal again

Unsuitable for Children Under 36 Months Contain Small Parts

People who love people also give blood

Police get stoned by teen-age mobs

The most embarrassing typos seem to occur inevitably in headlines. All the examples on this page are authentic. Disasters happen. (So help me, we once forgot the logo off the cover of an issue of the architectural magazine I was involved with—and nobody even noticed! Perhaps the cover format was so strong that we didn't need it?)

Whatever happened to THE GREAT AMERCIAN JOB?

Town prepares for for the Big Crunch

Each pronoun should agree with their antecedent.

Verbs has to agree with their subject.

Between you and I, case is important.

A writer must not shift your point of view.

When writing, participles must not be dangled.

In formal writing one shouldn't use contractions.

Do not write run-on sentences you got to punctuate them.

Don't never use no double negatives.

You gotta avoid slang.

No sentence fragments.

One-word sentence? Eliminate.

In letters themes and reports use commas to separate items.

Do not use commas, that are not necessary.

Its important to use apostrophe's in the right places.

Eschew ampersands & abbrevs., etc.

Check to see if you any words out.

Always avoid annoying alliteration.

One should never generalize.

Be careful to never split infinitives.

Never use a preposition to end a sentence with.

And don't start a sentence with a conjunction.

Be more or less specific.

The passive voice is to be avoided.

Kill all bangs—i.e., exclamation points !!!

Parenthetical remarks (however relevant) are (usually) superfluous.

Foreign words and phrases are not apropos.

Use words correctly irregardless of how others use them.

Never use a big word when a diminutive one will suffice.

Shun mixed metaphors, lest they kindle a flood of anger.

There is no excuse for spelling misteaks.

Last but not least, avoid clichés like the plague. They're old hat.

Also, too, never, ever use repetitive redundancies.

Do not use more words than are necessary; that is unnecessary.

Lousy English, bad spalling, misteakes in grammer, careless readproofing are not cute bloopers or funny takeouts. They lower the standard and jeopardize the magazine's credibility. Excellent writing bespeaks not only careful craftsmanship but, more important, accuracy of thought. It is essential for transmitting ideas clearly. Unfortunately, something will inevitably go wrong somewhere, given the complexity of the product and the rush in which it is normally produced, but there's little excuse for carelessness. How is the harried, overwhelmed reader likely to react?

Traps to look for

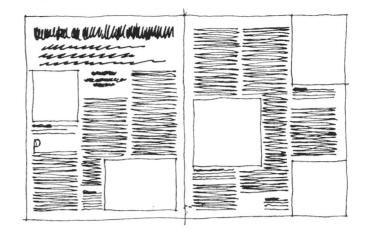

Pictures crammed into the text "to break it up." Examine the shape of the text columns. How many indents and wiggles and column-top starts are there? Is the text area so cut up that it is a puzzle? Does it encourage continuity of reading or are the interruptions so disruptive that the reader is likely to give up halfway through?

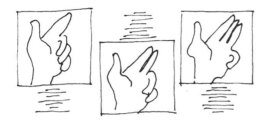

NO   YES

Checkerboard patterns without functional reason (or just for the fun of it because "it looks nice" that way). Arbitrary patterns of any kind are suspect because they can destroy the vital, if simple, relationships pictured *inside* the rectangles.

Big numbers in color that 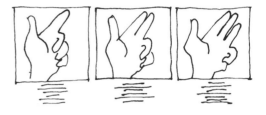 attract attention to themselves. Looking cute is usually not enough reason for their being that important—but if the story is about "5 ways to..." then 1, 2, 3, 4, 5 deserve screaming.

Clip-art picked to fill holes in the layout. What's wrong with empty space?

Pictures blown up out of all proportion just to fill the space or regardless of the scale of the image just to align with its neighbor.

Disaster? Relax. Mistakes are inevitable, despite the greatest of care. They'll be forgotten by the next issue.

Face it: we have to prove to them-out-there that they **need** our publication, no matter what form it takes. Once they do realize that, they'll pay attention—maybe. To succeed, we must see our work from their viewpoint, not ours. That is a huge leap of the imagination, because we know what we're trying to say, so its excellence and utility are obvious to us. Unfortunately, they don't know, and it isn't obvious to them. To get them to **want** it, its value must jump out at them at first glance.

How do you start? When people send a postcard, most first write the name and address, which makes them focus on the recipient. Once they visualize the person, the message is easy. That's what we professionals must do.

We have to crystallize the idea, so we can transmit it fast and concisely. "If you can't write it on my business card you haven't a clear idea," said the great theatrical impresario David Belasco a century ago. It must be easy to enter, to follow, to understand, and to return to.

Furthermore, its value had better be dramatic or they won't notice it, and it had better be edited with the what's-in-it-for-me value right on top, or they won't even bother to start.

Other tricks of the trade. I've grouped them by topics of the typical Q's following my lectures. (A consultant is supposed to have all the A's.) I've worked with all sorts of journalist groups and designers' organizations, from eager pink-faced students to grizzled cynical veterans; in major publishing houses and individual publications; newsletters, tabloids, glamorous international magazines; girliebooks to tech-docs. 1800 seminars in twenty-seven countries. Amazingly, the problems are universal, no matter the language or the kind of publication. These worries seem endemic to our profession as communicators.

How can I get on better with the editors? They don't understand.

 ## How can I get on better with my designer? She bullies me.

Learn to understand and perhaps even laugh at them. They feel vulnerable about "art," and they are scared of sticking their necks out. They need a protective carapace, so they intuitively tend to say "NO" to your best, freshest ideas. If something hasn't been done before is an ideal reason to say "So why start now, if it hasn't been proved effective?"

Show how well your solution serves the editor's purposes. Don't present your solutions as "good design"—only you consider design as vital (you are right: so it is, but, alas, few editors understand that).

Become as verbally skilled as you are visually, so that you can explain and persuade them to accept your ideas on reasoning, not just beauty.

Become as broadly cultured as the writers and editors. Being an "artist" is not enough. It is restricting, boring to them. Read… learn… grow…

Persuade management to send you out on trips with the reporters. Insist on being in on editorial meetings and planning conferences, because you need to be just as fully involved in the substance as you need to be involved in the form of your common product.

Make your work space as similar as possible to the writers'. You aren't strange, so be un-strange in manners, dress, appearance, and surroundings. It is a question of perception and class.

Stop scaring people with weird typeface showings and shocking avant-garde art on your walls. Being cutting-edge is fine—but costs you a lot. It is no excuse for being untidy, working in a mess, losing stuff, or dressing like a weirdo.

Being a designer is no excuse for being late, either. Unfortunately designers are traditionally the last to receive the material, squeezed between writers' lateness and deadlines. So you are doubly visible.

Never admire layouts as works of art, hanging on the wall with medals and awards. See pubdesign for what it is: a fleeting impression in a sequence of impressions in an issue soon followed by the next. Accept the fact that what you do is temporary, impermanent, and evanescent. It is still *vital*.

•

Garamond

> The answers are set in different text fonts to show how the color and texture of type varies. All are set in 10/11 (i.e. 10 point, with 1 point additional line spacing).

Foster friendship and intellectual rapport over lunch on your expense account. When designers achieve high enough status to have expense accounts of their own, you have the makings of a team at last.

Realize designers are your partners and that their contribution is as vital to the combined success of the product as incisive editing and limpid writing.

Make up your mind why a story is worth publishing (i.e., where its significance to your readers lies.) Then *explain that* to your designers, so they understand and are involved.

Never send a story to the art department with a note, *"This is important, make it look exciting."* Explain it in person, so they can do it brilliantly. Together, decide what elements are worth emphasis, so the designers can bring them to the reader's attention. That will help create excitement using worthy material instead of superficial decoration.

Never reject a layout just because *"I don't like it."* Such subjective bullying just raises hackles. Train yourself to explain the reason why the layout isn't working for the story—and thus for you. Only when they understand can the designers fix it to make sense.

Stop thinking visuals secondary. They are often better information-carriers than words. Words and pictures complement each other. Blend them to make 1 + 1 = 3.

Realize that pictures are what the viewer looks at first, so edit the story with them in mind. Judge pictures not as "art" but for their value in terms of content, besides adding visual excellence to the issue as a whole. Base your choice on objective logic, not subjective "liking"—and reveal that rationale like all other reasoning to your designers.

Manipulating pictures is permissible: it is the story that matters. Be generous in crediting (and paying) photographers, especially when you crop or tamper with their images.

Understand that typography can reflect your tone of voice. Don't just *look* at type: *Listen to it.* Don't be satisfied with the monotonous drone of body text in column after column. Encourage your designer to turn your manuscript into modulated, expressive form, interesting to look at. Study what makes exciting stories in other publications so successful. It is seldom the subject alone. Figure out how you were captured by the design/edit team's clever blending of the content with the form.

Accept the fact that designers will always lack expertise (and probably interest) in your specialty. It is up to you to guide them to its fascination and significance. Don't make them guess at it. Tell'em.

•

Centaur

I'm an editor—
I'm scared by "Design"
—what can I do?

In junior high you were taught to center the title on the cover page of your report… skip two lines and center your name… skip ten lines and center the name of the school… skip a line and center the address… skip a line and center the date… and you were judged on *correctness*. This idea of Visual Rightness became embedded in your subconscious like spelling, paragraphing, and not splitting infinitives, presenting bibliographies, cross references etc., etc. Then you gave up "Art" because you couldn't draw a straight line. So now you know nothing about art but know what you like. Forget it.

Design is an integral part of the editing process. If you can edit with confidence, you can design with confidence. Of course it matters what a publication looks like. But it matters much more if it makes sense.

Communication in print is a one-to-one conversation in which you write instead of speaking and your audience reads instead of listening. So type is not an abstract artform, but speech made visible. Concentrate on the idea and how you would use your voice to tell it—and its typographic expression will follow. Open your eyes and listen.

Pictures are so important because they are a parallel language that speaks to emotion and curiosity. The right image catches the viewers' attention and pulls them into the text by means of the most important words on the page: the caption.

Color's greatest value is that it isn't black. It is different, therefore it should be reserved for the elements that you need to emphasize, classify, separate, organize. It is also pretty. But its main advantage is clarification of the message.

The medium is not the message, the message is. Concentrate on the content and the form will follow. Forget design as Beauty. See it as Utility.

The art of designing is exactly the same as that of editing: controlling relationships and emphasizing some elements while downplaying others. They use the same thinking.

Every action has a price. Something has to be sacrificed in order for something else to be accomplished. Weigh the cost/benefit ratio. Decide on both the cost and the benefit by their comparative editorial utility.

Nobody knows what you had intended to do, so they don't know how badly you goofed. Learn to forgive yourself. The next issue awaits.

•

Times New Roman

Why, when, and how
do we redesign?
Who does it?

Don't try to be artificially different just to be "creative." Worthwhile originality grows out of the special circumstances dictated by the needs and the materials at hand.

Don't redesign to show off how clever and with-it you are… to solve problems other than visual character… because *you* are bored with the product.

Redesign only when you have a new editorial policy or new publishing technique… or the competition is gaining and forcing you to look at yourself… or you suspect that your typography is beginning to look a bit old-fashioned… or you need an infusion of fresh energy… or the sales people are trying to impress ad agencies… or you are trying to appeal to a new group of subscribers.

Don't try to do it yourself. Even an expert surgeon can't take out his own appendix. Turn to a professional. The investment will pay off with new approaches, because he doesn't know all your reasons why not.

Professionals perform a functional service in devising active means to catapult stuff off the page into the reader's mind fast and effectively. That is only tangentially artistic.

Explain in as much detail as you can what editors and publishers are attempting—and why—so they can solve for deeper purposes than merely dressing up the product more fashionably. They ought to show genuine interest in what *your* magazine is trying to accomplish editorially.

They mustn't use your product to build monuments to themselves, but make the product worthy of a monument to itself.

The right re-designers will proudly display whole stories in their portfolios, instead of only single-page units or spreads. You want someone oriented towards flow rather than one-shot effect (which is fine for ads, but not magazine-making).

They should submit complete issues and explain how their design scheme helped to fulfill editorial purposes. Yes! That's the secret.

Hire designers who communicate well in words. They are likely to be sympathetic to writers, instead of thinking of type as that dull, grey stuff. They will be more than page-decorators. Besides, they must persuade the team to understand and sign on enthusiastically to use their new scheme. That demands verbal skills.

•

Hoefler

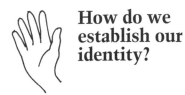

How do we establish our identity?

If you don't carry advertising which dictates standardized sizes, and if you can afford it, change shape: 8 $\frac{1}{2}$" x 11" is boring but most economical. Go taller, like the metric A4 size, or widebody, 9" x 12". Bigger is more expensive, so its value may be questionable. 6" x 9" is efficient paper use. 5 $\frac{3}{8}$" x 7 $\frac{1}{2}$" fits in the pocket and is good for heavy text.

Tabloid size is hard to handle: it is too big to be small, too small to be big. It has the advantages of neither except that it can accommodate island halves with runaround edit.

Can you recognize which magazine a page is from, if it is torn out and hung on the wall by itself?

Count the number of typefaces used for all the attention-getting wording. No wonder the magazine looks like a fancy costume party. Ideal number of fonts: one.

Logo and department headings are interconnected serial signals that must echo throughout. They are an integral part of the graphic personality and should be styled in conjunction with the display typography.

Let the logo stand out on the cover in its own clean space, without surrounding visual clutter. Make the inescapable small stuff smaller, so the logo looks bigger by contrast.

Separate the logo from the other cover words by ample space.

Non-text elements are always examined first and are a major part of the visual character-creating continuum. Establish and follow a consistent style for all charts, graphs, and diagrams.

Devise a styling and stay consistent in everything that repeats. Signals: (front logo/TOC/dept heads). Text type. Display type. Headings on boxes. Handling of byline. Handling of bio. Handling of photo credits.

Establish a two-tiered color palette. Color palette: foreground (for attention-getting splashes) and neutral background (for boxes, tint areas, to go with color photos, etc.). Don't depart from it.

•

Trump Mediæval

How do we establish authority?

Know your audience's interests. Direct the writing and layout to them—that is the best audience-luring technique. You can't write too short. They are in a hurry, so respect their time-poverty. When in doubt, cut it out.

Nothing draws like the feeling of being served. Tag important stories with a topic title, and amplify the heading with a deck that articulates why your friend (the reader) should be interested. Or set the first sentences in larger type, run them in color—anything that will display the relevance and utility of the information powerfully.

Speak directly to the reader: use language and tone of voice appropriate to the readership. Use the word "you" or imply it in the display.

Never overpromise by overinflating an opening image (maybe because it is a glorious picture and you haven't got that many in the issue) and then following it up with a puny story. Overselling, like crying wolf, disappoints and angers.

Publish lists of the ten best, or the fifty worst.

Establish and publicize your Anything of the Year or Hall of Fame.

Research statistics and publish comparisons. Who gets paid how much?

Run stories on important individuals and show large portraits or—better—incisive cartoons of them.

Run surveys to gather and opinions and organize Round Tables to generate controversy.

Let readers in on how, where, when you got the things you are telling them, and why you think they are significant.

Establish links by developing a personal relationship with them—make them realize that each copy is a one-on-one conversation with a particular reader. Introduce yourself with more a informative bio than "Joe Doakes, Managing editor"—give them a reason to know and learn to trust you as professionals.

Illuminate character and personality by replacing passport mugshots of contributors and editors with realistic alive snapshots at work or on the road.

Let editors become individuals with handwritten comments in margins, notes on post-its, disagreements on notepads, explanatory footnotes, annotations.

•

Gill Sans Light

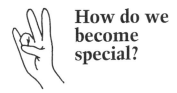

How do we become special?

Make the individuality and quality of your service stand out. Don't take it for granted that it will be noticed, but show it off. Trumpet it.

List major contents on the spine.

Number items to show off how many you have gathered on cover... in story... in items. Big.

Place short bits, which are always more popular than long-looking items, where they are most visible: on the outsides. They are easy to enter.

Compile a fast Executive Summary to follow the TOC.

Make the most of audience participation. In the New Products section, put in open squares at the end of each item to encourage readers to check off the items they want to send for on the bingo cards in back.

Draw explanatory diagrams that show what to look for in complicated photographs.

Draw direction arrows on plans to show where pictures were taken from and which direction they look.

Run an annual index, even though it is a pain to assemble and uses precious space. It is an investment in shelf-life and implies serious utility for the product.

Highlight special database services your readers can't find anywhere else but here, such as:
e-mail addresses of people or firms mentioned.
Your own e-mail page for more information.
Pictures and e-mail addresses of editors.
List of advertisers.
List of advertising agencies.
List of peoples' names the first time they occur.
List of firms the first time they occur.
Index of subjects like illnesses in a health mag.
Index of books.
Index of anything that is a useful service.

•

Helvetica Neue Light

How do we get them to pay attention?

Psychology of curiosity: people are catalog shoppers and will expend effort if they sense a reward, so promise one and deliver on it—or else. Highlight advantages or positive attributes.

The reader's self-interest must be served. By clearly persuading them of "why" and showing them "how" will make them want the product. That's the "pull" rather than "push" technique.

Headlines must be long enough to promise a benefit. Cow lays eggs = news. Cow lays golden eggs = news + possible enrichment. Cow that lays golden eggs for sale = extraordinary opportunity.

Edit and design so that the story works on both levels: the immediate summary scan in 2.5 seconds, and the detailed scrutiny up to 5 minutes.

Visual appearance helps to point out what's vital in the scanning. It is a combination of type, pictures, boxing, callouts, white space, color, composition, scale, etc.

A clear entrance and flow from element to element—"layout"—and parts of message highlighted by boldface that are read first are controlled by typography.

The picture opens the mind to want information. Place the headline under it like a caption. One/two punch.

Pics must say something, not just show what something or somebody looks like. Picture editing searches for the image that reveals inner meaning.

Use the TOC to get the browser to linger long enough to scan. It is a sales tool, so make it as big as possible. It is a persuader, make it look Proud. Enticing, not cramped. Organize it consecutively, or by topics rather than Features and Departments (which are categories significant only to us).

•

Palatino

See how it doesn't matter that the columns don't align at the foot of the page?

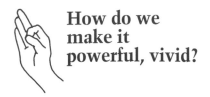

How do we make it powerful, vivid?

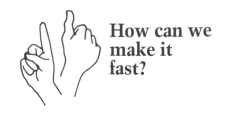

How can we make it fast?

"You never have a second chance to make a first impression," said Aaron Burns, the great typographic designer. Plan for immediate understanding. Readers stay with you 2.5 seconds, then turn the page, unless you capture them NOW.

Combine the opening picture and the headline into a one/two punch. The words and image should be intimately allied in both meaning and placement. Best place for the headline is below the photo.

Edit pictures at the same time as you edit the words and incorporate them into a unified message. This is the opposite of "breaking up the text," though it may possibly result in a similar look. Here it improves sense.

Write all boldfaced words as though they were standalone heads. That forces you to define the valuable gist, which scanners will be able to gather fast. See them as curiosity-arousing hooks.

Start stories on spread with big pic at left. Stories that start on the right-hand page are weakened by the fact that they are vying for attention with whatever story appears on the left side of the spread.

Place heads at top of pages because that's where people look for them. If heads are down in comparative obscurity at the foot of the page, make them bigger to ensure their noticeability.

Avoid tall columns because they look daunting. Breaking text into short columns next to each other looks less of a chore to plough through.

Layouts should project the contents. They should never just be passive coffins into which the stuff is fitted.

Make the most of contrasts:
Size: big/small, important/unimportant.
Texture: smooth/rough, airy/dense.
Shape: horizontal/vertical, box/freeform.
Balance: symmetrical/asymmetrical.
Amount: one/group, full/empty.
Placement: high/low, left/right.
Scale: large/small.
Weight: heavy/light, thick/thin.
Value: dark/pale, color/black and white.
Definition: separate/combined.

Pictures add drama to the story and the page. Diagrams, charts, and graphs add interest and knowledge. Always start with something familiar in describing statistical facts. A dinosaur isn't big when you say he is sixteen feet tall, but he looks terrifying compared to a man.

•

Oficina Sans

Everyone first quickly scans the document to decide whether the knowledge gained is worth the effort invested. Is it interesting enough for me?

Scanning is fast, erratic, vertical—needs elements that stand out. Reading is slow, steady, horizontal—needs neat, smooth, steady flow. Edit and design to accommodate both.

Never repeat in the deck what you said in the headline... never repeat in the text what you said in the captions. Never repeat the pullquote in the text. Never repeat.

Rewrite slow-reading textblocks as fast-scan lists.

Make lists look like tabulated pictures and distinguish them from running text by geometry, alignment, different typeface.

Introduce each list with a headline. Separate it with extra space and insert extra space between items.

Set bullets or numbers flush left, indent everything else. Make lists look like tabulated pictures.

Turn statistics into visual form as charts and graphs.

Write captions so they say something interesting. Use big type: they are important.

Use strong, dark type for display so it pops out... and write it so it says something.

Pick type that creates strong contrast between the emphasized bold black display and the surrounding pale grey text.

Use all-lowercase for headings for fastest reading and to allow Proper Names to stand out and be noticed. Restrict ALL-CAPITALS to a few words, and Never, Ever Use Up-And-Down-Style Like This Anywhere.

Leave a wide margin at left, poke heads into it for fastest, easiest scanning.

Get in close when taking photos (or crop supplied photos tight). It is like editing verbal information: exposing the significant.

•

Century Schoolbook

We haven't got much to work with.

Make the most of what you've got. Get more impact for less investment: control what you're stuck with; don't hanker for the unattainable.

Define the what's-in-it-for-me value and spotlight it for first-glance noticing.

Strengthen the story: make them notice they're looking at something worth while by giving it more visibility. Not by more color and fireworks, but by patterning, repetition, same color. Less is more—if it is repeated over and over.

Invest some space by making the head margin deeper than normal ("deep sinkage") so the material beneath that white space gets an aura of specialness.

Avoid fireworks: they skew attention from the story to themselves. Falling in love with one's own cleverness (which is often tangential to the story) is a dangerous will o' the wisp.

Number things. There's magic in numbers: twenty-four something-or-others, ten best thingumajigs…

Get more impact from the layout by forgetting to make it beautiful. Make it meaningful and clear so it gives service fast, smoothly, easily. It has to be fast so that a 2.5 second overview communicates the gist and why the reader should bother.

Tabulate the information as clearly as you can: horizontal layouts makes it easier to arrange the menu sideways for easier scanning. Link things by closeness, overlapping, mortising, alignment.

Break the page into information-units each in its own rectangular zone. Each story becomes special that way. Construct pages block-on-block rather than up-and-down in chain sequence in columns.

Indents and exdents explain hierarchy, so use the left-hand edge of the column actively.

Ruled lines of various weights add color and organization for free.

Don't be afraid to leave space at end of items. Don't fill holes by expanding text or inserting clip-art. Leave them empty. Don't clutter.

Use clip art only if it both enriches the product's overall image and adds meaning to a story. Don't decorate, because readers doesn't want a candy box.

Invest in one subtly different typeface and make it your own. If you are stuck with Helvetica or Times, you have to work too hard on everything else in order to have a unique visual personality.

•

Syndor

How can we get more for less?

Squeeze more into a smaller area: concentrate the type, squeeze out the excess space from within it and add it to the headlines. Then make the headlines bigger, bolder, and longer, so they can say something irresistible.

Make the product look big and full but not daunting. Bits of extra white space are invaluable.

Two half-columns of text alongside each other look less daunting than one full-page-high.

Use ample white space to frame and separate units from each other; that way each appears unique and valuable.

Pick provocative pullquotes, to rile up the reader into paying attention. They cost no extra.

Make big things out of little ones by clustering them under an umbrella topic head. That looks like a special service.

Break big daunting things into smaller units under an umbrella headline.

Emphasize boxed material by larger type size (rather than the usual smaller) and cast a shadow to make it stand out from its background.

Contrast the formality of large and justified text in wider columns against the informality of smaller size in narrower columns set ragged-right.

Play feather-edged pullquotes and picture captions against geometric regularity of text type in the columns.

Use typographic elements (like outsize letters, descriptive words) as illustrations to add color, visual variety, and even meaning.

Don't reinvent the design wheel each issue or story in order to enrich the issue. Stick to style because that strengthens your image. Then, when you do decide to depart from it, the contrast will carry more surprise.

•

Bookman Light

How do we encourage reading?

Advantage of print: page-flipping tells people quickly how much there is. Placement, layouts, and signals show what sort of material it is and how long it might take to read. (On screen it is hard to tell without scrolling, which is a pain.)

They start with a goal in mind: is this worth bothering with—am I interested enough? If they think they have had enough, they stop reading and there's little we can do about it.

Use the standard traditional fonts even if they are boring, because they are comfortable, proven, easy to read (i.e., not like this).

To improve acceptability of text, use a bigger type size, shorter lines, more space between the lines, and set ragged right to retain rhythm of spacing.

Avoid reversing (white on black or color) because it cuts readership by 40%. If it is unavoidable, then increase the size, set it in bold in even shorter lines with more space between them, and keep the text as short as possible.

Readers' aims are different: retain detail, or find out if they can just dip into it, or browse, or search, or skim, or scan, or study closely, or dip in for occasional help.

Decide whether the piece is made to impress, to reveal information, to store information, to support an argument, to accompany explanations... each deserves its own special format.

Most readers prefer material broken down into small scale quantities or procedures they can manage in bite-size chunks.

Don't confuse by weird makeup. Lead the eye deliberately; align tops of columns and avoid breaking up the text arbitrarily with inserted pictures.

Don't place hurdles between the head and text, but lead from one to the other smoothly.

Retain consistent spacing between things that are the same.

Don't colorize or enlarge words just to decorate without logical some strategy to emphasize meaningful words.

Don't angle type, compress type that should be normal, or fuss with drop shadows and embellishments. Keep it simple.

•

Franklin Gothic Condensed

How do we guide readers?

Not finding what they are looking for infuriates readers. Always repeat the exact words used as coverlines on the TOC and on the story itself.

To keep them reading, don't give them a chance to stop: break pages in mid-sentence; break columns in mid-paragraph when inserting pullquotes; make the second line of headlines shorter than the first so the eye is led into the text.

Make sure subheads say something worth knowing (teasers are skipped and ignored).

Don't misuse type fonts that are designed for display like this one for text. Unless, of course, you are trying to turn readers away.

Tell them what you're going to tell them, tell them, then tell them what you told them. Insert subsidiary tables of contents on the first page of an article that is a cluster of related stories. On the next x pages you will see...

Give them a clue where to start each page or spread: have a clear and inviting entry point using a dominant picture, an interesting headline thought, a startling image, anything that is connected with what's-in-it -for-me.

Help them know where they are in the issue: establish clear, logical, easily seen and noticed "continued on" and "continued from" lines and standardize their use.

Make the page numbers big enough to see easily and put them everywhere you possibly can.

Help them navigate through the issue by establishing and standardizing roadsigns... always in the expected place.

Use a starting and ending "bug" for each story. Perhaps a drop-cap initial for the start and a personalized icon or mini-logo for the end.

•

Techno

How do we appeal to kids?

Forget the s'posed-to rules and do the opposite. Youth wants to revolt against whatever is accepted as normal. Therefore question whatever you would do that might be expected and go as far as you dare the other way.

Break everything into bite-size chunks: attention span is short, and fast-cut is what they are used to. Single-page units are deemed very large.

Exploit color: use black-and-white where color would be expected, use color where black-and-white would be normal. And wherever possible, use unnatural colors.

Play with the type, even though you know that type's purpose is to be *read*: set it ragged instead of justified, ragged-left is OK. Set it angled instead of straight, curved instead of aligned, large instead of small, or tiny instead of normal.

Contrast exaggerated sizes with tiny ones: enormous instead of large, huge close-ups with long shots.

Play with headline type: aligned letters at the top instead of bottom to make them skip around, overlap letters, make some words bigger than others. Weave them with pictorial elements in rebus fashion.

•

Skia

How do we fight the ads? They're so ugly.

Be grateful for them, they pay the bills. The uglier they are, the better the editorial looks by comparison. Unless they buy preferred positions, bury them in the back. Don't worry, there's nothing you can do about them. You have enough troubles making what you can control—the editorial—as good as it can be.

Ignore the gorgeous large-space ads: don't try to outscream them. Instead, be happy they give the product glamor (and income). Depend on the interest inherent in the editorial material to attract and hold readers.

Let advertisers have the right-hand pages in the front of the book: accept the lefts gladly. They are better for us, because their left-hand edge is the ideal place to start headlines in, especially if the pages are successively and regularly organized.

Never let an ad halve the impact of a story-start on the first spread of the story. Insist on putting it on the second spread.

Don't fight small-space ads: they pay the bills. You can't outshout them, so outwhisper them instead. Create a contrasting quiet typographic texture and steady color. Avoid pictures in scattered columns because they blend with the ads to the detriment of both the editorial matter and the ads.

Bring readers into the classified ads: insert little paragraphs of cute information among them. A small investment enriches the wasteland and adds interest. Add fascinating background bits in short sentences in the foot margin.

Take advantage of the rhythm in the front of book. The spaces left over between the ads — whether full-page or small-space—are small scale. Fill them with deliberately small-scale material, in order to contrast with big-scale feature stories.

•

Optima

Color is a complex, technical subject, but the purpose of this book is how-to-use-color, not its esoteric technicalities. However, there are some words and concepts that must be mentioned. They are related here by sense, not in alphabetical glossary order.

Chroma: The degree of purity, brilliance, intensity, or saturation.

Luminance: Degree of lightness or darkness of colors seen on-screen, created by mixing light.

Saturation: Degree of purity, brilliance, chroma.

Shade: Color resulting from black pigment being added to a pure hue ("neutralized").

Tint: Color resulting from white pigment being added to a pure hue ("pastel").

Value: Degree of lightness or darkness of colors printed on paper, measured against a scale of white to black.

Hue: the characteristic of a color created by a wavelength of light and distinguished by a name such as "red" or "blue."

Chromatic: any color other than black, gray, or white.

Monochromatic: single hue varied in value and chroma.

Nonchromatic: neutral hue black, gray, or white.

Polychromatic: using many hues.

Cool and warm colors: Dangerous generalizations, because every effect is the result of the relationships and proportions of colors to each other. **Cool** colors subdue: hues from the blue, green and violet families; pale yellow, light pinks. **Warm** colors excite: hues from the red, yellow, orange families; also intense greens and violets.

Bright and somber colors: bright colors with pure and high chroma shimmer and delight; by contrast, somber colors are dark and probably mixed with black (sombra is shadow in Spanish).

Color, additive. The primary colors (red, green, and blue, RGB) that form white light, when added together on-screen.

Color, subtractive. The three ink colors (yellow, magenta, and cyan) used in process color printing on paper. Each primary is created by absorbing (i.e., "subtracting") one of the additive primaries from white light.

Color, process. The three subtractive primary colors used, together with black, in process color printing (CMYK). Process yellow reflects red and green and absorbs blue light. Cyan (or process blue) reflects blue and green and absorbs red light. Magenta (or process red) reflects blue and red light and absorbs green.

Color separations: A colored original transformed into four halftone printable segments ("seps"): the three subtractive primaries (yellow, magenta, and cyan) and black. They print on top of each other to create the illusion of full color.

Color wheel: clock-face of colors originally created by bending Sir Isaac Newton's spectrum of the rainbow into a circle. Red is at 12, blue at 4, yellow at 8. Between red and blue lie red-violet, violet, blue-violet. Beween blue and yellow lie green-blue, green, and yellow-green. Between yellow and red lie orange-yellow, orange, and red-orange.

Complementary colors: Lie opposite each other on the color wheel.

Secondary color: made by mixing two primary colors.

Tertiary color: made by mixing a primary with an adjacent secondary color.

Tint builds: Superimposing screens of process colors to match desired hue (see Spot color).

Metameric color shift: apparent change of hue under various lighting conditions.

Moiré pattern: Undesirable star or other patterns resulting from superimposing dotted screens at wrong screen angles.

Color ramp or **gradient fill** or **graduated tint** or **fountain.** The illusion of gradual change of one color to another created by a series of discrete steps.

Spot color: Area of flat color added to black. Usually a special ink rather than a combination of process color inks ("tint build").

Posterization: mechanical process converting continuous tone images (e.g., photos) into a variety of flat areas.

Alphanumeric: mixture of letters and numbers.

Ampersand: The character & that combines "e" with "t" and means "and" in Latin. The word probably comes from the way children were taught to memorize it: "And per se and."

Anamorphic scaling: Altering the size of an image in one direction resulting in squeezing or stretching.

Ascender: The part of the lowercase letters b, d, f, h, k, l, and t that protrudes above the body of the type (its x-height); the opposite of descender.

Back matter: Pages following the main text of a publication, devoted to reference matter such as index, appendix, glossary.

Bleed: A visual element, usually an illustration or screened area, that prints to the edge of the paper. A sliver is cut off when the publication is trimmed—hence it "bleeds."

Batch processing: When similar tasks are delayed and grouped for combined handling.

Block: Group of words handled as a unit.

Blow-in insert: See Insert.

Blow up: enlarge.

Blurb: Any wording whose purpose is promotion, usually on the back cover or inside flaps of a bookjacket. In a periodical it can be run in conjunction with an article, like a **deck** (which differs only in that it is less blatantly sales-oriented).

Body: The x-height of the lowercase letters a, c, e, m, n, o, r, s, u, v, w, x, and z that lack ascenders and descenders.

Body copy: Text of an article.

Body type: Type used in the the text, as distinguished from display type.

Bodyline capacity: Number of lines per page.

Boldface: Darker version of the regular type formed from heavier wider strokes.

Bullet: Black dot • (used indiscriminately and too often).

Callout: Wording placed ouside the illustration but attached by a line or arrow to that part of the illustration it describes.

Caps: Short for "capitals" (see Uppercase letters).

Caption: Wording appearing in conjunction with a visual; also called cutline or legend.

Carry-over line: Words placed in top-left corner of spreads identifying them as belonging to what precedes them (see Running head).

Character set: Collection of all characters available in a font: alphabetic, numeric, symbolic, punctuation, and special swash letters.

Color: See Color-related words on page 240.

Condensed type: Narrow, compact version of the normal typeface. Good ones are specifically designed. Less good ones are artificially produced by setting the computer at an abnormal horizonal scale.

Continued line: Words usually placed in lower-right corner, instructing reader where the continuation of a story may be found. Used only when it is "jumped" beyond overleaf.

Copy: The words of a manuscript; all the material to be printed.

Cropping: Chopping off edges of an illustration to make it fit or to concentrate attention onto the important area.

Dash: Em-dash is long — and used primarily to indicate a break in thought. **En-dash** – is half the length of the em-dash and used mainly to represent the word "through" as in A–Z. The **hyphen** is the shortest of the three - and is used as a link and to indicate word break at line ends (see Em and En).

Deck: Wording following the headline and expanding on its subject, but preceding the text (see Blurb).

Department slug: In hot-metal days, a **slug** was an often-used word or symbol precast and standing ready for insertion. The name of a **department** (i.e., section of a publication) dropped into its normal position on the page.

Descender: the part of the lowercase g, j, p, q, and y that drops below the body of the type (the x-height); the opposite of ascender.

Dingbats: Technical term for printers' flowers and other ornamental (as opposed to punctuation) symbols such as ✱ ☛ ◯ ❀ ✿.

Display type: Type used for headlines, decks, pullquotes, subheads, captions, and all other attention-getting words, as distinguished from "body type" used for text.

Double-truck: The material that extends over both pages of a spread. The term is misused if it is synonymous with "Spread."

Downstyle: Headlines and display set in lowercase, capitalizing only the first initial and the first letters of proper names and acronyms. Sometimes called Sentence style (see Up-and-Downstyle).

Dropout: Type appearing in white on black or in pale color against a dark colored background. Also called "reverse."

Ellipsis: Three dots used to indicate missing word ... words (see Leaders).

Em: Measurement in typesetting; the square of the type size. The Em in 12–point type is 12 points high and 12 points wide.

En: Measurement in typesetting; one-half the width of the Em. The En in 12–point type is 12 points high but only 6 points wide.

Exclamation point: "Bang" in journalese! Originated from manuscripts, in which IO, the Latin for Wowee!, was squeezed into less space by shrinking the O into a dot and writing it under the I.

Expanded type: wide, extended version of the normal typeface. Good ones are specifically designed. Less good ones are artificially produced by setting the computer at an abnormal horizonal scale.

Figures (numerals): **Lining** figures have no descenders and align with the capital letters of a type font. Also called Modern. **Oldstyle** figures correspond to the x-height and have ascenders and descenders.

Flag: See Logo.

Flush-left, flush-right: Even or aligned on the left edge or the right edge of the column, the opposite side remaining deliberately uneven. Written f/l, f/r. Also called **ranged left**, **ranged right**.

Folio: Page number.

Font: Complete collection of one size of a named typeface consisting of capital and lower case letters.

Footline: (**Footer** in documents.) Name and date of publication, often run in conjunction with the folio or page number.

Form: An assembly of 4, 8, 16, or 32 pages printed simultaneously in one pass through the press. When it is folded and trimmed, it is called a **signature**. When signatures are grouped in sequence to make up a publication, they are said to be **gathered**.

Format: The elements that combine to give a product its individual character: size, shape, color, margins, typefaces, binding, display typography, color, etc. Also called **styling**.

Front matter: Pages preceding the main text of book, devoted to title, table of contents, preface, foreword, etc. ("Foreword," never "forward"!)

Gutter: Inner space between two facing pages. Crossing it with an element from one side to the other is **jumping the gutter**. Also the gap between two adjoining columns of type.

Halftone: Continuous tone original (e.g., photo) made reproducible in print by converting it into tiny dots whose size simulates the darkness and lightness of the original (see Screen).

Hanging punctuation: Typographic refinement in which punctuation is placed outside the left or right-hand border of the column, allowing characters themselves to create a precise edge.

Indent: Notch cut in usually from left-hand edge of a block of type, but also possible from the right or both edges. **Paragraph indent** appears in first line of each paragraph (though it should not do so in the first one). **Hanging indent** cuts in all except the first line, which is flush left. **Runaround indent** parallels the edge of a neighboring illustration.

Infographic: Report transformed into a combination of interconnected pictorial and verbal explanations.

Information unit: Verbal and visual material combined into a self-contained story, with its own headline; component of a larger article.

Insert: A piece printed on different stock and bound into the publication. Loose elements such as postcards are **blow-in inserts**.

Interrobang. This punctuation mark doesn't exist, but it should, to be used in situations such as "What? No kidding!" It combines the startling quality of an exclamation point with the asking capacity of the question mark.

Italics: Type originally resembling handwriting and slanting to the right. Most text fonts have both roman (vertical) and italic (slanted) versions. *The italic* is often paler (see Oblique).

Justify: Aligning left and right edges of a column of type for traditional neatness. Don't justify with fewer than eight words (forty characters) per line to avoid force-justifying or "opening up" by word-spacing or, worse, character-spacing and thus jeopardizing smooth, rhythmic reading.

Leaders: Dots set in succession to lead the eye from left to right......... (see Ellipsis).

Lead-in: First few words of text or picture caption, usually set in contrasting type size or boldness (Boldface lead-in). Must be written to be worthy of such attention-getting treatment.

Leading pronounced LEDDING: Additional space added between lines of type ("linespacing"). Name comes from ancient metal days, when an actual sliver of lead alloy of a specific thickness was so inserted.

Letterspacing: Space artificially i n s e r t e d between characters. Don't; harder to read. Is the effect worth it?

Live matter page: The printable area of a page within the margins.

Logo short for Logotype: From Greek LOGOS, word. Originally any pre-set word, but now that word manipulated into a recognizeable trademark denoting the name of the publication ("nameplate" or "flag").

Lowercase: The small version of the alphabet as contrasted to CAPITALS. Also called Minuscules.

Mugshot: Standard passport-type photo of a person. Jargon for police portraits of possible probable perps.

Nameplate: See Logo.

Numerals: See Figures.

Oblique: Type slanted to the right, simulating italics. True Italics are specially designed, whereas oblique is a mechanically altered version of vertical "roman."

Picas and points: Americn type measurement. Six picas to the inch. European (but not metric) system is based on Didot's ciceros, which are a hair bigger than picas. In time the current mess in sizes and nomenclatures may yet all be standardized by the needs of the computer with its spots per inch... or —what? Don't go by mathematical measurements. Print it out, look at it, and judge whether it is big enough to read comfortably.

Question mark: Originated from the Latin QUESTIO ("I ask"). To save space, scribes shortened it to QO, shrank the O to a dot and wrote it beneath a squiggle that vaguely resembled a Q.

Ragged type: Lines of type with one or both side margins left deliberately uneven or "unjustified."

Ranged left and **ranged right**: (See Flush left and Flush right).

Recto: Right-hand page (see Verso).

Roman: Type with vertical emphasis, as contrasted to italic or oblique. The material we are all used to for normal reading.

Runaround: Type set to follow the contour of an element that intrudes into the column.

Run-in: Closing a gap between type elements, allowing them to follow directly.

Running head or **title**: Words placed in top-left corner of spreads in books, repeating the chapter title (see Carry-over line).

Screen: Pattern of dots or lines into which continuous tone (like a photograph) is converted to make it printable. The eye is fooled into thinking that a pattern of black dots looks like a shade of grey. The smaller the dots and the wider their spacing, the paler the grey; the bigger dots and the tighter the spacing, the darker the grey. White is 0%, black 100%. The finer the paper, the higher the resolution of the screen can be (see Halftone).

Serif: Cross-lines at the ends of the strokes of letters. **Sans serif** (sometimes known as Gothic) is without them.

Sidebar: Short, separate but related story with its own headline, run in conjunction with main article, usually boxed.

Signature: See Form.

Sinkage: Area of white space at top of pages created by an unusually deep head margin.

Slug: See Department slug).

Smallcaps: Letters in the alphabet that have the form of capitals, but smaller, aligning with the x-height. CAPITALS SMALLCAPS and lowercase.

Spine: Binding edge of a multi-paged printed publication, where the pages are folded and assembled. Sometimes known as the "backbone." Its inside is the "gutter."

Spread: Two facing pages in a publication. Never say double-page spread—that's duplication, like pizza pie (see Double truck).

Styling: See Format.

TK: Note inserted in middle of a hole on the page reserved for material not yet received. Short for "to kum," deliberately mis-spelled "to come" to prevent it from being published.

Tombstoning: Undesirable unintended alignment of elements horizontally across page (like three subeads in three adjacent columns of type).

Turnover line: Second line of an item in a list or table, usually indented.

Typeface: See Font.

Umbrella headline: Overall title of a piece consisting of several components (see Information unit).

Underscore: A line set beneath a line of type as underlining to be avoided, because it can interfere with descenders and affect the type's legibility.

Up-and-Downstyle: Outmoded Tradition That Capitalizes the First Letters of All Important Words in Titles and Display. Harder to read than Downstyle.

Uppercase: CAPITAL letters or caps. (When in metal, they were stored in a type-case placed above the lower case that contained the lower-case letters.) Also called Majuscules.

Verso: Left-hand or *reverse* page (see Recto).

Weight: Relative thickness of the strokes of letters. "Bold" type is blacker with thicker, thus heavier, strokes than pale or "light" type.

Wordspacing: Inserting extra space between words to stretch out a line artificially to a desired length or to justify the column. Not recommended: not only are such gaps unsightly, but reading rhythm is disturbed (see Justify).

x-height: The height of the main portion of lowercase letters. Its bottom edge is the baseline of the type. Ascenders tower above the x-height, descenders dip down below it (see Ascender).

Books from Allworth Press

The Elements of Graphic Design: Space, Unity, Page Architecture, and Type
by Alexander W. White
(paperback, 6 ¹/₈ x 9 ¹/₄, 160 pages, $24.95)

The Graphic Designer's Guide to Clients: How to Make Clients Happy and Do Great Work
by Ellen Shapiro
(paperback, 6 x 9, 256 pages, $19.95)

Inside the Business of Graphic Design: 60 Leaders Share Their Secrets of Success
By Catharine Fishel
(paperback, 6 x 9, 288 pages, $19.95)

Business and Legal Forms for Graphic Designers, 3rd edition
by Tad Crawford and Eva Doman Bruck
(paperback, 8 ¹/₂ x 11, 160 pages, includes CD-ROM, $29.95)

Design Management: Using Design to Build Brand Value and Corporate Innovation
by Brigitte Borja De Mozota
(paperback, 6 x 9, 256 pages, $24.95)

AIGA Professional Practices in Graphic Design: The American Institute of Graphic Arts
edited by Tad Crawford
(paperback, 6 ³/₄ x 9 ⁷/₈, 320 pages, $24.95)

The Graphic Designer's Guide to Pricing, Estimating, and Budgeting, Revised Edition
by Theo Stephan Williams
(paperback, 6 ³/₄ x 9 ⁷/₈, 208 pages, $19.95)

Starting Your Career As a Freelance Illustrator or Graphic Designer, Revised Edition
by Michael Fleishman
(paperback, 6 x 9, 272 pages, $19.95)

Careers By Design: A Business Guide for Graphic Designers, Third Edition
by Roz Goldfarb
(paperback, 6 x 9, 232 pages, $19.95)

Licensing Art and Design, Revised Edition
by Caryn R. Leland
(paperback, 6 x 9, 128 pages, $16.95)

Graphic Design and Reading: Explorations of an Uneasy Relationship
edited by Gunnar Swanson
(paperback, 6 ³/₄ x 9 ⁷/₈, 256 pages, $19.95)

Design Issues: How Graphic Design Informs Society
edited by DK Holland
(paperback, 6 ³/₄ x 9 ⁷/₈, 288 pages, $21.95)

Looking Closer 4: Critical Writings on Graphic Design
edited by Michael Bierut, William Drenttel, and Steven Heller
(paperback, 6 ³/₄ x 9 ⁷/₈, 304 pages, $21.95)
